ISO 42001 and Legal Compliance

A Principled Implementation of the AI Management System

Matthew Seet

apress®

ISO 42001 and Legal Compliance: A Principled Implementation of the AI Management System

Matthew Seet
Singapore, Singapore

ISBN-13 (pbk): 979-8-8688-2098-4
https://doi.org/10.1007/979-8-8688-2099-1

ISBN-13 (electronic): 979-8-8688-2099-1

Copyright © 2025 by Matthew Seet

This work is subject to copyright. All rights are reserved by the Publisher, whether the whole or part of the material is concerned, specifically the rights of translation, reprinting, reuse of illustrations, recitation, broadcasting, reproduction on microfilms or in any other physical way, and transmission or information storage and retrieval, electronic adaptation, computer software, or by similar or dissimilar methodology now known or hereafter developed.

Trademarked names, logos, and images may appear in this book. Rather than use a trademark symbol with every occurrence of a trademarked name, logo, or image we use the names, logos, and images only in an editorial fashion and to the benefit of the trademark owner, with no intention of infringement of the trademark.

The use in this publication of trade names, trademarks, service marks, and similar terms, even if they are not identified as such, is not to be taken as an expression of opinion as to whether or not they are subject to proprietary rights.

While the advice and information in this book are believed to be true and accurate at the date of publication, neither the authors nor the editors nor the publisher can accept any legal responsibility for any errors or omissions that may be made. The publisher makes no warranty, express or implied, with respect to the material contained herein.

Managing Director, Apress Media LLC: Welmoed Spahr
Acquisitions Editor: Susan McDermott
Development Editor: Laura Berendson
Project Manager: Jessica Vakili

Distributed to the book trade worldwide by Springer Science+Business Media New York, 1 New York Plaza, New York, NY 10004. Phone 1-800-SPRINGER, fax (201) 348-4705, e-mail orders-ny@springer-sbm.com, or visit www.springeronline.com. Apress Media, LLC is a Delaware LLC and the sole member (owner) is Springer Science + Business Media Finance Inc (SSBM Finance Inc). SSBM Finance Inc is a **Delaware** corporation.

For information on translations, please e-mail booktranslations@springernature.com; for reprint, paperback, or audio rights, please e-mail bookpermissions@springernature.com.

Apress titles may be purchased in bulk for academic, corporate, or promotional use. eBook versions and licenses are also available for most titles. For more information, reference our Print and eBook Bulk Sales web page at http://www.apress.com/bulk-sales.

If disposing of this product, please recycle the paper

I would like to dedicate this book to my mother, S.K. Tan, and to the Sandbox community.

Table of Contents

About the Author xi

About the Technical Reviewer xiii

Acknowledgments xv

Preface xvii

Chapter 1: INTRODUCTION 1
    The problem: use, misuse and abuse of AI 1
    The solution: AI governance 3
        Emerging AI disciplines 4
        AI governance 5
    Summary and Key Takeaways 7
    Reference 7

Chapter 2: ISO 42001: THE STANDARD 9
    Organizations 9
    Standard 10
        Overview 10
        Clauses 11
        Controls 12
    Approaches 14
        Process Approach 14
        Risk-Based Approach 15
        Harmonized Approach 16
    Solution? 16
    Summary and Key Takeaways 17

Chapter 3: ISO 42001 AND THE LAW 19

The Legal Status of ISO 42001 19

Law —> ISO 42001 21

    Organization's External Context (Clause 4.1 Note 2a) 21

    Relevant interested parties' requirements (Clause 4.2) 21

    Determination of risks and opportunities based on external context (Clause 6.1.1) 22

ISO 42001 —> Law 27

    Direct contribution: Safe harbor 27

    Indirect contribution: the subject of this book 28

Summary and key takeaways 29

References 30

Chapter 4: ACCOUNTABILITY 31

A. Principles 31

    (1) Oversight 32

    (2) Assurance 32

    (3) Contestability 33

    (4) Traceability of input - with copyright as a case study 33

    (5) Traceability of output (Responsibility) 34

B. Provisions 34

    (1) Oversight 34

    (2) Assurance 35

    (3) Contestability 37

    (4) Traceability of Input (Copyright) 39

    (5) Traceability of Output (Responsibility) 40

C. Practices 41

    (1) Assurance 41

    (2) Reporting and feedback 42

    (3) Traceability of Input (Copyright) 43

    (4) Traceability of Output (Responsibility) 44

Summary and key takeaways 46

Chapter 5: SECURITY AND SAFETY 49

   A. Principles 49

      (1) AI security 49

      (2) AI safety 50

      (3) Insecure AI 50

      (4) Unsafe AI and resulting harms 53

   B. Provisions 53

      (1) Security 53

      (2) AI safety 55

      (3) Manipulation, disinformation and deepfakes 56

   C. Practices 60

      (1) Integrated security-specific approach 60

      (2) Data Governance 61

      (3) Operational safeguards 63

      (4) Assurance Measures 64

      (5) Transparency and accountability 65

   Summary and key takeaways 66

Chapter 6: PRIVACY 69

   A. Principles 69

      (1) Security safeguards 72

      (2) Purpose specification 72

      (3) Data minimization 72

      (4) Use limitation 73

      (5) Openness 74

      (6) Individual participation 75

      (7) Data quality 75

      (8) Accountability 76

   B. Provisions 76

   C. Practices 82

      (1) Integrated privacy-specific approach 83

      (2) Data governance 86

TABLE OF CONTENTS

    (3) Transparency and accountability 88

  Summary and key takeaways 91

Chapter 7: FAIRNESS 93

  A. Principles 93

    (1) Fairness 93

    (2) Bias 96

  B. Provisions 98

  C. Practices 102

    (1) Team diversity 102

    (2) Data governance 103

    (3) Assurance measures 105

    (4) Transparency and accountability measures in relation to fairness 106

  Summary and key takeaways: 107

Chapter 8: TRANSPARENCY AND EXPLAINABILITY 109

  A. Principles 109

    (1) The black box problem 109

    (2) Transparency 110

    (3) Explainability 111

    (4) Consequences 111

  B. Provisions 112

  C. Practices 119

    (1) Data governance 119

    (2) Documentation 121

    (3) Disclosure 124

  Summary and key takeaways 126

Chapter 9: ROBUSTNESS 127

  A. Principles 127

    (1) Accuracy 127

    (2) Consistency 128

  B. Provisions 130

C. Practices	131
(1) Data governance	131
(2) Computing infrastructure	136
(3) Operational safeguards	137
(4) Accountability and transparency measures	139
Summary and key takeaways	140

Chapter 10: CONCLUSION 143

Appendix 147

Index 269

About the Author

Matthew Seet is the lead author of the forthcoming book, *The Risks of Artificial Intelligence in Law*, to be published with Globe Law and Business. He is also the founder of LAIRisk (https://www.lairisk.com/), the world's first legal AI risk management edtech (education technology) company. LAIRisk's mission is to guide legal professionals and technologists in managing AI risks by using the framework of ISO 42001 (the international standard on responsible AI). It is a Microsoft for Startups partner (Level 3), and is registered in both Singapore and the European Union (Estonia) - both signatories of the EU-Singapore Digital Trade Agreement.

Matthew obtained his Master's in International Law from the Graduate Institute of International and Development Studies in Geneva on a Swiss Government Scholarship, and is certified as an Artificial Intelligence Governance Professional (IAPP), ISO/IEC 42001:2023 Artificial Intelligence Management Systems Lead Auditor, ISO/IEC 27001:2022 Information Security Management Systems Lead Auditor and ISO 31000:2018 Lead Risk Manager.

He was formerly an international law lecturer at the National University of Singapore where he taught law for 7 years. His human rights writings have been published in the Cambridge Law Journal, Journal of International Criminal Justice, Citizenship Studies and International Journal of Refugee Law, cited in the Financial Times, and awarded the 2017 Foundation for the Development of International Law in Asia Prize for Young Scholars.

He also recently served as the board secretary of Sandbox, managing all legal and compliance matters of the Switzerland-registered global community of over 1600 entrepreneurs and creators. He previously conducted research on human rights and data privacy at the Office of the United Nations High Commissioner for Refugees headquarters in Geneva for over a year, and represented Switzerland in the Philip C. Jessup International Law Moot Court Competition.

About the Technical Reviewer

Alvin Antony is the Chief Compliance Officer of GovernAI, where he leads capacity building in compliance, standards, audits, and legal governance. A trained lawyer with specialization in intellectual property, he has litigated disputes across fashion, pharmaceuticals, and rogue digital platforms, while also handling IP prosecution, licensing, and enforcement.

An early scholar in the field of artificial intelligence, Alvin has been writing on AI and law since 2021, beginning with his piece on intellectual property in AI-generated creations. His advisory practice today spans AI governance, compliance, and client consultancy on auditing frameworks, laws and regulations.

He holds professional accreditations as a Certified Data Protection Officer, Chief AI Officer, AI Compliance Professional, and Auditor on ISO/IEC 42001:2023 AI Management Systems. A frequent speaker and contributor to national and international platforms, Alvin continues to shape discourse at the intersection of law, policy, and emerging technologies.

Acknowledgments

I would like to thank the technical reviewer, Alvin Antony, for his helpful feedback, and the Apress editorial team (Susan McDermott and Jessica Vakili) for their patience and meticulousness.

Preface

WHO THIS BOOK IS FOR: This book is for anyone (not just lawyers) implementing an AI management system under ISO/IEC 42001:2023 (which this book will refer to as ISO 42001), given that this standard explicitly applies to organizations of all sizes and in all industries - provided they develop, provide, or use AI-based products or services.

A PRINCIPLED APPROACH: This book adopts a distinctive principled approach to serve all of these organizations, rather than providing step-by-step implementation guidelines. By focusing on the relationship between principles, regulations, and clauses and controls of ISO 42001, this book supports your organization in implementing the standard in a principled and legally compliant manner.

STRUCTURE: The structure of this book reflects this approach. Chapter 1 defines the problem (AI risks) and considers several solutions. Chapter 2 introduces ISO 42001. Chapter 3 elaborates on the standard's relationship with the law. Chapters 4-9 discuss the applicable regulatory and ISO provisions according to AI ethical principles: security and safety, privacy, fairness, transparency and explainability, robustness, and accountability. Each chapter is structured based on principle, followed by provisions, followed by practices. The regulations covered in this book are largely from the EU, the US, and China. Chapter 10 concludes by summarizing the relationships between the AI ethical principles.

LEGAL DEVELOPMENTS: This principled approach provides durable foundations for implementing the standard effectively, even as specific legal requirements change in the continuously evolving AI regulatory landscape. The final manuscript was submitted to the production team on 28 September 2025, and hence the information in the substantive chapters reflects the state of law and practice as of 28 September 2025. There have been several noteworthy legal developments since then:

1. California's Governor Newsom has signed into law a dozen AI-related bills, most notably SB 53, the first frontier AI law in the US, and AB 853, which delays the implementation of the AI Transparency Act (discussed in this book) and imposes additional obligations on large online platforms and capture device manufacturers.

PREFACE

2. The European Commission has proposed a Digital Omnibus simplifying the relevant EU legal provisions related to cybersecurity, privacy, data, and AI. Of the many proposed amendments in the Digital Omnibus, the most relevant to this book are the amendments providing that AI model training is a "legitimate interest" justifying the processing of personal data, and allowing for the processing of sensitive data for bias detection and correction. The Digital Omnibus has been submitted to the European Parliament and Council for discussion, before "trilogue" negotiations between all three EU institutions (Commission, Parliament, and Council) take place.

3. The White House has reportedly drafted an Executive Order, "Eliminating State Law Obstruction of National AI Policy", directing federal agencies like the Department of Justice to file lawsuits against states for AI regulations deemed "onerous" by the administration, and to adopt a new uniform federal law that preempts state-level AI regulations. This Executive Order is currently on hold.

For my analyses of legal developments (including those mentioned above) after 28 September 2025 that are relevant to this book's content, please refer to: `lairisk.substack.com` (subscription not required).

THE ISO TRILOGY: This book is intended to serve as the first volume of a planned trilogy on the ISO digital governance framework, with subsequent volumes anticipated to provide guidance on the information security management system (under ISO/IEC 27001:2022) and privacy information management system (under ISO/IEC 27701:2025). Together, they form the integrated architecture referenced several times in this book - necessary for your organization to address evolving challenges of the AI era.

SCOPE AND DISCLAIMERS: This book is for educational purposes only, and does not constitute legal advice or give rise to any attorney-client relationship. You are also advised to purchase your own copy of the standard for reference purposes, because this book analyzes the standard but is not intended to be a substitute for that.

CHAPTER 1

INTRODUCTION

This chapter provides the necessary context for the book by highlighting the problems of AI for organizations and the several emerging disciplines (particularly AI governance) which aim to address these problems.

The problem: use, misuse and abuse of AI

The increased use of AI across the world has resulted in tremendous concern and skepticism amongst the general population, where AI is viewed as a threat particularly in the West (as compared to Asian countries like China). As per a Pew Research study, the percentage of American adults who are more concerned than excited about AI increased from 37% in 2021 to 52% in 2023. Concerns span a full range of issues (malicious cybersecurity attacks, privacy breaches, algorithmic bias, job displacement, hallucinations, and deepfakes), and how they affect a whole range of stakeholders (individuals, groups, society at large, and the environment). However, given the readership of this book, I'll focus on the concerns of organizations (especially businesses) relating to economic risks related to the use (and misuse and abuse) of AI, where the faulty AI product or system costs your organization money.

The more straightforward economic risks are *legal*. These can be subdivided into both liability risks (where your organization faces litigation, such as class action lawsuits for harm caused by AI) and regulatory compliance risks. As this book on ISO 42001 and legal compliance will demonstrate, while AI-specific regulations are still being enacted across the world, organizations developing or using AI must still comply with existing laws in related areas such as privacy and non-discrimination so as to avoid harm to individuals, groups, and other entities. Non-compliance may result in enforcement actions by regional/national administrative bodies, which include fines and injunctions. Other less well-known economic risks include systemic AI-induced job redistribution and displacement, and investments in AI systems and talent that may not remain with your organization.

CHAPTER 1   INTRODUCTION

The more concerning indirect economic risks to your organization are *reputational*. These include loss in trust (by the public or consumers or partner organizations) and brand value—and hence loss in revenue. Your organization's share price may plunge due to a PR disaster. Your organization may get "canceled" on social media. As organizations increasingly use or even develop AI products and systems, they put themselves in new situations they may not be prepared for; any AI practices or output which causes harm to stakeholders (individuals, groups, society at large or the environment) would affect their reputation. If the harm results from your organization's technical deficiencies in safely developing or using AI, it would be regarded as incompetent. Even worse is your organization's actions or omissions resulting in harm, despite evidence suggesting its knowledge of the potential harm; in such cases, your organization may be regarded as unethical.

Nowhere is the latter point clearer than in the context of *online manipulation*. Two unfortunate examples involve Facebook's mishandling of user data. In the high-profile Cambridge Analytica scandal, a British firm scraped the data of Facebook users, created personality profiles of these users based on their online behavioral patterns (without these users' consent), and used this data to target them with political advertisements to influence their voting decisions. In a lesser-known case, Facebook researchers sought to test whether "emotional contagion" (reactions to others' emotions) could take place on social media, specifically by altering users' Facebook feeds to show more "positive" or "negative" updates by their Facebook friends and assessing if their own updates became more "positive" or "negative"—all without user informed consent. This problem is magnified by AI: AI algorithms collect information on us, determine what we see on social media and the Internet more generally, and predict and impact our future actions. In short, they increasingly control the virtual world we live in. AI-generated content has the potential to mislead and result in misinformation/disinformation at such a scale that is near impossible to control, given the capabilities of AI bots.

Even if not regarded as unethical, technical deficiencies in your organization's use or/and development of AI that arise from your organization's lack of expertise and result in harm to individuals and groups may still engender reputational costs for responsible parties. An example of this is *algorithmic bias* discriminating against certain subsets of society, such as women in this case concerning Amazon. Its resume-screening algorithm was trained with data compiled primarily from resumes of men, with few (if any) women's colleges listed in the successful applicants' data. Amazon's algorithm regarded applicants who graduated from women's colleges to be unqualified and hence effectively discriminated against female applicants. Another public incident involved the Dutch prime minister's resignation after it was publicized in 2021 that the Dutch government's algorithm detecting fraudulent claims for children's benefits had resulted in thousands of incorrect re-claims and denials.

What makes some cases concerning algorithmic bias especially challenging is the *opacity* and *inscrutability* of AI systems, particularly deep learning systems, where the input and output are known but the decision-making process is unknown. Such "black box" systems are fundamentally antithetical to trust, and organizations that develop or use these AI systems without addressing the lack of transparency and explainability carry reputational risks. Consumers may lose trust in your organization if they are not informed—not only of their being subject to the algorithm but also of the specifics of the decision-making process itself, such as the automatic denial of their claims.

Such opacity and inscrutability can result in *AI/algorithmic exceptionalism* or *automation bias*: the assumption that computers are infallible and 100% accurate and better than human beings, such that there is little need for human verification of the output. Such over-reliance on an AI system, which appears to be competent and confident at the same time, leads us to surrender our own judgment. This complacency can lead to outcomes which are embarrassing (such as recent cases of lawyers being sanctioned by courts for citing false cases made up by ChatGPT) or tragic (such as the fatal accident caused by an Uber self-driving vehicle in Arizona, which was later found to be a result partly of the human safety driver's slow reaction at a critical juncture due to over-dependence on AI). All of these problems may be compounded by *acceleration risks*, best illustrated by the phrase in the startup world, "Move Fast and Break Things", with businesses engaged in a race, without putting in place guardrails necessary to ensure the safe development and use of AI.

The solution: AI governance

Several disciplines have been developing in response to these challenges posed by AI. These disciplines are often referred to interchangeably, so it is important to differentiate them.

CHAPTER 1 INTRODUCTION

Emerging AI disciplines

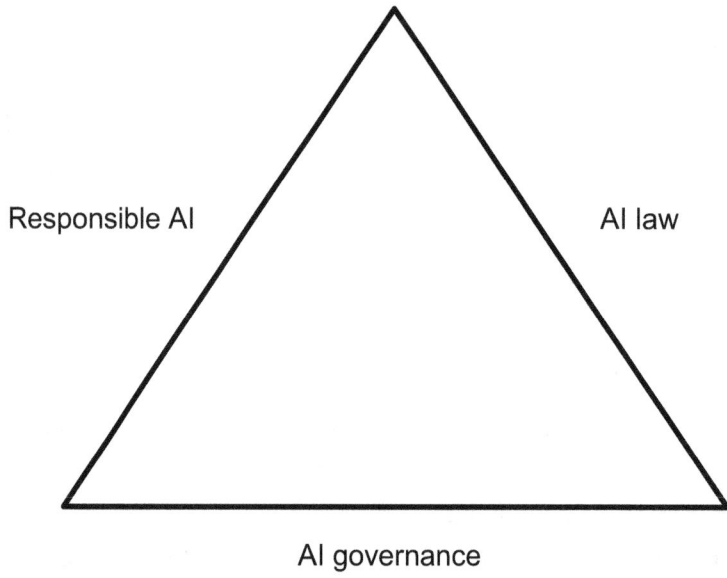

Figure 1-1. *Emerging AI disciplines*

The first discipline is *responsible AI*. **This entails developing and using AI in a way that is consistent with principles and ethics such as security and safety, privacy, explainability and transparency, fairness, robustness, and accountability—all of which will be comprehensively fleshed out in this book with a chapter devoted to each.** Two well-known international documents of ethical AI principles are the UNESCO Recommendation on the Ethics of AI and the European Commission's Ethics Guidelines for Trustworthy AI.

Organizations can align their practices with responsible AI by designing their own ethical AI frameworks and guidelines. Given the speed of AI development and given that AI regulations may or may not clearly apply to their specific situation, ethical AI frameworks can provide stakeholders with necessary guidance (Benraouane, p. 69), and to a certain degree, prevent the incidents described in the previous section. However, the limitation of ethical AI frameworks is that they are often too high-level and insufficiently precise, which is not particularly helpful for organizations seeking to handle cases which are not clear-cut.

The second discipline is *AI law*, which includes international, regional, and domestic laws and regulations pertaining to the development and use of AI. Legal compliance in this context entails ensuring that your organization's practices abide by these laws and regulations. Laws and regulations are usually more concrete than nebulous ethical AI principles and frameworks, with clearly stipulated enforcement bodies and penalties for non-compliance. However, this field faces a couple of limitations.

One limitation is the difficulty of international coordination about what is a relatively new technology (notwithstanding the history of AI dating back to the early 1950s at Dartmouth). The development and use of AI is largely unconstrained by national borders or industries (export controls on the hardware for AI is the exception to this rule). Laws and regulations are largely specific to domestic legal jurisdictions, hence ineffective in anticipating and addressing challenges and incidents resulting from AI use, misuse and abuse. As the next chapter will demonstrate, attempts at multilateral treaties have faced challenges in adoption, and countries have a long way to go in developing bilateral treaty arrangements on AI coordination (as compared to other inter-state issues like extradition of criminals), given the relative newness of AI.

Another limitation is the difficulty of enacting timely legislation to effectively respond to the exponential rate of progress and innovation in AI. This is due to several factors—one being bureaucratic delays, which the European Union has been criticized for in its enacting of EU regulations and directives on the changing digital landscape. Another is the competency gap: not all regional and national legislatures have trained experts on a wide range of AI-related subjects (bearing in mind the multi-disciplinary nature of AI). This impedes the ability of regulators to either amend the existing legal frameworks on AI-adjacent subjects such as privacy and non-discrimination, or design new guardrails which would sufficiently address AI challenges.

A particularly notable limitation is political divisiveness. AI is an extremely political subject, given that the development and use of AI would ostensibly increase mass unemployment and widen the wealth disparities between states and within states. Both California's AI Safety Bill SB-1047 (which was previously passed but vetoed) and the recent One Big Beautiful Bill Act (which previously imposed a 10-year moratorium on state-level AI regulation that has since been withdrawn) have attracted fierce debate.

AI governance

The third emerging discipline is *AI governance*. It is best described as a system to deal with the AI system. An AI system is defined in the EU AI Act (a regulation you will see many times in this book) as "a machine-based system that is designed to operate with varying levels of autonomy and that may exhibit adaptiveness after deployment, and that, for explicit or implicit objectives, infers, from the input it receives, how to generate outputs such as predictions, content, recommendations, or decisions that can influence physical or virtual environments" (Article 3(1)).

AI governance sets up checks and balances for these systems, providing for their proper planning, design, development, deployment - the main stages of the AI life cycle (Figure 1-2).

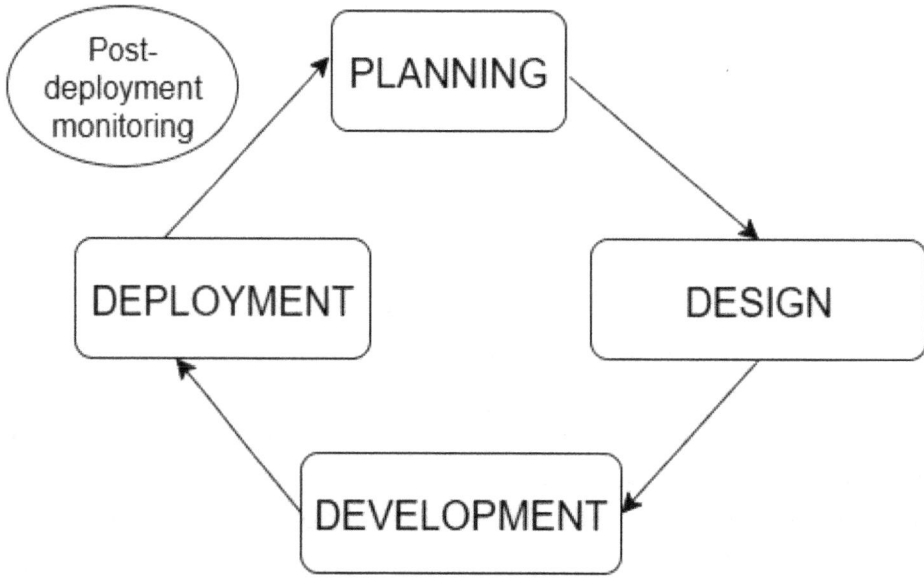

Figure 1-2. *The complete AI life cycle*

Throughout all this, there would have to be sufficient human oversight (such as regular updates, audits and evaluations, and monitoring), and regular engagement with the necessary stakeholders (such as employees, customers, vendors, and enforcement agencies). These AI governance processes ensure alignment.

These AI governance processes also ensure that AI systems operate safely and ethically. Hence, AI governance is distinct from—yet inextricably linked with—responsible AI and AI law. While responsible AI is the ultimate goal, AI governance codifies its processes in laws and regulations, and also non-binding principles, frameworks and standards. AI governance is hence broader than AI law, and organizations (especially multi-national corporations) can design an AI governance program that applies throughout their offices in various legal jurisdictions. Yet AI governance simultaneously ensures that the AI system complies with AI law. **The relationship between the three disciplines—responsible AI, AI law and AI governance—will be fleshed out throughout the course of this book.**

Non-binding frameworks and standards are less nebulous than ethical AI principles and provide stakeholders with the necessary guidance to operationalize AI governance. An important AI framework document is the NIST AI Risk Management Framework. (In contrast, standards provide not just technical specifications but also objective thresholds and benchmarks for organizational performance to be assessed against - whether by their own employees or external stakeholders. For a relatively new technology like AI which brings about a whole range of risks and much distrust, standards provide quality assurance, consistency, and trustworthiness - not only for your organization developing or using the AI system but its stakeholders too. **And as this book will demonstrate, standards allow organizations to demonstrate compliance with laws and regulations in different legal jurisdictions.**

Summary and Key Takeaways

This chapter has provided the necessary context of this book by highlighting the economic risks posed by AI to your organization, both legal (direct economic loss) and reputational (indirect economic loss), It has outlined three emerging disciplines which have developed in response to the increasing threats created by AI: responsible AI, AI law, and AI governance—and elaborated on what AI governance constitutes, which includes non-binding standards. **One standard in particular, ISO 42001, will be the focus of this book.** It is this standard that I shall now draw your attention to.

Reference

Sid Ahmed Benraouane, *AI Management System Certification According to the ISO/IEC 42001 Standard* (Productivity Press, 2024).

CHAPTER 2

ISO 42001: THE STANDARD

In this chapter, I discuss the standard that is the subject of this book: ISO/IEC 42001:2023 (which this book will refer to as ISO 42001 for ease of reference).

Organizations

ISO/IEC 42001:2023 is co-published by both the ISO and IEC and developed by member states of the ISO/IEC JTC 1 SC 42. If these acronyms are unfamiliar to you, no worries—I will briefly cover these organizations before turning to the standard itself.

(a) ISO stands for the International Organization for Standardization. ISO is an international non-governmental organization which independently publishes international standards, and which is made up of representatives from national standards development organizations of its member states. It is the member states and not ISO itself which draft the standards through participating in technical committees. ISO has published over 25000 standards to not only ensure safety, quality control and consumer protection, but also promote innovation and process improvement for a wide range of products and services, across a wide range of sectors and industries.

(b) IEC stands for International Electrotechnical Commission. Like ISO, IEC is also headquartered in Geneva, Switzerland and is an international non-governmental organization which independently develops and publishes international standards with the aim of balancing technological advancement and innovation with safety and sustainability. However, IEC focuses specifically on electrical and electronic technologies.

(c) ISO/IEC Joint Technical Committee 1 was jointly established by both ISO and IEC to develop standards in the fields of information technology (IT) and information and communications technology (ICT). The JTC 1's aim is to ensure that technological innovations in these fields are aligned with global norms regarding security and data privacy. Its Sub-Committee 42 is a specialized body which decides on the roadmap for future standardization in AI, and has published many international standards on AI, most notably:

- ISO/IEC 22989, which elaborates on the foundational concepts and terminology regarding AI and machine learning, including the AI life cycle discussed above.

- ISO/IEC 23894, which provides guidelines on managing risks related to AI applications.

- ISO/IEC 42005, which is a recently released guidance standard on assessing the impact of AI systems.

Standard

Overview

In contrast to the previous standards, ISO/IEC 42001:2023 is the first (and only) management system standard for AI, which over 100 ISO/IEC member states participated in developing—in collaboration with a wide range of external stakeholders: small-medium enterprises, academia, and civil society. A management system is a system of organizational elements that relate and interact with each other to put in place processes and responsibilities necessary to achieve its objectives—in this case, those related to AI. The year at the end of the standard indicates that the current version of the standard was published in 2023.

This standard can be tailored to and used by any organization which develops, provides, or uses products or services that involve AI, regardless of the organization's size (even sole proprietors) or industry (from technology companies to government agencies) or legal jurisdiction. (As the sub-section on controls below will demonstrate, developers are likelier than users to find the implementation and maintenance of ISO 42001 complex, given that more of the controls would be applicable.) By embedding responsible AI considerations (such as security, privacy, transparency and explainability, fairness, reliability and accountability) into AI governance and ensuring both human oversight over AI systems and reporting/complaint mechanisms, the main objective of ISO 42001 as a voluntary standard is to provide best practices for organizations to develop, provide, or use AI products and services in an ethical way while also meeting their strategic objectives efficiently.

The standard is structured as follows: The requirements of the standard are laid out in the 10 clauses. There are four annexes. The first two annexes include the controls—Annex A listing them and Annex B providing guidance on their implementation. Annex C includes potential AI related organizational objectives and sources of risks, and Annex D focuses on the applicability of AI management systems to various industries.

Clauses

The first three clauses (1. Scope, 2. Normative References, 3. Terms and Definitions) are self-explanatory: they lay out the scope and definitions of the standard. In particular, Clause 2 refers to the previously mentioned standard, ISO 22989, which defines the concepts and terminology used in ISO 42001, provides a conceptual framework of the processes in AI systems, and briefly discusses the ethical considerations of AI. Hence, these two standards complement each other with a slight overlap. However, ISO 22989 is a guidance standard, unlike ISO 42001 which is a certifiable standard (the next section will discuss certification), and the next seven clauses (4-10) are mandatory requirements (indicated by the word "shall") for organizations seeking to be certified under ISO 42001. These requirements are generic and only provide the "what", not the "how"—such that each organization will have to decide how to interpret these clauses to implement the standard. While the clauses most relevant to the book will be fleshed out in Chapter 3, a brief, high-level summary of each clause/requirement is as follows:

- Context (clause 4) lists both internal and external AI-related factors for your organization to take into account. Specifically, it must decide on its role - whether it is a developer or deployer or even another participant (like an importer or distributor) of AI systems. It must also determine who its stakeholders are and what they need.

- Leadership (clause 5) requires your organization to establish policies on the roles and responsibilities of your organization's management team, thereby ensuring their commitment.

- Planning (clause 6) requires that organizations define their AI-related objectives and establish their processes for both risk management, which entails identifying, assessing and treating risks, and impact assessments, which entail assessing the effects of the AI system on various stakeholders (individuals, groups, society at large, the environment).

- Support (clause 7) mandates that your organization has the necessary resources, ensures that its employees involved in AI governance has met the necessary competency requirements in the form of qualifications and awareness training, and establishes proper internal and external communication channels.

- Operation (clause 8) details the operational requirements of the two processes listed in Clause 6: risk management and impact assessment, and requires documentation of these processes.

- Evaluation (clause 9) requires your organization to monitor, measure, analyze, and evaluate the performance of the AI management system, including through internal audits and periodic reviews - according to its own metrics.

- Improvement (clause 10) ensures continual enhancement of the AI management system to achieve its purpose of balancing its strategic objectives with responsible AI.

Controls

To be fully compliant with ISO 42001 and obtain the certification, your organization must implement not only the 7 requirements above but also the controls from Annex A that are applicable to your organization. There are a total of 38 controls in Annex A, structured in nine categories. Given that not every single one of these controls will necessarily apply to your organization, your organization should come up with a Statement of Applicability listing which controls it applied, excluded, and explanations for such exclusions. Your organization is also free to include additional controls as part of its AI management system. Documentation and record-keeping are essential for the implementation of the controls (and the standard more broadly). While the controls most relevant to the book will be fleshed out in Chapter 3, a brief, high-level summary of each category of controls is as follows:

- AI policies (A2). Your organization should establish policies relating to AI development and use.

- Internal organization (A3). Your organization should define the roles and responsibilities, for example regarding incident response and the AI system's impact on your organization.

- Resources (A4). Your organization should map out the resources necessary for the whole AI life cycle, in regard to expertise, hardware, software, and data.

- Impact assessment (A5). Your organization should establish and document the process of assessing the impact of the AI system on various stakeholders (individuals, groups, society at large, and the environment).

- AI system life cycle (A6). Throughout the AI development life cycle (planning, design, development and deployment), organizations should keep the necessary technical documentation while ensuring that the AI management system is functioning as intended.

- Data (A7). Your organizations should put in place a data governance process, which covers data acquisition and provenance, quality and preparation.

- Information for third parties (A8). Such information includes technical specifications and general notifications for users of the AI system.

- Use of AI systems (A9). Your organization can take into account a range of considerations as to whether to use an AI system, and should clarify what these considerations are and develop policies addressing them.

- Relationships with customers and others (A10). Your organization should assign responsibilities to relevant parties throughout the supply chain.

Approaches

ISO 42001 can be characterized by three approaches: process, risk-based, and harmonized (Figure 2-1).

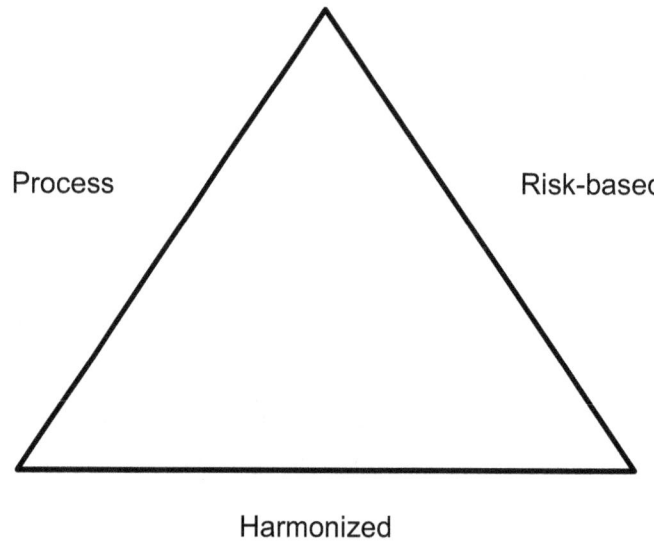

Figure 2-1. *ISO 42001's approaches*

Process Approach

Plan-Do-Check-Act is the basis of the process approach, whereby the PDCA cycle applies to all of the moving parts of the AI management system. This approach aims at continuous improvement of processes and measurable results. The Plan-Do-Check-Act cycle is not explicitly included in ISO 42001 itself, but the standard's clauses can be mapped onto the four distinct stages of this cycle (Figure 2-2).

CHAPTER 2 ISO 42001: THE STANDARD

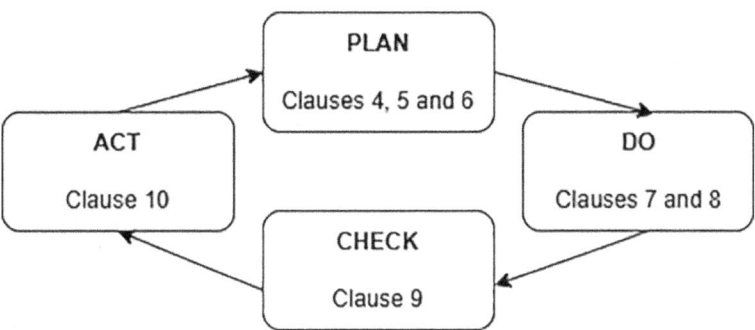

Figure 2-2. *The Plan-Do-Check-Act cycle*

The four parts are as follows:

1. Plan: Establishing the AI management system's scope, resources and objectives in response to stakeholders' concerns

2. Do: Carrying out the necessary steps, including implementing the relevant and appropriate controls

3. Check: Conducting internal audits and reviews to assess if stakeholders' concerns have been addressed

4. Act: Assessing results and refining processes with the aim of improving and maintaining the AI management system. The cycle of continual improvement repeats.

Risk-Based Approach

A risk-based approach is relevant throughout the above Plan-Do-Check-Act cycle. ISO 42001 incorporates risk management into AI governance, specifically requiring your organization to identify potential risks arising from the development and use of AI and to implement the necessary and relevant controls to address them. While ISO 42001 does not explicitly set out risk categories (unlike the EU AI Act as you shall see in the next chapter), the risk-based approach is inherent in its clauses/requirements - especially Clauses 6.1 (actions to address risks and opportunities), 8.2 (AI risk assessment) and 8.3 (AI risk treatment). ISO 31000 defines risk as the effect of uncertainty on one's objectives, with such a deviation being positive or negative.

CHAPTER 2   ISO 42001: THE STANDARD

Harmonized Approach

The harmonized approach is the common feature of all ISO management system standards. This means that ISO 42001's clauses and sub-clauses share the same high-level structure, titles and common text, including terminology and requirements, as other ISO management system standards. For example, compare ISO 42001 with 27001 (the information security management system standard): similar harmonized structure, annex containing a list of controls with the Statement of Applicability required. Where the standards differ is in the inclusion of topic-specific additions to or deviations from the core text—that are deemed necessary to satisfy the scope of the respective standards.

For example, ISO 42001 contains impact assessment requirements, that are not included in ISO 27001 because these are specific to AI. Further, ISO 42001 includes in Annex B guidance on the implementation of its controls listed in Annex A; whereas such guidance in the case of ISO 27001 is included in an entirely separate standard: ISO 27002. The purpose of the harmonized approach is to ensure consistency of the ISO management system standards, and to simplify the integration of various management systems (AI, information security, and others) into their existing operational infrastructure, thereby enhancing their effectiveness and efficiency.

Solution?

There are three ways in which implementation of ISO 42001 enables your organization to address the economic risks discussed in the first chapter. There, I categorized economic loss as direct and indirect. ISO 42001 implementation helps an organization avoid direct economic loss in the form of penalties (including sanctions, fines and injunctions) for non-compliance with AI regulations. **This book will primarily focus on how ISO 42001 is aligned with and provides a structured framework supporting an organization's efforts to ensure regulatory compliance prior to being assessed or even investigated by enforcement bodies conducting conformity assessments.** Reducing legal risks also reduces economic risks.

Second, as mentioned at the start of the chapter, even when an organization is not in breach of any regulations, its mishandling of AI risks can also result in reputational damage and hence indirect economic loss. ISO 42001 incorporates the ethical principles of privacy, security and safety, fairness, transparency and explainability, robustness and accountability—all into its AI governance system, thereby helping organizations manage the whole range of AI risks related to the aforementioned ethical principles, ensuring compliance with not just legal standards but also ethical standards.

Third, ISO 42001 certification goes beyond implementation and compliance, and goes beyond helping an organization address economic risks to even providing economic benefits for your organization. ISO 42001 is a "Type A" standard which allows organizations to be certified by an accredited third party, with such a certification evidencing that your organization satisfies the requirements of the standard. ISO 42001 is also a management system standard, stipulating requirements for both management and governance regarding AI; it does not include requirements specific to products or services or technologies and cannot be used to certify these.

How ISO 42001 certification works is as follows. Auditors of a third party certification body (preferably accredited by an established accreditation body part of the International Accreditation Foundation) conduct an initial certification audit. The auditor provides the findings. After the non-conformities have been addressed, your organization's management is deemed certified, and your organization receives a certificate valid for three years, during which annual surveillance audits are conducted, and after which your organization can seek recertification. The certificate can be suspended or withdrawn if the certification body finds out (perhaps through complaints received) that your organization's AI management system is non-compliant with ISO 42001 or if your organization misses its annual surveillance audits.

Trust is in limited and decreasing supply in the age of AI-generated misinformation, disinformation and deepfakes. ISO 42001 certification by an external, accredited third party validates that your organization is committed to responsible AI practices. Such enhancement of trust attracts customers, business partners and investments.

Summary and Key Takeaways

This chapter has expounded on the essential elements of ISO 42001, co-published by ISO and IEC and developed by the ISO/IEC JTC 1 SC 42. It has outlined the structure of the standard, broken down into its clauses (which are mandatory requirements) and controls in Annexes A and B, where controls may either be applicable or excluded with justification. This standard is characterized by its process, risk-based, and harmonized approaches. Finally, this chapter has explained the several ways in which ISO 42001 implementation and certification will help your organization reduce economic risks. The next chapter will examine the relationship between ISO 42001 and the law.

CHAPTER 3

ISO 42001 AND THE LAW

Given that this book is on ISO 42001's relationship with legal compliance, this chapter provides the background on ISO's relationship with the law in general and starts with a discussion of ISO 42001's legal status.

The Legal Status of ISO 42001

ISO 42001 is a voluntary standard published by a non-governmental organization with an international membership, and does not have the status of law and is not legally binding.

However, some international law (and, to a lesser extent, domestic law) scholars consider several types of documents to constitute "soft law." Several have suggested that ISO standards are in fact international "soft law", with examples such as ISO 14001 as the environmental governance soft law standard (Conglianese, 2020) and ISO 26000 for corporate social responsibility (Sheehy, Tuslian and Lie, 2021). Can the same be said of ISO 42001?

ISO's mission is to connect people, groups and countries to form a global consensus regarding emerging technologies, bridging national and regional regulatory differences. The ISO/IEC JTC 1 SC 42 is perhaps one of the only international bodies (if not the only one) made up of a broad range of 39 participating members from different countries, including major players in AI such as both the US and China, and several EU states and smaller countries like Singapore. Because ISO 42001 is developed from the process of consensus-seeking and harmonization, there is a strong case for this standard to be deemed international "soft law".

Contrast that with a more clear-cut case of binding international law. Article 38(1) of the Statute of the International Court of Justice lists treaties as one of the sources of international law. The Council of Europe Framework Convention on Artificial Intelligence is the first international legally binding treaty on AI which aims to "ensure that activities within the life cycle of artificial intelligence systems are fully consistent with human rights, democracy and the rule of law" (Article 1(1)). It currently has 17 signatories (including the EU) but its signatory base is far less diverse than the membership base of the ISO/IEC JTC 1 SC 42, largely comprising Western states (and Japan). Far less specific than ISO 42001, this framework convention is very high-level, with just the Conference of the Parties as the dispute resolution mechanism (Article 23).

Moreover, this treaty holds states accountable for what private organizations do (long accepted under human rights doctrine) but not for anything related to national defense (Article 4), making it simple for states to claim that all of their activities in the AI race are covered by their national defense interests. If anything, this treaty's impact is indirect, where individuals in states which are parties to the European Convention of Human Rights (ECHR, which is also a Council of Europe treaty) can bring AI-related cases before the European Court of Human Rights, which has the mandate to rule on the interpretation of ECHR provisions; those ECHR cases would probably refer to this new treaty and extend the interpretation of its provisions, and national courts in these member states may then rely on such interpretations in their rulings. As you will see in this book, ISO 42001's impact is more concrete.

The next two sections of this chapter tease out the symbiotic relationship between ISO 42001 and the law (Figure 3-1). On one hand, consideration of the applicable legal requirements is necessary for ISO 42001 implementation and certification. On the other hand, ISO 42001 implementation itself helps an organization with compliance with the law.

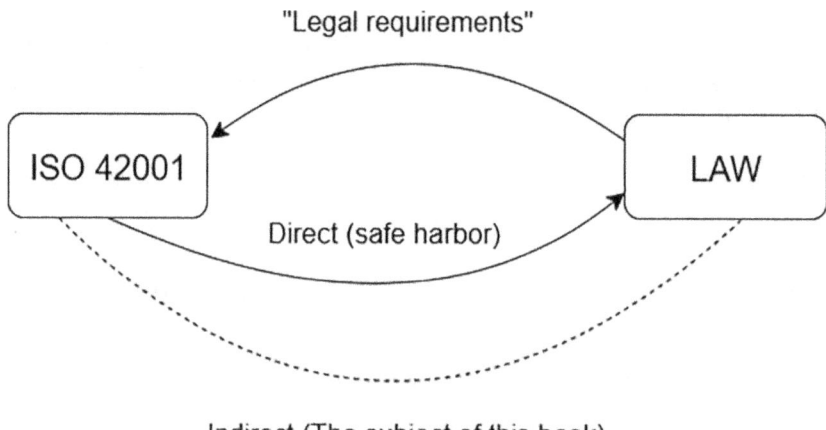

Figure 3-1. *The symbiotic relationship between ISO 42001 and the law*

Law —> ISO 42001

This section expounds on the portions of the ISO 42001 implementation process where legal considerations will feature. The substantive content of the "legal requirements", the applicable regulatory provisions, that are mentioned in the relevant clauses and controls of the standard, are elaborated on in the rest of this book. What this section does is to explain the surrounding contexts of such instances.

Organization's External Context (Clause 4.1 Note 2a)

When considering both the internal and external issues relevant to your organization's objectives and its ability to ensure that its AI management system functions, your organization must understand the potential liability specific to its use of AI as a new technology. This means taking into account the applicable laws (including specific restrictions or prohibitions on AI development or use), and supporting documents issued by the regulatory authorities (e.g. administrative decisions, executive policies, guidance frameworks) concerning these laws, their enforcement and interpretation.

In practice, given the significant impact of AI on many industries and aspects of our lives, organizations would have to account for a wide range of legal consequences: from outsourcing work to third party vendors, to climate change. This clause notably requires organizations to determine the relevance of climate change. Given the increasing energy consumption and cooling of data centers inherent in AI development, organizations may be under greater regulatory scrutiny in relation to environmental laws - sustainability in general, and, more specifically, reporting of carbon emissions.

Relevant interested parties' requirements (Clause 4.2)

Related to the previous requirement of context examination is the determination of the "interested parties" relevant to your organization's AI management system. Who affects the AI management system? Who is affected (or thinks they are affected) by the AI management system? And what do they need and expect from your organization? Both lawmakers and regulators enforcing these laws are clearly external "interested parties," both imposing specific legal obligations on these organizations, and providing other stakeholders with rights which can be enforced against these organizations, such as rights of redress for violations of data privacy and non-discrimination.

CHAPTER 3   ISO 42001 AND THE LAW

Further, in the overall assessment of whether—and which of—the requirements of all of your organization's "interested parties" would be addressed by your organization's AI management system, the legal compliance obligations (outlined in the rest of the book) will probably be a key factor, as you will see in the rest of this section.

Determination of risks and opportunities based on external context (Clause 6.1.1)

Hence, lawmakers and regulators, as "interested parties", are significant in shaping the risks and opportunities of the development and use of AI. This is bolstered by your organization being required, at the AI management system planning stage, to identify the risks and opportunities of its AI management system based on the external context (which includes the legal context, as previously discussed).

There are, of course, a whole range of risks and opportunities. In particular, regulatory non-compliance is, in itself, a substantial risk for your organization. On the spectrum where we have civil wrongs on one end and criminal wrongs on the other hand, such non-compliance is deemed less civil (involving two private parties, with the aggrieved one seeking redress) and more criminal (where the state punishes the wrongdoer for the harm adjudged to have affected society at large, and that condemnation contains a moral message). Such a non-compliance finding (and accompanying penalty) in turn carries reputational risks for your organization. The changes in the applicable regulations, which strive to adapt to the changes in the technology, increase the uncertainty, thereby adding to the risks.

Employee awareness of non-compliance (Clause 7.3)

Your organization's employees are required to be made aware of and understand their roles and responsibilities regarding the AI management system. This entails your employees understanding the implications of not complying with the AI management system's requirements - and this also includes the applicable legal standards. This is crucial given that an organization can be liable for the acts of its employees; it can, for example, be sued for discrimination if its employees do not abide by the relevant anti-discrimination laws when using AI-powered tools for hiring or approvals, resulting in unfair outcomes. So, the awareness requirement can be addressed by not only monitoring regulatory changes and consulting with the in-house legal team or external lawyers from the early stages, but also by conducting role-specific training educating relevant employees (like risk managers) on what is required of the AI management system to comply with the applicable regulations.

Internal audit (Clause 9.2.1)

This subsection focuses on where legal considerations apply to internal audits; the details of how internal audits are to be conducted for ISO management systems are elaborated on in ISO 19011. Internal audits are to be conducted at planned intervals decided by your organization (possibly longer or shorter than a year) and by an impartial auditor (possibly an employee) who cannot audit processes which involved them directly. The internal audit is intended to assess compliance with your organization's own requirements for its AI management system - and as stated in the previous paragraph, these can include the applicable legal standards. For example, if your organization intends to audit its regulatory compliance, the AI regulations of the legal jurisdiction your organization is in serve as additional criteria for the internal audit. As compared to other functions like marketing, regulatory compliance has a more significant impact on the AI management system and should thus require more frequent and extensive internal audits.

AI policy (Clause 5.2) - and its documentation (Control A.2.2) and review (Control A.2.4)

Your organization must have an AI policy defining how the AI management system is incorporated into its operations. Implementation Guidance B.2.2 mentions that a portion of the AI policy is to elaborate on how your organization meets the necessary requirements, which includes legal requirements which apply to your organization.

The documentation of the AI policy entails listing all of the applicable laws and regulations—in their most updated form. If your organization cannot meet those obligations (either temporarily or permanently), it should provide details on how it can handle such exceptions, the risks of such non-compliance and the necessary controls to be implemented to address those risks, and the roles and responsibilities of the relevant parties such as the legal/compliance team (discussed in the next control below). More broadly, the AI policy should also include the principles (such as privacy and transparency) necessary to support your organization in its compliance with its legal requirements.

It is important for your organization to periodically review its AI policy at a planned interval of its choice to assess its continued effectiveness, relevance to and alignment with your organization and its AI management system. Bearing in mind how the legal landscape changes relatively quickly in response to technological changes in AI and its adjacent disciplines (such as privacy and cybersecurity, and emerging technologies like quantum computing), such developments may require updates to the list of applicable laws and regulations or even other sections in the AI policy.

Defining roles and responsibilities in your organization (Control A.3.2)

Implementation Guidance B.3.2 explicitly lists the fulfillment of legal requirements as a specific area requiring your organization to define roles and responsibilities. This is where legal/compliance teams are clearly involved. Outside of this specific objective, defining roles and responsibilities for the effective management of AI systems throughout the AI life cycle and regularly re-assessing and updating these roles and responsibilities would support your organization in adapting to the changing legal landscape and ensure continued compliance with applicable laws and regulations. And outside of legal/compliance teams, other roles in your organization are relevant in ensuring legal compliance - for example, privacy and data protection roles in ensuring compliance with laws like the GDPR.

AI system impact assessment (Clause 8.4) - and its process (Control A.5.2) and documentation (Control A.5.3)

Your organization should conduct impact assessments of its AI system(s) either periodically at a planned interval of its choice, or when key changes are anticipated. These changes could include the coming into force of new regulations (such as the fundamental rights impact assessment requirement in the EU AI Act), or when the purpose of your organization's AI system itself has changed, such that its new legal implications warrant a re-assessment of its compliance with relevant legal standards. Even without these changes, it is nonetheless good practice for AI system impact assessments to be performed by your organization prior to its risk assessments, given that the findings of the impact assessment enable a more thorough assessment of legal risks.

Establishing the process of the AI system impact assessment entails defining the roles and responsibilities of key personnel—which should include legal/compliance officers.

Implementation Guidance B.5.2 highlights both the legal status of individuals and human rights as key factors for consideration when assessing the potential consequences of the AI system. This is especially relevant to industries like the immigration and criminal justice system where AI algorithms in automated decision-making tools can incorrectly profile individuals (which results in dire consequences), and/or do so in an improper way (which raises questions about accountability, transparency and fairness).

Your organization should retain the results of the AI system impact assessment as documentation. The details of such retention (including the duration of retention) may be governed by the applicable laws. Those should be reflected in your organization's data retention policy.

AI system life cycle (Control A.6.2) - specifying and documenting requirements (Control A.6.2.2), operation and monitoring (Control A.6.2.6), and event log recording (Control A.6.2.8)

Your organization should define the requirements for AI systems which are new or undergoing major changes, and should cover the entire life cycle. These requirements may include legal requirements. To ensure not only alignment with your organization's AI policy but also its compliance with legal regulations, the AI system's requirements should also be reviewed if legal concerns which surface during certain phases of the AI life cycle (such as development or testing) render the originally established AI system requirements infeasible or improper.

Related to specification and documentation, monitoring the system entails ensuring compliance with legal requirements and providing necessary updates for that purpose. Changes in the legal landscape (such as newly enacted data protection laws) should warrant updates to the system to ensure its continued legal compliance.

Finally, as per Implementation Guidance B.6.2.8, the applicable legal requirements concerning data retention would govern the keeping of records of event logs in the AI system life cycle. These should be reflected in your organization's data retention policy.

Determining and documenting how the data is obtained (A.7.3)

The purpose of this control is to ensure that organizations understand the data's history and provenance and ensure that its use in the AI system (including for the development of AI models) abides by both ethical and legal requirements regarding data use. Implementation Guidance B.7.3 suggests including details on prior use of the data, and on whether (re)use of such data complies with privacy and security laws. This necessarily entails examining whether, at the time the data was collected, the data subject's consent for such (re)use was obtained, or/and whether such collection/(re)use was provided for under contract. Implementation Guidance B.7.3 also suggests taking into account the rights of individuals if the data is determined to contain personally identifiable information of data subjects or copyrighted material of third parties; in such instances, specific legal obligations apply, such as obtaining consent or a license.

Reporting to stakeholders - generally (Control A.8.5) and specifically for incidents (Control A.8.4)

The reporting obligations of your organization regarding its AI system are likely to be shaped by the applicable laws in its jurisdiction. These laws require the sharing of information with necessary parties including regulatory and law enforcement authorities, usually with specific requirements as to the format, content, and timelines. High-risk AI systems in particular are likely to require the submission of technical documentation (concerning data use, model training, and other details) to regulators prior to deployment of such systems. This would require legal/compliance teams to coordinate with technical teams. All of these requirements should be determined and documented by your organization.

A crucial subset of such reporting obligations is incident reporting, which requires organizations to have a plan in place. The AI system (be it an autonomous vehicle system or medical classification system) may malfunction or behave unpredictably or indicate larger ethical concerns (such as privacy breaches). Again, the applicable laws of your organization's jurisdiction may stipulate requirements regarding the format, content and timelines of such reporting - not just to regulatory or law enforcement authorities but especially the users of the AI system. Such accountability is a key aspect of your organization's credibility and reputation regarding responsible AI.

Ensuring that the use of AI systems is both responsible (Control A.9.2) and as intended (Control A.9.4)

As part of the responsible use of AI, your organization should clarify its considerations in deciding whether to use an AI system. Implementation Guidance B.9.2 lists applicable legal requirements as one such consideration in such a decision. Depending on the jurisdiction and industry (especially heavily regulated industries like healthcare), regulatory approval or other compliance requirements (such as the reporting requirements mentioned above) may apply prior to and throughout deployment of AI systems. Your organization should establish policies for addressing such considerations, which may include approval by the legal/compliance team.

As per Implementation Guidance B.9.4, your organization should monitor the operation and use of the AI system (by your organization and its users) to ensure strict alignment with the AI system's purpose as reflected in its technical specifications and user instructions. This should entail human oversight in order to reduce a range of risks, including legal risks; excluding such human oversight may lead to greater liability exposure. If the appropriate use of the AI system as intended raises legal concerns (such as potential violation of non-discrimination laws), the relevant parties, such as the legal/compliance team and the third-party vendor, should be informed. Finally, the applicable legal requirements concerning data retention would govern the AI use documentation. These should be reflected in your organization's data retention policy.

ISO 42001 —> Law

There are two ways in which ISO 42001 implementation and certification can contribute to legal compliance: direct contribution ("safe harbor") and indirect contribution.

Direct contribution: Safe harbor

The most direct way is through "safe harbor" provisions in the law. Colorado is the first US state to enact comprehensive legislation on AI. This legislation enters into force on 30 June 2026. It provides that, in the event that Colorado's Attorney General commences an enforcement action under the legislation, a developer or deployer can raise the affirmative defense that it discovered and cured a violation through (1) feedback that the developer, deployer, or other persons encouraged others to provide, or (2) adversarial testing or red teaming (as defined by the National Institute of Standards and Technology) or (3) an internal review process, and is also in compliance with both the NIST AI Risk Management Framework and ISO 42001 (Section 6-1-1706). Further, the legislation requires deployers of high-risk AI systems to implement a risk management policy and program which must be "reasonable" when considering ISO 42001 as one of the standards (Section 6-1-1703, 2(I)(A)).

CHAPTER 3 ISO 42001 AND THE LAW

Indirect contribution: the subject of this book

In the following chapters, you will see how ISO 42001 indirectly helps organizations (especially multinational corporations with operations across legal jurisdictions) comply with the changing legal landscape regarding AI. The following chapters will focus on the specific legal provisions and how ISO 42001 relates to them. Here, a brief list of the regulations covered in this book would provide the necessary context.

EU AI Act: This landmark legislation is the first comprehensive AI legislation in the world, intended to provide certainty while enabling innovation, and ensure the development and deployment of trustworthy AI that respects fundamental rights. It was published in the EU's Official Journal in July 2024, entered into force on 1 August 2024 and will be fully applicable on 1 August 2026, with several exceptions: prohibitions and AI literacy obligations entered into application from 2 February 2025; rules regarding governance and general-purpose AI models obligations apply from 2 August 2025 onwards; rules regarding high-risk AI systems have until 2 August 2027 an extended transition. This legislation is extraterritorial, applying not only to providers and deployers in the EU but also to providers and distributors outside the EU if their AI system is in the EU, and providers and deployers outside the EU if their AI system's output may be used in the EU.

Organizations that enjoy an exemption from the legislation include non-professional organizations, military and national security organizations, international organizations, public authorities in non-EU countries, and research and development agencies for non-commercial, public and private reasons, open-source AI software that is not high-risk and not prohibited. The EU AI Act adopts a risk-based approach, defining risk as the severity of harm combined with the probability of occurrence (Article 3.2), and identifies four risk levels: 1. Unacceptable risk and prohibited, 2. High risk, 3. Limited risk, and 4. minimal risk. The obligations for developers and deployers depend on the risk levels their product or system falls under, and much of the legislation focuses on high-risk systems.

General Data Protection Act: The GDPR was adopted in May 2018, as a comprehensive regulation on data privacy in the EU and European Economic Area, focusing on the collection and use of personal data, which is information regarding identified or identifiable natural persons. Like the EU AI Act, it has extraterritorial reach and is risk-based. It is intended to be technology-agnostic to adapt to emerging technologies like AI and quantum computing, and defines many concepts relevant to AI systems.

Digital Services Act: An EU regulation seeking to update the Electronic Commerce Directive 2000 regarding illegal content, transparent advertising, and disinformation. It was adopted by the European Parliament and the Council of the European Union in October 2022 and came into force in November 2022. This regulation applies to online intermediaries and platforms, including marketplaces, social networks, content-sharing platforms, app stores, and online travel and accommodation platforms. The DSA overlaps with the GDPR regarding platform transparency, as you will see in the chapter on Transparency.

The other EU laws briefly touched upon in this book include the recently enforced EU Data Act and EU Cyber Resilience Act, Network and Information Security Directive 2, General Product Safety Regulation and Product Liability Directive.

The Chinese regulations covered in this book include the Provisions on the Management of Algorithmic Recommendations in Internet Information Services ("Algorithmic Recommendations Provisions"), the Provisions on the Administration of Deep Synthesis Internet Information Services ("Deep Synthesis Provisions"), the Interim Measures for the Management of Generative Artificial Intelligence Services ("Generative AI Interim Measures"), and the Measures for Labeling of AI-Generated Synthetic Content ("Content Labeling Measures") which have just recently entered into force.

One UK law will be briefly referred to by way of comparison: the UK Data (Use and Access) Act. Several US laws will be discussed in this book. At the federal level, we have Title VII of the Civil Rights Act prohibiting employment discrimination, Affordable Care Act, and Americans with Disabilities Act. At the state level, this book covers Colorado SB 205, the Texas Responsible AI Governance Act, California Generative AI Training Data Transparency Act, differentiated from California Transparency Act, California Bot Act, and Utah AI Policy Act. The New York City Local Law 144 is the only local-level law covered.

Summary and key takeaways

In this chapter, I have explained the different ways in which ISO 42001 related to the law in general, first by examining ISO 42001's legal status as a non-binding voluntary standard which arguably constitutes international "soft law" given how representative it is of the global consensus on responsible AI. I have then expounded on the symbiotic relationship between ISO 42001 and the law, where consideration of legal requirements is necessary for ISO 42001 implementation and certification, and where ISO 42001 implementation can contribute to your organization's compliance with the law—both directly (though "safe harbor" provisions) and indirectly—as I shall demonstrate in the following six chapters structured around the responsible AI principles of security and safety privacy, transparency and explainability, fairness, robustness, and accountability.

References

Cary Coglianese, "Environmental Soft Law as a Governance Strategy" (2020) 61 *Jurimetrics* 19-51.

Benedict Sheehy, Widya Tuslian and Luther Lie, "The Use of International Soft Law for Corporate Social Responsibility Reporting in the Retail Industry: A Study of Four Major Retailers in the Asia-Pacific" (2021) 18(1) *Canberra Law Review* 60-80.

CHAPTER 4

ACCOUNTABILITY

This chapter on accountability starts with a discussion of the principle of accountability and several related concepts, examines the applicable regulations, and analyzes the relevant ISO 42001 clauses and controls.

A. Principles

Accountability is the overarching principle in this book. This book covers six different principles, and accountability directly relates to the five others. Here, accountability involves the obligation to develop and use AI systems in a manner that is safe, secure, robust, fair, transparent, and explainable, while also protecting privacy.

ISO 42001 Annex C paragraph 2.1 lists accountability as an objective, noting that AI use can alter current frameworks of accountability, where individual actions determining one's accountability can be based upon or supported by AI use.

It is important to note that the principles in the remainder of this book, security and safety, privacy, fairness, transparency, and explainability, robustness, are listed in Annex C as objectives to be taken into account for both the responsible development controls in Annex A and the responsible use controls in Annex A. Annex C also lists the principles in this book as risk sources to be taken into account under Clause 6 of the ISO standard.

Several key concepts in accountability require further examination (Figure 4-1): 1. Oversight, 2. Assurance, 3. Contestability, and 4. Traceability of both input and output.

Chapter 4 Accountability

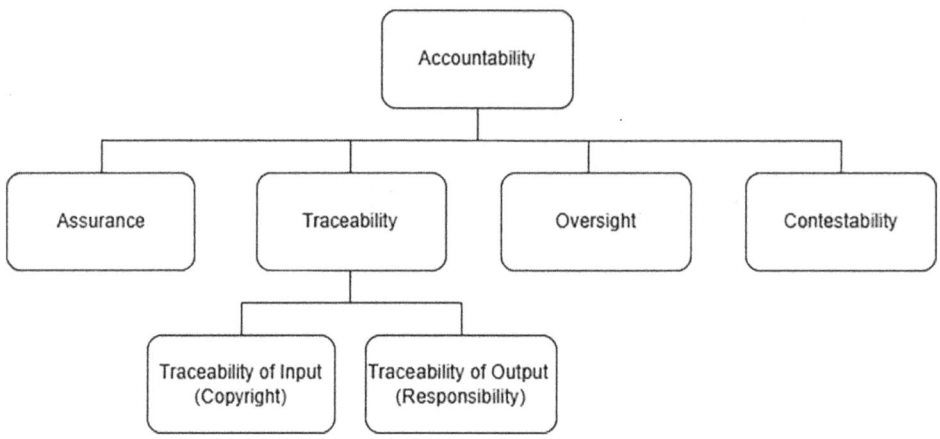

Figure 4-1. Accountability concepts

(1) Oversight

The point is that while AI systems can operate autonomously and produce outputs on their own, they should not control how human beings behave. Human beings should always exercise oversight over AI systems. The underlying concern of this principle of oversight is that of autonomy. Human autonomy is still valued, notwithstanding the increased autonomy with which AI systems operate. As such, AI systems should be developed in a human-centric way. Human beings should also monitor AI systems.

The concept of human-in-the-loop is relevant here. Human-in-the-loop refers to a scenario where an individual reviews the AI system's decision before it takes effect. By way of contrast, a human-on-the-loop is where the individual may choose to alter the outcome of the AI system where necessary. The human-out-of-the-loop system is where no human beings are involved in the AI system's process at all. Human-in-the-loop arrangements serve as critical oversight for the development and deployment of AI systems.

(2) Assurance

Related to oversight is this concept of assurance. AI assurance aims to evaluate and measure the performance of AI systems, thereby enhancing their trustworthiness and reliability. This includes various forms of assessments and audits: conformity assessments, risk assessments, impact assessments, internal audits, certification audits, and testing and validation in general. Section C (Practices) of this chapter outlines the various types of assurance measures specified in ISO 42001.

(3) Contestability

Another related concept to oversight is that of contestability. Contestability enables individuals to scrutinize the output of AI systems and challenge them to ensure that the systems are functioning as intended. This directly contributes to accountability. It is also linked to transparency. Transparency involves the communication of information from the organization creating the AI system or deploying it to the users. Contestability allows users to provide feedback to the organization regarding the AI system. This is crucial in high-risk AI systems. Therefore, if individuals wish to challenge the output of AI systems, they should be allowed to do so and provide feedback.

(4) Traceability of input - with copyright as a case study

Traceability relates to both input and output. When it comes to traceability of input, the focus is on the data fed into the AI system. The concept of provenance is key to understanding the traceability of data. This involves tracking the sequence of data ownership. Data provenance is concerned with the origin of the data, specifically how it was created. It maintains a record of who created the data and modified it. This ensures the validity and integrity of the data. This can be contrasted with data lineage. Data lineage is primarily concerned with the movement of data and how various data elements relate to one another. It focuses on the end-to-end data journey. This also relates to the traceability of data. A case study in the traceability of input, specifically the traceability of data, raises the issue of copyright law. When it comes to AI systems, the concern involves ownership of the input data that is fed into these systems.

In the context of AI, developers of AI systems often scrape data from the web. The question is whether such publicly available data is protected by copyright and whether training AI models on this data constitutes an infringement of the copyright. This is where data provenance is relevant. A historical record of the data, providing information about its origins, would address questions regarding whether such training data is protected by copyright or licensed to the developer of the AI system. Section B (Provisions) on legal provisions provides an in-depth explanation of copyright law.

(5) Traceability of output (Responsibility)

Regarding the traceability of output, concerns include responsibility and liability for harm caused by AI systems. The AI system's output should be traceable to a responsible party in the supply chain, allowing for the determination of exactly where the harm originated. Accountability involves assigning liability and responsibility to the correct individual, whether it is the third-party vendor, the AI provider, or the user. Every single link in the supply chain would need to be accounted for. Traceability of output is limited to the extent that the AI system is explainable. Explainability directly assists organizations in tracing the origin of harmful output by the AI system.

All of these concepts in accountability ensure that the AI systems operate as expected.

B. Provisions

This section covers the legal provisions related to the previously mentioned aspects of accountability: 1 Oversight, 2. Assurance, 3. Contestability, 4. Traceability of Input, and 5. Traceability of Output.

(1) Oversight

EU:

- **EU AI Act:** Article 14 requires human oversight for high-risk AI systems, with human operators well placed to disregard, override, or reverse any output of the AI system (Article 14(4)(d)), or even intervene and interrupt the system if necessary (Article 14(4)(e)) with a "kill switch". The aim is to minimize risks to health, safety, and fundamental rights (Article 14(1)), and the oversight measures should be "commensurate with the risks, levels of autonomy and context of use" of the AI system (Article 14(2)). This provision forms the basis of:
    1. Deployers' obligations to:
        a. Monitor high-risk AI systems based on the instructions of use (Article 26(1)); and

b. Assign human oversight to individuals with the "necessary" competence, training, authority, and support (Article 26(2)).

c. Providers' obligation to implement a post-market monitoring plan "in a manner that is proportionate to the nature of the AI technologies and the risks of the high-risk AI system" (Article 72(1)) to ensure the continuing safety of the high-risk AI system after deployment.

US:

- **Colorado SB 205:** The deployer is required to conduct:

  1. Regular and systematic reviews and updates of the risk management policy and program it has put in place "over the life cycle of a high-risk artificial intelligence system" (Section 6-1-1703 (2)(a)).

  2. Reviews of the deployment of each high-risk artificial intelligence system "at least annually" to ensure that the high-risk artificial intelligence system is not causing algorithmic discrimination (Section 6-1-1703 (3)(g)).

(2) Assurance

EU: The **EU AI Act** provides for several forms of AI assurance: conformity assessment, risk assessment and fundamental rights impact assessment.

a. Conformity assessment (Article 43):

- It is defined as the "process of demonstrating whether the requirements set out in Chapter III, Section 2 relating to a high-risk AI system have been fulfilled" (Article 3(20)). These include:

  - Risk management system (Article 9; discussed next in this sub-section)

  - Data and data governance (Article 10)

  - Technical documentation (Article 11)

  - Record keeping (Article 12)

CHAPTER 4   ACCOUNTABILITY

- Transparency and provision of information to deployers (Article 13)
- Human oversight (Article 14)
- Accuracy, robustness and cybersecurity (Article 15)

- Its purpose is to ensure a high level of trustworthiness before high-risk AI systems are placed on the EU market or put into service (Recital 123). Chapter III, Section 5 of the EU AI Act (entitled "Standards, Conformity Assessment, Certificates, Registration") details the procedures for the conformity assessment – and is included in the Appendix.

b. Risk assessment (part of the risk management system under Article 9):

- The high-risk AI system provider must establish and implement the risk management system - a "continuous iterative process planned and run throughout the entire lifecycle of a high-risk AI system" (Article 9(2)).
- The risk assessment involves identifying and analyzing known and reasonably foreseeable risks (Article 9(2)(a)) and estimating and evaluating them (Article 9(2)(b)-(c)). (Article 9(2)(d) discusses risk treatment which follows risk assessment.)

c. Fundamental rights impact assessment (Article 27):

- In contrast with risk assessments, fundamental rights impact assessments need only be conducted once prior to the deployment of the high-risk AI system by deployers of only a select group of high-risk AI systems: specifically bodies governed by public law or private entities providing public services (Article 27(1)) or AI systems intended to be used to evaluate the creditworthiness of natural persons or establish their credit score (except AI systems used for the purpose of detecting financial fraud), or intended to be used for risk assessment and pricing in relation to natural persons in the case of life and health insurance (Annex III, paras. 5(b)-(c)).

- At a minimum, fundamental rights impact assessments include:
    - individuals or groups likely to be affected (Article 27(1)(c));
    - specific risks of harm that are likely to affect them (Article 27(1)(d));
    - descriptions of the high-risk AI system's use (such as the frequency) (Article 27(1)(a));
    - human oversight measures and complaint mechanisms (Article 27(1)(e)).

US: Under Colorado SB 205,

- Deployers of high-risk AI systems must conduct both risk and impact assessments, whereby they must identify and document "reasonably foreseeable risks of algorithmic discrimination" as part of their risk management policy and program which is to be an "iterative process" (Section 6-1-1703 (2)(a)) with regular reviews and updates - as discussed in the above sub-section on Oversight).

- Specifically, they must conduct impact assessments "at least annually and within ninety days after any intentional and substantial modification to the high-risk artificial intelligence system is made available" (Section 6-1-1703 (3)(a)), with records of the impact assessments kept for at least three years post-deployment (Section 6-1-1703 (3)(f)) - in contrast to the EU AI Act.

(3) Contestability

EU:

- **EU AI Act:** If the output from a high-risk AI system "produces legal effects or similarly significantly affects individuals in a way that they consider to have an adverse impact on their health, safety or fundamental rights", such affected persons have the right to an explanation from the AI system's deployer, which entails clear and meaningful explanations of the AI system's role in the decision-making process and the main elements of the decision taken (Article 86(1)).

- **GDPR:** The data subject has the right of access to meaningful information from the data controller regarding the existence of automated decision-making (including profiling), the logic underpinning the automated decision, and the significance and envisaged consequences of such data processing for the data subject (Article 15(1)(h)). In such cases of automated individual decision-making (including profiling), the data subject retains the right to obtain intervention by the data controller, and to express their point of view and contest the decision (Article 22(3) and Recital 71).

China:

The following organizations are required to establish effective complaint mechanisms:

A. Algorithmic recommendation service providers (Article 22 of the Algorithm Recommendation Provisions)

B. Deep synthesis service providers (Article 12 of the Deep Synthesis Provisions)

C. Generative AI service providers (Article 15 of the Generative AI Interim Measures)

The obligations under these three legal provisions are the same:

1. Set up portals that make it convenient for the user to submit complaints or appeals;

2. Publicly disclose the process (including the time limits) for the handling of such complaints or appeals;

3. Accept and address the complaints and appeals;

4. Provide feedback on the outcome.

US:

- **Colorado SB 205:** Deployers of deploy high-risk AI systems that make or substantially contribute to a "consequential decision" that is "adverse to the consumer" must provide the consumer with the right of appeal in the form of human review if technically feasible, unless such an appeal is not in the consumer's best interests (such as potentially affecting their life or safety) (Section 6-1-1703(4)(b)(III)).

(4) Traceability of Input (Copyright)

EU: Under the **EU AI Act**,

- General-purpose AI model providers should "put in place a policy to comply with Union law on copyright and related rights" according to Recital 106 of the EU AI Act, which will be monitored by the EU AI Office (Recital 108).

- Article 53(1)(c) requires providers to comply with Article 4(3) of the EU Copyright Directive. Briefly:

    - Article 4(1) of the EU Copyright Directive allows for "reproductions and extractions of lawfully accessible works and other subject matter for the purposes of text and data mining".

    - Article 4(3) qualifies this by requiring that the use of such "works and other subject matter" has not be reserved by their rightsholders explicitly and appropriately, including via machine-readable means for publicly available online content.

- This obligation applies to all general-purpose AI providers placing their models in the EU market "regardless of the jurisdiction in which the copyright-relevant acts underpinning the training of those general-purpose AI models take place" (Recital 106).

- Article 53(1)(d) bolsters this by further requiring providers to make available to the public a "sufficiently detailed" summary regarding the training content based on the EU AI Office's template.

China:

- **Generative AI Interim Measures:** Providers that carry out pre-training, optimization training and other activities concerning training data must ensure that no infringement of third-party intellectual property occurs (Article 7(2)), and that data and models are obtained from lawful sources (Article 7(1)).

CHAPTER 4   ACCOUNTABILITY

(5) Traceability of Output (Responsibility)

US:

- **Utah AI Policy Act:** Companies are responsible for the output of generative AI, such that the use of generative AI which "made the violative statement", "undertook the violative act", or "was used in furtherance of the violation" "is not a defense" to liability (13-2-12 (2)).

In contrast, **Colorado SB 205** more clearly delineates the responsibilities of both developers and deployers regarding their duties to avoid algorithmic discrimination:

- The developer is required to provide extensive documentation to deployers and other developers concerning the high-risk AI system, including its uses and purposes, risks and benefits, and any other information "reasonably necessary to assist the deployer in understanding the outputs and monitor the performance of the high-risk artificial intelligence system for risks of algorithmic discrimination" (Section 6-1-1702(2)).

- If the developer provides the AI system to an "unaffiliated entity acting as a deployer" (Section 6-1-1702(3b)), the developer must provide documentation necessary to conduct impact assessments (including model cards and dataset cards and other impact assessments) (Section 6-1-1702(3a), unless the developer "also serves as a deployer" (Section 6-1-1702(3b)).

- In determining whether the obligations regarding risk management, impact assessment, and transparency in Section 6-1-1703 (2), (3) and (5) apply to the deployer, Section 6-1-1703 (6) of the Colorado SB 205 also considers whether the AI system continues "learning based on data derived from sources other than the deployer's own data" (Section 6-1-1703 (6)(b)(II)) and whether the deployer does "not use the deployer's own data to train the high-risk artificial intelligence system" (6-1-1703 (6)(a)(II)) - in addition to other conditions.

C. Practices

This subsection is divided into four components: 1. Assurance, 2. Reporting and feedback, 3. Traceability of input (with copyright as a case study), and 4. Traceability of output (focusing on responsibility).

(1) Assurance

Risk assessment (Clause 6.1.2) and impact assessment (Clause 6.1.4 and Controls A.5.2-A.5.5)

Regarding assurance, the risk and impact assessments in ISO 42001 are the clearest examples of assurance measures strengthening the accountability of your organization and the AI system. Here, the relevant clauses are 6.1.2, which pertains to AI Risk Assessment, and 6.1.4, which relates to AI System Impact Assessment. These are two complementary processes that aim to assess the implications of developing and using AI systems.

A risk assessment, as per Clause 6.1.2, focuses on identifying and analyzing specific risks associated with the development, deployment and use of AI systems, including strategic, operational, and technical risks. AI impact assessments go beyond that to understand the broader societal implications of AI systems beyond traditional risk analysis. A good example of this is included in the category of controls, A.5, Assessing the Impacts of AI Systems. A.5.2 requires your organization to establish the process of assessment, A.5.3 requires your organization to document the results of the AI system impact assessment, and A.5.4 concerns the assessment of the AI system's impact on individuals or groups of individuals. Going even further, A.5.5 is concerned with assessing the societal impact of AI systems. This demonstrates the breadth of AI system impact assessments as compared to AI risk assessments.

To clarify, there is significant overlap between risk assessments and impact assessments regarding AI, where the results of one inform the other. AI risk assessments require your organization to identify, analyze, evaluate, and prioritize possible risk treatments. AI risk assessments, as per Clause 6.1.2, require organizations to identify AI risks, analyze them, evaluate them, and prioritize the risks to be addressed, whereas AI system impact assessments require your organization to define the process for such an assessment, taking into account the relevant socio-technical context in which the AI system is deployed, and to determine the consequences of the AI system's deployment and use, as well as possible misuse on individuals, groups of individuals, and societies. The AI Impact Assessment under Clause 6.1.4 of ISO 42001 is broader than the Fundamental Rights Impact Assessment under the EU AI Act, as it encompasses not only fundamental rights but also considers broader aspects such as security, disinformation, and other relevant considerations. Yet, AI system impact assessments under Clause 6.1.4 provide a solid foundation for the Fundamental Rights Impact Assessment under the EU AI Act.

Monitoring, measurement, analysis, and evaluation (Clause 9.1)

Apart from risk and impact assessments, another form of assurance under ISO 42001 is the monitoring, measurement, analysis, and evaluation outlined in Clause 9.1. This assurance measure is necessary, given that new AI risks may emerge even after the AI system has been deployed. This clause requires organizations to decide on the appropriate monitoring and measurement approaches. The adversarial testing exercises mentioned in Chapter 5 (Security and Safety) are one such monitoring method. This allows your organization to track its performance in relation to security amongst the other principles discussed in this book. The results of any monitoring measure taken by your organization must be documented.

Internal audits (Clause 9.2)

Going beyond monitoring, Clause 9.2.1 states that the organization shall conduct internal audits at planned intervals to provide information on whether the AI management system conforms to its own requirements for its AI management system, conforms to the requirements of this document, and is effectively implemented and maintained. ISO 42001 is a clear example of the criteria against which your organization can conduct an internal audit of its AI system. It can go beyond that to utilize criteria such as the NIST AI Risk Management Framework, if desired.

(2) Reporting and feedback

Reporting is a key aspect of accountability as provided for in ISO 42001. The relevant controls here are A.3.3 and A.8.3.

Reporting of concerns (Control A.3.3)

Your organization should define and implement a process to report concerns about its role in relation to an AI system throughout its life cycle. This internal reporting ensures that internal stakeholders can provide input and feedback.

External reporting (Control A.8.3)

Your organization should provide capabilities for interested parties to report adverse impacts of the system. Establishing feedback loops, which enable both internal and external stakeholders to provide input, enhances the accountability of an AI system by facilitating two-way communication.

As you will see in Chapter 8 (Transparency and Explainability), transparency involves disclosing information and communicating information to stakeholders. Here, accountability involves allowing internal and external stakeholders to provide information to your organization, enabling it to improve its processes. In subsequent chapters, we will revisit Control A.8.3 in relation to external reporting and its impact on the other principles.

(3) Traceability of Input (Copyright)

In terms of traceability of input, using copyright as a case study, the relevant control here is A.7.3 concerning the acquisition of data.

Data acquisition (Control A.7.3)

Implementation Guidance B.7.3 states that details for data acquisition can include data rights such as copyright. Such details should be determined and documented by your organization. In this specific case, especially when it comes to data scraped from the web, it can be challenging for organizations to determine the data owner. A relevant question here is whether the data acquired and selected for use in the AI system is protected by copyright. If so, the question arises as to whether your organization needs to obtain a license from the data owner to use the data for the AI system. Your organization will need to conduct legal due diligence to review licenses and obtain the right to use the data lawfully through a licensing agreement, thereby gaining a clear understanding of the data's ownership and its rights as a licensee.

(4) Traceability of Output (Responsibility)

Regarding the traceability of output, this chapter focuses on allocating responsibility both internally and externally.

a. Internal accountability

Allocating roles and responsibilities within the organization (Control A.3.2)

Focusing on internal organization, the relevant category of controls is A.3, which pertains to internal organization. This entails establishing accountability within your organization to uphold its responsible approach to the implementation, operation, and management of the AI system.

Specifically, Control A.3.2 involves assigning AI roles and responsibilities according to your organization's needs. Implementation Guidance B.3.2 for this control explicitly states that defining roles and responsibilities is crucial for ensuring accountability throughout your organization for its role in the AI system's life cycle. Other roles include risk management and impact assessments, security and safety, supply chain relationships, and data management, amongst other areas.

The subject of documentation will be expounded upon in Chapter 8 (Transparency and Explainability).

b. External accountability

Control over external processes (Clause 8.1)

Regarding accountability to external stakeholders, the starting point is Clause 8.1, which concerns operational planning and control. It clearly requires that your organization retains control over external processes, products, or services relevant to the AI management system. In reality, most organizations rely on external providers for various components of AI systems, including AI models, training data, AI platforms, AI risk management solutions, and others. What is required under this clause is for your organization to specify criteria for evaluating third-party vendors, products, and services, as well as to monitor them.

Several controls buttress this clause. The category of controls most relevant to this clause is A.10, which pertains to third-party and customer relationships. The objective of this category of controls is to ensure that your organization understands its responsibilities and remains accountable, and that risks are appropriately apportioned when third parties are involved at any stage of the AI system's life cycle. I shall discuss the three controls in turn: A.10.2 on allocating responsibilities, A.10.3 on suppliers, and A.10.4 on customers.

Allocation of responsibilities – internally and externally (Controls A.3.2 and A.10.2)

According to A.10.2, your organization should ensure that responsibilities within the AI system life cycle are allocated between your organization, its partners, suppliers, customers, and third parties. Implementation Guidance B.10.2 acknowledges that responsibilities can be split among various parties, including those providing data or algorithms and models, as well as those developing or using the AI system. Such a distribution of responsibilities should be documented to ensure traceability. Your organization's contracts with various parties, including its partners, suppliers, customers, and other third parties, should clearly outline the apportionment of risks. This is especially true if these third parties play critical roles, such as maintaining the security of the AI infrastructure or building the AI models. Your organization is also obligated to ensure that the third party's systems meet its own standards regarding the responsible development and use of AI. This relates to Control A.3.2, which lists supplier relationships as one area requiring defined roles and responsibilities within an organization itself.

Supplier relationships (Control A.10.3)

According to this control, your organization should establish a process to ensure that its use of services, products, or materials provided by suppliers aligns with your organization's approach to the responsible development and use of AI systems. This necessitates that your organization obtains information and documentation related to the AI component provided by the supplier.

Implementation Guidance B.10.3 extends to consider contingencies where an AI system or system components from suppliers do not perform as intended or negatively impact individuals or groups of individuals and societies, such that the AI system or system components are not aligned with the responsible approach to AI systems adopted by your organization. In such a scenario, according to Implementation Guidance B.10.3, your organization should require the supplier to take corrective actions. What is not explicitly stated in Implementation Guidance B.10.3 is that if the supplier is unable to meet this objective, your organization may need to replace the supplier to avoid further negative impact.

In agreements with suppliers, organizations must clearly define the guardrails of the AI system or its components to ensure transparency and accountability. Your organization would need to know about the training data that the AI model was trained on by the supplier, including whether such data is copyrighted, as discussed in the previous subsection. The technical documentation in Chapter 8 (Transparency and Explainability) is what your organization should obtain from the supplier.

Internally, your organization should have clear policies and benchmarks in relation to assessing and evaluating suppliers. These considerations underscore the challenges of working with third-party vendors in terms of visibility. It is necessary to conduct risk assessments based on the available documentation that third-party suppliers are to provide.

Customer relationships (Control A.10.4)

Under this control, your organization should ensure that its responsible approach to the development and use of AI systems considers their customer expectations and needs, Implementation Guidance B.10.4 for this control acknowledges the complex nature of supplier and customer relationships, noting that your organization should understand not only these complex relationships, but also where responsibility lies with the provider of the AI system and where it lies with the customer. This relates to the objective in this category of controls concerning the apportionment of risks. When it comes to customers under Control A.10.4, Implementation Guidance B.10.4 suggests that your organization should identify the risk and provide the appropriate information to its customers so that they can treat the corresponding risks.

Summary and key takeaways

1. Conduct risk assessments and impact assessments regularly in accordance with Clause 6.1.2/6.1.4 and Controls A.5.2-A.5.5, and determine the appropriate monitoring and audit mechanisms (such as adversarial testing) under Clause 9.1/9.2, including their criteria (including those outside of ISO 42001 such as the NIST AI Risk Management Framework if desired) and frequency.

2. Establish mechanisms accessible to employees, users, and other stakeholders to provide feedback on AI systems to ensure that AI systems operate as intended. [Controls A.3.3 and A.8.3]

3. Conduct a thorough inventory of the training data (including that of the supplier, if relevant) to trace their origins and ownership, and legal review of licensing agreements (if relevant) to avoid copyright infringement. [Control A.7.3]

4. Define clear benchmarks regarding the responsible development and use of AI in evaluating third parties including suppliers and other partners - prior to contracting with them and while working with them. [Control A.10.3]

5. Draft and negotiate agreements clearly allocating risks and distributing responsibilities between your organization, third parties (including suppliers and other partners), and users/customers - covering the entire AI life cycle (planning, design, development and deployment) and the AI system's various components (data, algorithms, models). [Control A.10.2]

The next chapter will examine the principles, provisions, and practices related to security and safety.

CHAPTER 5

SECURITY AND SAFETY

This chapter on security and safety starts with a discussion of the principles and several related concepts, examines the applicable regulations, and analyzes the relevant ISO 42001 clauses and controls.

A. Principles

There are four parts in this subsection: 1. AI security, 2. AI safety, 3. Insecure AI, 4. Unsafe AI.

(1) AI security

This book focuses on security specifically in the context of AI. This is to be distinguished from general cybersecurity, which focuses on protecting information systems and networks from cyberattacks. Therefore, Annex C paragraph C.2.10 identifies security as an objective, noting that novel issues of security in the context of AI and machine learning should be looked at beyond the current lens of information and systems security.

AI security is specifically concerned with the actions of malicious actors. The AI system may be subject to attacks by these malicious actors at any point in time. They can choose exactly when and how to attack the AI systems, putting them at a significant advantage compared to defenders who must protect the AI system from all conceivable types of attacks. So, here, AI security specifically involves guarding the AI system and its various components, such as its data, model, and output. Regarding the protection of data integral to the AI system, I will address this in Chapter 6 (Privacy).

AI security should also be distinguished not only from general security, but also from privacy. As mentioned, the protection of the data component of AI systems is to be discussed in Chapter 6 (Privacy). Note that security is one of the eight key privacy principles, which will be expounded upon in Chapter 6 (Privacy). There, I will examine the relationship between AI security and privacy.

(2) AI safety

After distinguishing AI security from general cybersecurity and privacy, this chapter also distinguishes AI security from AI safety. Safety in the AI context can be defined as avoiding the harms that AI may cause. Such harms include harms to individuals, groups, society, and the environment. ISO 42001 Annex C paragraph 2.9 lists safety as an objective whereby the AI system does not jeopardize the life and health of individuals, their property, or the environment.

AI safety can also involve minimizing the harms of AI resulting from misinformation, disinformation, and deepfakes, which are outputs of AI systems. This narrower definition of AI safety is the one adopted by this book. In contrast to broader terms of AI safety, including the existential risks posed by AI and the governance of computing power, these broader terms of AI safety will not be the subject of this book, which is specifically designed for organizations seeking compliance with AI regulations.

To explain the relationship between AI safety and AI security, it is helpful to note that an AI system, in itself, may be unsafe due to the harm it causes to individuals, groups, society, and the environment. An insecure AI system can lead to an unsafe AI system. Harm resulting from the compromised security of an AI system overlaps with the compromised safety of an AI system. Hence, this chapter discusses both AI safety and AI security together.

(3) Insecure AI

AI systems are largely insecure due to adversarial attacks. Adversarial attacks are malicious, deliberate attempts to compromise the AI system, designed to result in malfunction or inappropriate, dangerous, or inaccurate output. This is an intentional manipulation of the AI model, resulting in such harmful output. Incorrect, harmful output is the goal of the malicious actor here, who may use deceptive or malicious input data to carry out such adversarial attacks or any other means. Such adversarial

CHAPTER 5 SECURITY AND SAFETY

attacks may or may not require technical knowledge and expertise. All that is necessary is knowledge of how to manipulate the AI system's input and output, along with a basic understanding of the AI system's overall architecture. This makes adversarial attacks particularly dangerous for AI systems.

In particular, open-source software or AI systems relying on various open-source tools are particularly vulnerable to adversarial attacks with a larger potential attack surface, which makes them susceptible to attacks by malicious actors. There are multiple forms of adversarial attacks (Figure 5-1). The five are data poisoning, model poisoning, model evasion, model extraction, and model inversion.

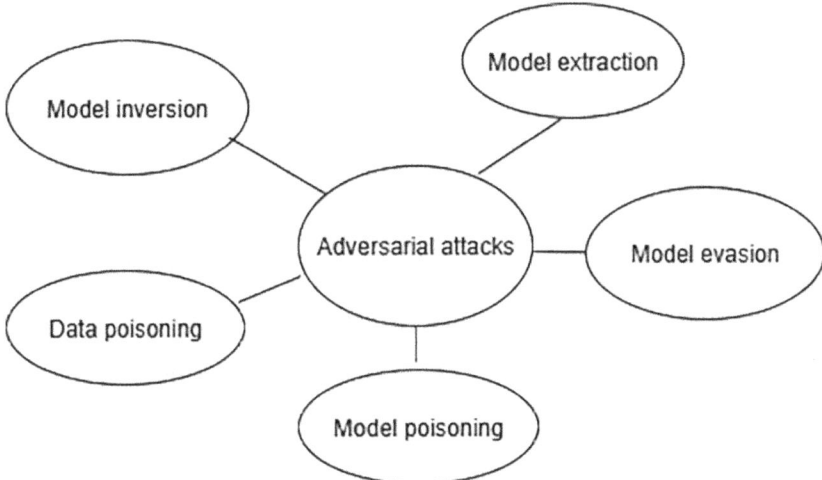

Figure 5-1. *Adversarial attacks*

(a) For data poisoning, the malicious actor is deliberately making changes to the training data. This could include introducing new data or altering the data's labels. The quality of the AI system's output depends entirely on the quality of the data on which it is trained. Data poisoning, which corrupts the training process, negatively impacts the model's performance. Here, the malicious actor would need to obtain access to the training data to compromise it and ultimately manipulate the model's operation, thereby adversely impacting the model's output.

(b) Model poisoning is distinct from data poisoning. Data poisoning involves intentionally skewing the data to impact the model negatively. Model poisoning involves manipulating a different component of the AI system, specifically the model's parameters, rather than the data, causing the model to behave in a way unintended by the AI model's creators, thereby adversely affecting its performance. These two forms of poisoning target different components of the AI system: the data versus the parameters.

(c) Model extraction occurs when the malicious actor obtains access to the model's parameters and weights. These parameters and weights may be proprietary. Model extraction is a form of theft that enables a malicious actor, who knows the model's weights, to create a model that replicates those parameters, thereby avoiding the entire training process and the associated costs. Model extraction may still be applicable for open-source software if the license agreements with the software's creators limit access to specific software components. Such model extraction occurs by sending specific prompts to the model to evaluate its output, reverse-engineer the parameters, and uncover the model's hidden mechanism, allowing a malicious actor to copy and replicate the model at the financial expense of the original model creator.

(d) Model evasion occurs when a malicious actor intentionally crafts input to cause the model's output to be incorrect, for example, by being misclassified. Adding noise to the input data confuses the model, resulting in a misclassification of the data and a wrongly classified output. All of this avoids mechanisms built into the model to ensure proper classification.

(e) Finally, model inversion occurs when the malicious actor reverse engineers the model, obtains sensitive information from it, determines the model's overall architecture, including its parameters, and uses that information to obtain even more information from it. A specific example of this is a membership inference attack, where the malicious actor obtains training data from the model.

(4) Unsafe AI and resulting harms

Such attacks on the AI system's security can result in significant physical and financial losses, mainly when AI is used in critical services such as medical diagnosis and autonomous vehicles. This, in turn, results in reputational damage to the organization.

Such attacks can also result in the manipulation of output, specifically in the form of disinformation and deepfakes. Disinformation is distinguished from misinformation, where such disinformation is a deliberate falsehood while misinformation is the result of a mistake. Deepfakes are another example of AI output being manipulated to cause harm, where generative AI produces audiovisual material that spreads deliberate falsehoods or when original images and videos are manipulated using AI. Deepfakes and disinformation are hence significant concerns, specifically in the context of unsafe AI.

AI systems may also be abused beyond their intended purpose. Generative AI models can be used to create harmful images and videos, and AI can also be leveraged to compromise cybersecurity systems. This is distinguished from adversarial attacks on the AI itself. Here, malicious actors are improperly utilizing AI and training it to launch cyberattacks on individuals, groups, and organizations. AI algorithms that rely on a significant amount of training data concerning individuals and groups, activities, behaviors, lifestyles, and preferences may be abused by individuals, allowing them to influence our behavior as predicted by the AI algorithm.

All of the above cybersecurity and safety risks are exacerbated by automation bias or AI exceptionalism, as mentioned in Chapter 1 (Introduction). Automation bias and AI exceptionalism, where human beings overly depend upon AI systems, create a false sense of security, reducing their autonomy and increasing the risk to the overall safety of individuals, groups, and society.

B. Provisions

This section is divided into three parts: (1) security, (2) safety, and (3) manipulation, disinformation, and deepfakes.

(1) Security

The **EU AI Act** sets out detailed requirements for providers of the following AI systems:

    A. High-risk AI systems:

- Adopt technical and organizational measures to ensure resilience against errors, faults, and inconsistencies (Article 15(4))
- Anticipate risks from third parties to safeguard their systems against unauthorized attempts by third parties to alter the use, outputs, or performance of these AI systems by exploiting system vulnerabilities. The technical solutions adopted to manage these risks should be tailored to the specific circumstances and the associated risks. These can include measures to prevent, detect, respond to, resolve, and control attacks, such as data poisoning, model poisoning, adversarial examples, model evasion, and confidentiality attacks, as well as model flaws (Article 15(5)).

B. General-purpose AI systems:

- Provide adequate cybersecurity, including physical infrastructure and protection for general-purpose AI models with "systemic risks" (Article 55(1)(d)).
- Evaluate models via adversarial testing, for example, and identify and mitigate risks (Article 55(1)(a)-(b)).
- Assess general-purpose AI models according to standard protocols, and monitor, document, and report serious incidents to the AI office (Article 55(1)(c)).

Two complementary EU laws expound upon the details concerning the implementation of such security measures in the EU AI Act:

A. **EU Cyber Resilience Act**

Article 12 of the EU Cyber Resilience Act explicitly focuses on high-risk AI systems and directly references Article 15 of the EU AI Act. Where "products with digital elements" falling within the scope of the EU Cyber Resilience Act are also classified as a high-risk AI system under the EU AI Act, they shall be deemed to comply with Article 15 of the EU AI Act if:

- The products satisfy the EU Cyber Resilience Act Annex I Part I essential cybersecurity requirements (Article 12(1)(a), EU Cyber Resilience Act). These requirements are included in the Appendix.

- The manufacturer's processes satisfy the EU Cyber Resilience Act Annex I Part II essential cybersecurity requirements (Article 12(1)(b), EU Cyber Resilience Act). These requirements are included in the Appendix.

- The declaration of conformity under the EU Cyber Resilience Act (as per Annex V) demonstrates that the level of cybersecurity protection which is required under Article 15 of the EU AI Act has been satisfied (Article 12(1)(c), EU Cyber Resilience Act).

B. **NIS 2 Directive**

While the NIS 2 Directive does not explicitly refer to AI systems like the Cyber Resilience Act, the cybersecurity measures listed in Article 21 apply to AI systems. Some of these include:

- Policies on risk analysis and system security (Article 21(2)(a))
- Incident handling (Article 21(2)(b))
- Supply chain security (Article 21(2)(d))
- Cyber hygiene practices (Article 21(2)(g))
- Cryptography and encryption (Article 21(2)(h))

(2) AI safety

- **EU AI Act**: Requirements concerning the security of general-purpose AI systems also entail regulating "systemic risks" (Article 55). Such risks are those emerging from high-impact general-purpose models that significantly impact the internal market and have actual or reasonably foreseeable adverse effects on public health, safety, public security, fundamental rights, or society as a whole that can be propagated at scale across the value chain (Recital 110).

Moving beyond the EU AI Act, the **General Product Safety Regulation** addresses the safety of all products, including new technologies, hence covering product digitization and safety. This ensures that the current safety regime in the European Union is updated and that the liability rules are in accordance with this new safety regime.

Further, the newly reformed **Product Liability Directive** now extends to artificial intelligence, software, and digital products, and includes the following:

- A strict liability approach to apportioning liability, which shifts the burden of proof to the defendant (Article 10(1))

- The defendant bears the presumption of defectiveness, assuming the organization has not complied with the liability rules (Article 10(2); Recital 48).

- In deploying the AI system, there is also the presumption of causation whereby the damage is presumed to be consistent with the product's defect (Article 10(3); Recital 48).

- Claimants only need to present "facts and evidence sufficient to support the plausibility of the claim for compensation", and defendants must disclose evidence when requested (Article 9(1)), such that it is up to defendants to demonstrate that they have complied with the Product Liability Directive.

(3) Manipulation, disinformation and deepfakes

EU:

A. **EU AI Act**

- Manipulation and deception: The EU AI Act prohibits AI systems that employ subliminal techniques on individuals or use purposefully manipulative or deceptive techniques, aiming to impair individuals' ability to make informed decisions and thereby distort their behavior. Such behavior causes, or is reasonably likely to cause, significant harm to such individuals (Article 5(1)(a)).

- Deepfakes: The EU AI Act defines deepfakes as AI-generated or places, entities, or events that would falsely appear to a person to be authentic or truthful (Recital 134), and explicitly states that deployers of AI systems that "generate or manipulate images, audio, or video content constituting a deep fake, shall disclose

CHAPTER 5   SECURITY AND SAFETY

that the content has been artificially generated or manipulated"; however, they may do so in a way that "does not hamper the display or enjoyment of the work" if such deepfake content "forms part of an evidently artistic, creative, satirical, fictional or analogous work or programme" (Article 50(4)).

- By itself, Article 50(4) appears inadequate in dealing with the significant harm resulting from deepfakes. However, Article 50(4) should be read in conjunction with Article 5(1)(a), which prohibits AI systems from deploying subliminal or purposefully manipulative or deceptive techniques. This means that AI systems generating deepfakes that cause significant harm may in fact fall within the prohibited category in Article 5(1)(a).

B. **Digital Services Act**

- While the provisions of the Digital Services Act do not explicitly cover the issues of disinformation or deepfakes, Article 45 provides for a Code of Conduct.

- The text of Article 45 does not explicitly mention these issues but encourages the Commission and the Board to draw up voluntary Codes of Conduct to tackle different types of illegal content and systemic risks (Article 45(1)).

- In relation to significant systemic risks, very large online platforms and very large online search engines, which are the subject of concern of such significant systemic risks, may be invited to contribute to the drawing up of Codes of Conduct (Article 45(2)).

- The Code of Conduct on Disinformation is now in force as of 1 July 2025, with its commitments auditable starting from that date. Adherence to the Code of Conduct on disinformation constitutes proof of compliance with the broader obligations imposed on very large online platforms and very, very large online search engines under the Digital Services Act.

CHAPTER 5   SECURITY AND SAFETY

- Commitment 15 of the Code of Conduct on Disinformation specifically references the EU AI Act and AI-generated and manipulated content including deepfakes, requiring signatories to establish and confirm their policies for countering "prohibited manipulative practices".

China:

A. **Deep Synthesis Provisions** (China's deepfake law)

- Deep synthesis services must not be used to "produce, reproduce, publish, or transmit" fake news (Article 6).

- Service providers must strengthen content moderation and review user input data and synthesis results through technical or manual measures; if they identify any false information, they must take prompt action such as reporting the matter to the authorities, issuing warnings, or suspending or closing accounts (Article 10).

- Further, they must establish and improve upon mechanisms for dispelling rumors (Article 11).

B. **Algorithmic Recommendation Provisions**

- Service providers are expressly prohibited from generating and synthesizing fake news and information (Article 13), falsely registering accounts, illegally trading accounts, manipulating user accounts or falsifying likes, comments or forwards, or using algorithms to block information, making "excessive recommendations", manipulating search results and rankings, controlling what is most searched or selected when presenting information to users, influencing network public opinions, or avoid supervision and administrative actions (Article 14).

- They are required to stop the transmission of, or remove, illegal information, keep records and submit reports to the relevant authorities, and establish a features library to screen illegal or harmful information and implement screening criteria, rules, and procedures (Article 9).

- They are encouraged to apply content management strategies, including the removal and fragmentation of content duplicates (Article 12).

C. **Generative AI Interim Measures**

Service providers must address two scenarios by employing various measures:

i. Illegal content: suspending the generation and dissemination of, or removing, any illegal content, or taking necessary steps, such as model optimization training.

ii. Abuse of generative AI for illegal activities: providing warnings, restricting user functions, suspending or terminating services, recording such conduct.

In both scenarios, service providers are to report such instances to the authorities.

D. **Measures for Labeling of AI-Generated Synthetic Content**

This most recent regulation supports the above three regulations in addressing disinformation and deepfakes by setting clear transparency requirements, which will be discussed in greater detail in Chapter 8 (Transparency and Explainability).

US:
There are various laws in the US concerning deepfakes.

At the federal level, the recent **Take It Down Act** addresses AI-generated deepfakes in the context of non-consensual intimate visual depictions. The state-level deepfake laws cover a range of contexts, from political communications (including **Texas SB 751**, Indiana HB 1133, and Oregon SB 1571) to child pornography (including **Florida SB 1798**, **Louisiana Act 457**, and **South Dakota SB 79**).

Focusing on an AI-specific US state law, the **Texas Responsible AI Governance Act** prohibits the development or deployment of AI systems to

- intentionally encourage physical self-harm, harm of others, or criminal activity (Section 552.052(1)-(3)), or

– produce or help produce or distribute images and videos violating laws regarding child pornography or material displaying non-consensual sexual activity (Section 552.057(a)(1)-(2)), with intent determined from the AI system's terms of use or marketing material (Section 552.057(b)).

C. Practices

This section covers five topics: (1) Integrated security-specific approach to ISO 42001, (2) Data Governance, (3) Operational Safeguards, (4) Assurance Measures, (5) Transparency and Accountability.

(1) Integrated security-specific approach

Regarding the integrated security-specific approach, the starting point is stated in Annex D, clause 1, which supports the comprehensive treatment of security, as opposed to separately addressing AI-related security issues. In the context of security, ISO 42001 should be integrated with ISO 27001 to form an Information Security Management System. Annex D, paragraph D.1 highlights the relevance of information security to AI, and paragraph D.2 notes the significance of security in an organization's meeting its AI-related goals in most contexts, and the shared high-level framework (discussed in Chapter 2 (ISO 42001: The Standard) of both ISO 27001 and 42001 – which facilitates implementing ISO 42001 controls in a manner which is integrated with ISO 27001 implementation. When it comes to ISO 42001, there are only 38 controls, compared to the 93 information security controls in ISO 27001. Additionally, ISO 27002 is a separate standard that provides guidelines on implementing the controls outlined in ISO 27001.

There are two ways in which ISO 42001 provides for the integration of information security governance and AI governance:

1. AI policy

AI policy (Clause 5.2 and Control A.2.3)

Clause 5.2 requires the organization's management to establish an AI policy, and Control A.2.3 states that the organization should determine where other policies can be affected by or apply to its objectives regarding AI systems. Implementation Guidance B.2.3

acknowledges that the security and safety domains intersect with artificial intelligence. Hence, your organization should thoroughly consider and analyze whether current policies, including information security policies, can be effectively integrated with AI policy. This may involve updating those policies, such as the information security policy, or incorporating provisions related to information security into the AI policy. This is one way in which information security governance and AI governance intersect in ISO 42001.

2. Impact assessment

Impact assessments (Clause 6.1.4 and Control A.5.2)

The second way in which both information security governance and AI governance intersect in ISO 42001 is in impact assessments. Clause 6.1.4 of ISO 42001 notes how AI system impact assessments focused on security (such as information security impact assessments) may need to be integrated into the organization's broader risk management program, specifically when it comes to AI systems where security is of utmost importance. This is buttressed by Implementation Guidance B.5.2, which repeats what was clearly stated in Clause 6.1.4 about performing security/safety-specific impact assessments as part of the organization's overall risk management program.

(2) Data Governance

Annex C paragraph C.3.4 lists as risk sources both the data quality and the data collection process, where data poisoning can affect safety. These risk sources should be accounted for in the risk management process, as outlined in Clause 6.1.2 of the ISO 42001 standard.

Data management (Control A.7.2)

Moreover, Control A.7.2 states that the organization should define, document, and implement data management processes related to AI development. Implementation Guidance B.7.2 states that such data management can include security implications due to the use of data, some of which may be sensitive in nature, and security and safety threats arising from AI system development, which is data-dependent. As such, data governance is a key aspect of the security and safety practices in ISO 42001.

To address the security and safety threats referred to in Implementation Guidance B.7.2, it is crucial that security controls are applied to prevent alteration of data in the data collection phase, the data storage phase, and the data processing phase. Such controls should also be implemented to prevent unauthorized access or data leakage. Poor data quality or malicious data in the development of AI systems is evident in the case of data poisoning, where malicious actors manipulate training data to adversely impact the output of AI models, as discussed in Section A (Principles) of this chapter. As such, when addressing security and safety threats in data management practices under this control, your organization should establish clear criteria for evaluating the quality of training data, specifically verifying whether there are anomalies that suggest the data has been compromised.

As for leakage of data, this is to be distinguished from a loss of data. A loss of data can occur due to human error or adversarial attacks, such as ransomware attacks, where the data becomes irretrievable. Regarding leakage, when data from the AI system is inadvertently sent to an unauthorized recipient, the AI system still retains a copy of the data. Although the data is not lost, it has been unintentionally leaked to someone. The security controls also cover data leakage.

To address the security implications associated with the use of sensitive data, a data management process that can be implemented is differential privacy. Not only is differential privacy a privacy-enhancing technique, but also it serves the interests of security. Adding controlled noise to the data, blurring individual details, and preserving individual privacy prevents malicious actors from tracing the data to specific individuals, thereby reducing risks to the safety of these individuals.

Therefore, a proper data management process should be defined, documented, and implemented under Control A.7.2.

Data acquisition (Control A.7.3)

As for the acquisition of data under Control A.7.3, your organization should determine and document details about how the data was acquired, and such information can include the compliance of such data with security requirements. This supports the consideration of Control A.7.2 regarding data management processes, taking into account the security implications of using data and the security and safety threats arising from the development of this data-dependent AI system.

(3) Operational safeguards

System infrastructure (Control A.4.5)

The starting point is securing the AI system's infrastructure. This includes considering the system and computing resources as per Control A.4.5. Securing the AI infrastructure entails evaluating the hardware and software to mitigate risks to the overall IT environment. A safety-by-design approach ensures an adequately robust safety infrastructure at the various levels of the AI system: the platform level, the model level, and the application level.

AI system design and development (Control A.6.2.3)

Another more specific safeguard is at the AI system design and development phases, where your organization should consider various security threats throughout the AI life cycle while documenting the AI system's design and development. Implementation Guidance B.6.2.3 lists data poisoning, model stealing, or model inversion attacks as such security threats, which must be documented at the AI system's design and development phases. These threats have been covered in Section A (Principles) of this chapter. Your organization should not only discuss these threats but also describe how it has addressed them. For example, how your organization restricts access to training data.

AI system deployment (Control A.6.2.5)

After performing a readiness assessment at the AI system deployment stage, as per Control A.6.2.5, which evaluates the security infrastructure, your organization should define and document its approach towards monitoring the AI system's operation. This should also take into account AI-specific security threats related to the AI system, including, once again, data poisoning, model stealing, and model inversion attacks.

As previously discussed, your organization should once again list the security measures in place to address such risks. Here, the human-in-the-loop approach supports the monitoring of AI systems for security threats by making the detection of and response to security incidents more efficient.

(4) Assurance Measures

Annex C paragraph C.3.3 notes that safety and security can be compromised by automation levels. AI systems that developers no longer control create security and safety risks.

Here, human-in-the-loop processes would be required to mitigate risks to safety, for example, in autonomous vehicles. Regarding risk treatment, as per Clause 6.1.3, it is essential to note that ISO 42001 does not include any controls for testing the security of an AI system against adversarial attacks. Therefore, additional controls beyond those listed in Annex A may be necessary.

AI system verification and validation (A.6.2.4)

Control A.6.2.4 is the starting point. This control requires your organization to define and document verification and validation measures for the AI system, including criteria for these measures. Such measures can include testing methodologies and tools. The evaluation criteria, which should be documented and defined by your organization, can be based on the safety requirements of the AI system. This control is just the starting point, and once again, it does not specify the exact tests to be used for AI safety and security threats. There are various forms of security testing (Figure 5-2), and the specific type of test depends on the particular AI system and its use case.

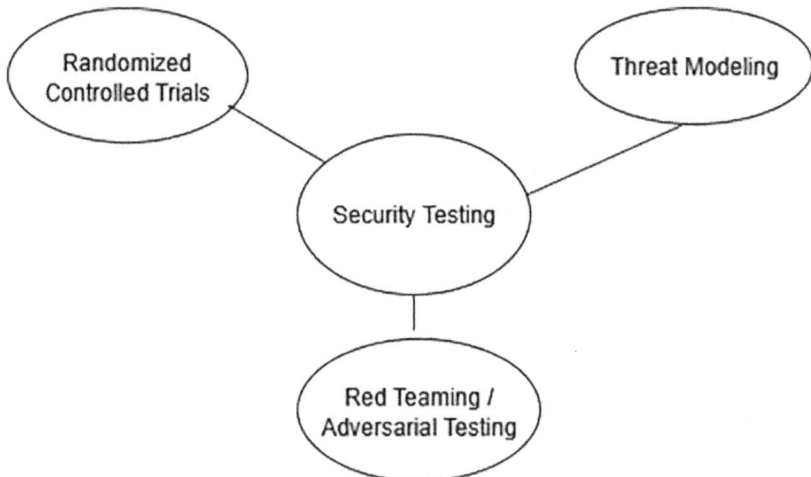

Figure 5-2. Security testing

One common test for AI systems in relation to security is adversarial testing, also known as red teaming. This entails including malicious input in the training data to attempt to cause the AI system to produce negative output. Conducting this test through an adversarial lens and simulating adversarial attacks on the AI system is intended to reveal the gaps and flaws in the AI system. What is interesting to note about this testing method is that defender bias is removed. So the results of adversarial testing are likely more accurate for developers of the AI system to rely upon in improving the security of the AI system before deployment.

Another testing method is threat modeling, which involves listing and identifying threats, enabling the prioritization of specific controls to address these threats. This is a more basic testing method regarding the AI system's security.

Randomized controlled trials also help in testing the safety of an AI system to reduce the risk of unpredictable output that could cause harm.

(5) Transparency and accountability

Finally, we examine how transparency and accountability measures support the objectives of security and safety as outlined in ISO 42001.

Incident reporting (Control A.8.4)

Communicating incidents related to the security of an AI system allows for greater transparency and control. A.8.4 requires organizations to determine and document such an incident communication plan. Implementation Guidance B.8.4 also refers your organization to ISO 27001 for more information on incident management for security.

External reporting (Control A.8.3)

Regarding accountability, Control A.8.3 states that organizations should provide capabilities for interested parties, including users, to report the system's adverse impacts. These impacts may include security vulnerabilities that malicious actors could exploit to compromise the system's security. Here, the reporting mechanism enables helpful feedback that contributes to the system's overall security.

Supplier relationships (Control A.10.3)

Importantly, when engaging with suppliers, Control A.10.3 requires alignment between your organization and suppliers to ensure the responsible development and use of AI systems, which entails ensuring security and safety. Your organization should establish a transparent process for this. The underlying concern of this control is that third-party vendors are not directly supervised by your organization, resulting in less control and visibility regarding the third-party vendor's security practices. This may result in your organization facing greater security risks, including system hacks, supply chain attacks, and other adversarial attacks.

This control requires due diligence especially in agreements with suppliers. Such contracts should address the question of alignment between your organization and the third-party supplier regarding security practices. This would include measures that the third-party supplier may or may not have in place to monitor the system's security through assessments and audits regularly. Whether the third-party supplier has an incident response plan in place is a factor.

Your organization should conduct regular audits to assess third-party risks and ensure compliance with your organization's security standards among third-party suppliers. This would entail reviewing the third-party supplier's technical documentation for security risks related to adversarial attacks and other forms of misuse, which could create safety risks.

Finally, your organization should restrict access to third-party suppliers only for the essential services.

Summary and key takeaways

1. Integrate AI-specific security measures with your organization's overall approach to information security by aligning the AI policy with your organization's information security policy, specifically by updating the information security policy to take into account AI-related issues and/or reproducing its language in the AI policies. [Control A.2.3]

2. Incorporate considerations regarding the security of AI systems into the security-specific impact assessments as part of your organization's overall risk management process [Clause 6.1.4 and Control A.5.2]

3. Evaluate training data in the data acquisition, storage and processing phases, to assess their quality and compliance with security requirements, and to check for anomalies such as compromised or leaked data or unauthorized access. [Control A.7.2]

4. Establish, conduct, and document the results of, testing, verification and validation of the AI system's security, whether it be in the form of adversarial testing, threat modeling or randomized controlled trials - on a regular basis. [A.6.2.4]

5. Review potential and current suppliers' technical and non-technical documentation regarding their security practices (especially regular monitoring and incident response), and restrict their access to what is necessary". [A.10.3]

The next chapter will examine the principles, provisions, and practices related to privacy.

CHAPTER 6

PRIVACY

This chapter on privacy starts with a discussion of the principles and several related concepts, examines the applicable regulations, and analyzes the relevant ISO 42001 clauses and controls.

A. Principles

Privacy is a fundamental right, even outside the context of AI. This right is enshrined in the Universal Declaration of Human Rights and in the constitutions of numerous countries worldwide. Privacy is an ethical issue in its own right, and privacy losses can harm both individuals and groups in various ways. ISO 42001 Annex C paragraph C.2.7 notes the potential harm suffered by individuals when their sensitive personal data is mishandled.

Individuals face a range of privacy harms, from economic to reputational, in more tangible forms of discrimination:

- Individuals can suffer emotional embarrassment when a sensitive medical condition, for example, is disclosed without their consent.

- This can subsequently lead to discrimination based on that specific piece of sensitive information.

- Individuals may suffer identity theft. For example, the leaked data may be used in an unauthorized or improper manner, leading to an individual's identity being stolen and causing significant financial harm to the data subject.

CHAPTER 6   PRIVACY

Organizations also suffer from privacy losses:

- Privacy losses may lead to liability faced by such organizations. Every single privacy breach can lead to a potential lawsuit or a fine from regulators. Therefore, collecting more personal data than necessary increases the risk of the above.

- Personal data, which is sensitive, can be costly for organizations to manage, requiring the essential expertise in such organizations to ensure compliance and proper data handling.

More broadly, privacy breaches can affect society as a whole. The leakage of sensitive data can lead to foreign adversaries blackmailing key individuals in countries. This would endanger national security.

Ultimately, the bottom line is that privacy, even outside the context of AI, is an ethical issue and a fundamental right.

What AI does is to raise the stakes of privacy breaches:

- First and foremost, there is a greater organizational incentive to collect more data. The amount of private data that AI algorithms are trained on has dramatically increased. This corresponds to increased privacy risks.

- Moreover, these AI algorithms have more access to sensitive information about their data subjects. They draw on large amounts of data regarding how individuals behave, act, and what they prefer. Additionally, these algorithms draw inferences from such data, which can threaten individual privacy. So the data of individuals holds clues to specific characteristics that individuals would rather keep private. With algorithms drawing inferences from such data, these inferences reveal private characteristics that individuals would prefer not to have disclosed.

- This, in turn, leads to the greater risk of manipulation as discussed in Chapter 4 (Security and Safety). As a recap, AI can be unsafe when malicious actors exploit AI to manipulate individuals, groups, and society as a whole. So, AI algorithms rely on data to manipulate individuals and groups and to shape their experiences.

CHAPTER 6 PRIVACY

All of the above make robust data privacy measures even more crucial to safeguard against algorithms that rely on and draw inferences from such personal data to shape our experience and manipulate us. Therefore, privacy as an ethical principle is even more crucial in the age of AI.

Eight principles form the basis of privacy as an essential right. These are the Fair Information Principles, which include: security safeguards, purpose specification, collection limitation, use limitation, openness, individual participation, data quality, and accountability. These eight principles are an expansion of the original five principles in the 1973 HEW Report, which included: no secret collection, access and amendment, consent, no secondary use, and appropriate safeguards.

The eight Fair Information Principles (Figure 6-1) also relate to other key ethical AI principles, including security, robustness, transparency, and accountability. I shall examine these eight Fair Information Principles one by one.

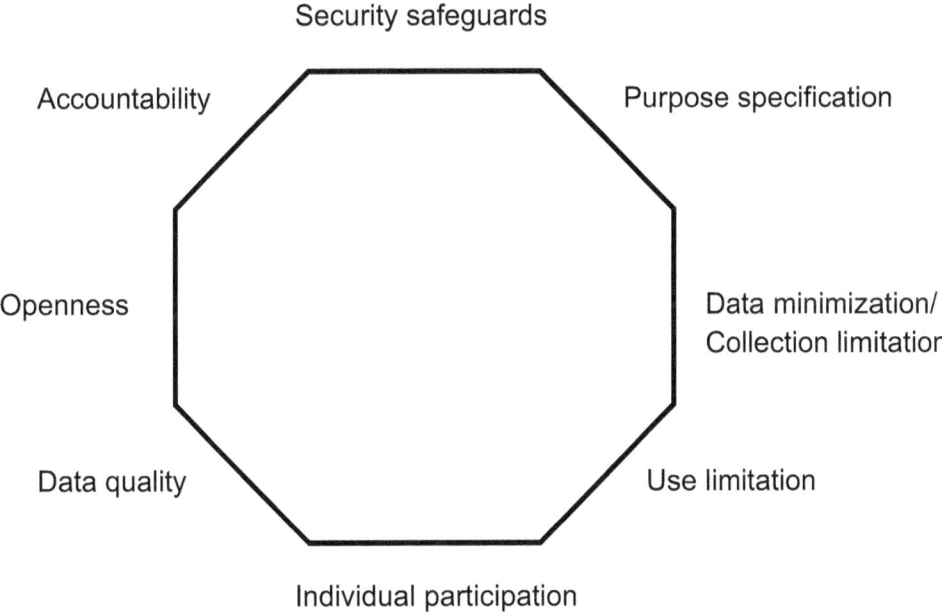

Figure 6-1. Fair Information Principles

71

(1) Security safeguards

The first is security safeguards. So AI security includes the protection of data because data is a component of the AI system. This principle mandates that an organization protect personal data using reasonable security safeguards, preventing such data from being lost, accessed in an unauthorized manner, destroyed, disclosed, modified, or used without authorization. Data security entails taking all necessary steps to prevent unauthorized access to this data. This entails securing not only the data itself but also the physical security of the hardware. It is essential that the network, systems, and all associated components are secured with the necessary administrative, technical, and physical safeguards to protect the data. Therefore, these security safeguards protect data from ransomware attacks, which can either destroy the data or encrypt it. They protect the data from theft or corruption. The section on practices will cover the whole range of data protection approaches, including encryption, anonymization, and cryptographic methods such as differential privacy.

The bottom line is that security safeguards require a holistic approach to protecting not only the data but also the physical security of hardware and storage devices, software applications, and the network. All of these must be protected for this principle to be satisfied.

The following three principles are linked:

(2) Purpose specification

After the purpose of data collection has been specified, the subsequent collection and use of the data should be limited to fulfilling those purposes only. For the principle of purpose specification, this entails that at the point of data collection, individuals should be informed as to why your organization is collecting the information, what data will be collected, and what your organization will do with that data. Your organization must clearly explain what personal data it is processing at every stage to meet the specified purpose.

(3) Data minimization

For the principle of data minimization, also known as the principle of collection limitation, this entails collecting data only when necessary for the business use case, specifically for the purpose specified. If a specific piece of information is not required for the particular business use case, then that information should not be collected.

Hence the principle of collection limitation also covers the data retention stage. Your organization should maintain the data only for as long as necessary. Otherwise, this data should be deleted. This data should not be collected with the intent of being retained perpetually. Here, an expiry date would be a good practice for this principle to be satisfied.

How the data is collected is also an aspect of this principle of data collection limitation, whether the data is collected in a fair and lawful manner, and with the data subject's knowledge or consent.

The organization collecting the data should conduct a cost-benefit analysis, bearing in mind that it is the data subject who bears the risk, for example, of embarrassment if the data is disclosed in an unauthorized manner. This means that the collection should only occur when the benefit of collecting the data outweighs the costs. In effect, the organization collecting the data should engage in a proportionality exercise, ensuring that only the necessary data is collected for the specific outcome, not more data than required, as this would increase the organization's risk of a privacy breach.

(4) Use limitation

The principle of use limitation ensures that the data subject's consent is paramount. When the data subject's information is being collected, they must be informed of exactly why that data is being collected and for what specific purpose. That organization should only use that information for that specified purpose, and not for a completely different purpose, because that would violate the use limitation principle. Only if the data subject has consented to your organization's use of that data for the other purpose, then that would be in conformity with this use limitation principle.

So there are three ways in which AI systems threaten the use limitation principle:

a. Secondary use

The first is when data collected from data subjects is repurposed and used in training new models without the subjects' consent. This is also known as secondary use. This violates the use limitation principle because when individuals provide their data in a specific context, they have clear expectations about how that data will be used. Now that that data has been transferred to a completely different context, the use limitation principle has been breached. Therefore, developers training AI models using training data should assess whether this training of the new model is consistent with the original purpose of the data collection, taking into account what data subjects who provided such information would expect. This secondary use is a form of data repurposing, which involves the usage of data outside of its original purpose. In the AI context, what is crucial is alignment between the training data collected and the AI system's purpose. The collection limitation principle is applicable here in addressing this possibility of secondary use. Collecting data only when it is required for the specified business purpose reduces the risk of secondary use.

b. Web-scraping

The second way in which AI systems threaten the use limitation principle is specifically in the case of web-scraping. Organizations that scrape data off the Internet risk violating the privacy of data subjects who have not expressly consented to having their data collected, despite such data being publicly available; when these data subjects provided such information, it is unlikely that they intended for it to be included as training data for an AI system.

c. Inference

The third way in which AI systems threaten the use limitation principle is inference. AI algorithms generate predictions based on the data they have been trained on. These inferences are logical conclusions derived from such training data, and they constitute a form of privacy harm to the individual affected, as AI algorithms can accurately predict what the specific individual will do. This constitutes a privacy harm because the individual has not provided such inferences, and the information has been obtained from the AI system.

The following two principles serve as possible solutions to the threats that AI systems pose to the use limitation principle.

(5) Openness

Openness is a solution because it provides individuals with transparent notice, clearly stating that the information provided to the organization will be used to retrain an AI model. This assures the individual that their autonomy has been respected, as they have been informed and can decide on their next course of action. A key aspect of the principle of openness is providing advance notice at the collection stage. Privacy policies on websites are an example of this, where the individual is notified of exactly what information will be collected, why it is collected, how it will be processed, and if the individual wishes to amend or have the data deleted, how they can do so. Openness as a principle endures throughout the data processing life cycle, beyond the advanced notice stage. Organizations would have to disclose exactly what data has been collected, how it is being used, and, in the context of AI, what the consequences of using such data by AI algorithms would be. Here, AI systems and this principle of openness may be in tension, given the inscrutability of AI systems, which serve as black boxes.

(6) Individual participation

Now, the second solution to the threats posed by AI systems to the use limitation principle would be the principle of individual participation. Here, the underlying tenet of this principle is preserving the data subjects' control over their data to avoid the breach or abuse of such data, allowing individuals to withdraw consent or to deny having their data collected or to obtain access to not only their personal data provided but also the inferences drawn from such personal data. One way in which data subjects can exercise such control is through an opt-out option. Specifically, this means that the data subject states they prefer not to have inferences drawn from the data they provide. Such access can also mean that data subjects can review and amend the data provided to your organization, as these actions are usually combined under the principle of individual rights. Given that access in itself is only helpful if the individual has the capacity and ability to amend the data, this is a logical consequence. Therefore, AI systems may not be entirely well-suited for this specific principle of individual participation, as once personal data has been included in a training dataset and introduced into the model, providing data subjects with access to that data may be challenging for organizations operating the data system. It may be difficult for such organizations to comply with requests to allow access or to delete the data.

(7) Data quality

The principle of data quality ensures that the personal data collected remains relevant to its specified purposes and is complete, updated, and accurate. This is linked to the earlier principle of individual participation, which ensures that individuals themselves provide the data, with such firsthand data being more accurate. Chapter 9 (Robustness) expounds on the importance of high-quality data.

(8) Accountability

As for the principle of accountability, it is included as a Fair Information Principle, and Chapter 4 (Accountability) expounds on what accountability as an ethical AI principle entails.

B. Provisions

This section focuses on aspects of privacy law as they specifically relate to AI, examining approaches in the EU, the UK, China and the US.

EU:

A. **GDPR**
- Personal data: By default, the GDPR prohibits the processing of personal data - unless such processing falls within one of the six categories for lawful processing (Article 6(1)):
    1. consent
    2. contractual performance
    3. vital interest
    4. legal obligation
    5. public task
    6. legitimate interest pursued by a controller or third party
- Data pseudonymization and anonymization (Recital 26). Anonymized data is not deemed personal information under the GDPR and therefore falls outside its purview; while pseudonymized data does not fully de-identify the individual and hence is still considered personal data under the GDPR.
- The special categories of personal data which require enhanced protection include (Article 9(1)):
    - race and ethnicity

- political opinions
  - religious and philosophical beliefs
  - trade union membership
  - genetic and biometric data
  - health data
  - and sexuality and sexual orientation

- However, there are exceptions where such data may be collected and processed (Article 9(2)), including but not limited to scenarios where:
  - the data subject has already made public that data (Article 9(2)(e) or provided explicit consent (Article 9(2)(a))
  - such data is being used for research or archiving purposes (Article 9(2)(j))
  - such data is collected and processed by a nonprofit organization or its affiliates (Article 9(2)(d)).

- Relationship with EU AI Act: Special categories of personal data (like those listed under Article 9(1) of the GDPR) may be required for effective bias testing and mitigation under Article 10 of the EU AI Act on data governance. Article 10(5) of the EU AI Act lists the six cumulative conditions for the use of such data – all of which have to be met:

  1. Other data (such as synthetic or anonymized data) cannot effectively serve the purposes of bias detection and correction;

  2. Such data is subject to technical limitations on the re-use of such data, and both security and privacy-preserving techniques (including pseudonymization);

3. Such data is subject to access controls and security safeguards which ensure strict confidentiality and avoid misuse;

4. Such data cannot be transferred to or accessed by third parties;

5. Such data must be deleted upon the conclusion of the bias correction or data retention period;

6. The data processing records explain why such data was strictly necessary for the detection and correction of biases, for which there was no alternative.

- Automated decision-making: The GDPR has a general prohibition against automated decision-making when there is a possibility that such automated decision-making will have significant effects on the individual (Article 22(1)), allowing the data subject to opt out. However, exceptions to this general prohibition include (but are not limited to):

    – explicit consent (Article 22(2)(c))

    – the fulfillment of a contract (Article 22(2)(a))

    – EU/member state law authorizing such automated decision-making while also safeguarding the data subject's rights (Article 22(2)(b)) - including the rights to human intervention, expression of their point of view, and contestation of the automated decision (Article 22(3)).

- Data protection impact assessment: The GDPR requires data controllers to conduct data protection impact assessments for "new technologies" (Article 35(1)). They are essential for identifying, assessing, and addressing privacy risks in the AI development life cycle, specifically in determining the data used to train and operate an AI system, and include the following components:

    – risk assessment in relation to the data subjects' fundamental rights and freedoms (Article 35(7)(c))

- assessment of necessity and proportionality in relation to the intended purpose for processing (Article 35(7)(b))

- systematic description of the planned processing, its purpose, and the pursued legitimate interest (Article 35(7)(a))

- measures to be adapted to safeguard against security risks and protect personal data (Article 35(7)(d)).

B. **EU Data Act**

This recent act supports the above GDPR provisions, restricting third parties receiving personal data from using it for purposes other than those agreed upon (such as the training of AI models):

- The third party must process the data "only for the purposes and under the conditions agreed with the user" and subject to EU and national law on protection of personal data (which ostensibly includes the GDPR), and must erase the data if such data is no longer necessary for the purpose (Article 6(1)). The exception to this (agreement with the user) applies to "non-personal data" only.

- Article 6(2)(b) of the EU Data Act qualifies the exceptions in Article 22(2)(a) and (c) of the GDPR: Both GDPR provisions allow for automated decision-making (including profiling) based on both the data subject's explicit consent and necessity for the contract between the data controller and data subject. The EU Data Act prohibits third parties from using data for "profiling" unless necessary for the service requested by the user.

UK:

By contrast, the recent **UK Data (Use and Access) Act** adopts a more lenient approach to automated decision-making.

- Previously in the UK, individuals retained the right not to be subject to a solely automated decision resulting in legal or similarly significant effects, unless the automated decision was necessary for entering into or performing a contract, required/authorized by law, or based on the data subject's explicit consent. In these scenarios, organizations would need to take steps to safeguard individuals, including the right to obtain human intervention, express their views, and contest the decision.

- Under the new legislation, "significant" and "solely automated" decisions (apart from those involving special category personal data or those based on "recognized legitimate interests") are generally permitted (amended Article 22A UK GDPR).

- This is subject to certain safeguards that enable data subjects to make representations, contest the decision, and require human intervention (amended Article 22C UK GDPR).

- A "significant" decision is defined as producing a legal effect or similarly significant effect for the individual (amended Article 22A(1)(b)).

- "Solely" is defined as the absence of "meaningful" human involvement in the decision (amended Article 22A(1)(a)), with the DUAA stipulating a key factor (among others) in assessing this: "the extent to which the decision is reached by means of profiling" (amended Article 22A(2)).

- However, the DUAA prohibits "significant" decisions involving special category personal data and based "solely" on automated processing, unless in the following scenarios (amended Article 22B):

    - consent by the individual
    - necessity for entering into or performing a contract between the individual and a data controller
    - necessity on public interest grounds
    - required by law

China:

While China has enacted several comprehensive laws aimed at protecting personal information, including the Personal Information Protection Law (PIPL), this subsection focuses on China's AI-specific regulations which cover privacy specifically in the context of AI.

CHAPTER 6   PRIVACY

A. **Generative AI Interim Measures** (Article 11)

- Service providers must "fulfill confidentiality obligations" regarding users' input data and usage records; this entails not collecting unnecessary personal information, not illegally retain any input data and usage records from which one can determine the user's identity, and not illegally providing the input data and usage records to third parties

- They must also promptly accept and respond to individuals' requests to access, reproduce, modify, supplement, or delete their personal information

B. **Deep Synthesis Provisions** (Article 14)

- Service providers and technical supporters must "employ necessary measures to ensure the security of training data", and specifically to comply with the regulations on the protection of personal information protection if the training data contains personal information.

- If service providers edit biometric information (such as faces and voices), they must notify the affected individuals and obtain consent from them regarding such secondary use.

C. **Algorithm Recommendation Provisions** (Article 17)

- Users of algorithmic recommendation services must not be targeted based on their personal characteristics.

- Users retain "convenient options", including the right to opt out.

US:
The US has established privacy laws at both federal and state levels:

A. **Federal level**: The **1974 Privacy Act (5 USC § 552a)** governs data protection by federal agencies, and the **1996 Health Insurance Portability and Accountability Act (HIPAA)** governs the privacy and security of sensitive patient health information.

B. **State level**: The **California Consumer Privacy Act** is the most comprehensive US state privacy legislation, enacted in 2018 and applicable to businesses that do business in California and collect or control personal information, providing consumers with rights regarding how companies use their data. Other US state-level privacy laws include **Illinois' Personal Information Protection Act** and **Biometric Information Privacy Act**, the **Colorado Privacy Act**, and the **Virginia Consumer Data Protection Act**.

As for privacy in the context of the AI-specific regulations in the US,

A. **Texas Responsible AI Governance Act**

- Government agencies are prohibited from developing or deploying AI systems to uniquely identify individuals using their biometric data (unless used in the context of the aforementioned HIPAA), or to gather their images or other media without their consent (Section 552.054(b)).

B. **Colorado SB 205**

- Where the high-risk AI systems make or substantially contribute to any "consequential decision" impacting consumers, the deployer must provide the consumer with information regarding their right to opt-out of the processing of their personal data for profiling purposes which affect them significantly (such as legal effects) (Section 6-1-1703(4)(a)(III)).

- Where such a "consequential decision" is "adverse to the consumer," the deployer must provide the consumer with the opportunity to "correct any incorrect personal data" used by the high-risk AI system in making or contributing to its decision (Section 6-1-1703(4)(b)(II)).

C. Practices

There are four aspects to consider in regard to privacy-related practices in ISO 42001. 1. The integrated privacy-specific approach. 2. Data governance. 3. Transparency. 4. Accountability.

(1) Integrated privacy-specific approach

Regarding the integrated privacy-specific approach, the starting point is stated in Annex D, clause 1 which supports the comprehensive treatment of privacy, as opposed to separately addressing AI-related privacy issues. In the context of privacy, ISO 42001 should be integrated with ISO 27701 to form a Privacy Information Management System. Annex D paragraph D.2 notes how AI systems process personally identifiable information in various settings, encouraging the integration of both management system standards, ISO 27701 and ISO 42001. Underlying this integration is the acknowledgment that adapting existing privacy governance structures to accommodate AI governance issues enables organizations to address AI governance issues responsibly and efficiently without significantly disrupting business operations.

There are three ways in which ISO 42001 provides for the integration of privacy governance and AI governance:

1. AI policy

AI policy (Clause 5.2 and Control A.2.3)

The first is in the AI policy. Clause 5.2 requires your organization's management to establish an AI policy, and Control A.2.3 requires your organization to determine where other policies can be affected by or apply to its objectives regarding AI systems. The Implementation Guidance B.2.3 acknowledges that the privacy domain intersects with artificial intelligence. Hence, your organization should thoroughly consider and analyze whether current policies, including privacy policies, can necessarily intersect with AI policy and either update those policies, like the privacy policy, or include provisions relating to privacy in the AI policy. So this is one way in which both privacy governance and AI governance intersect in ISO 42001.

2. Impact assessment

Impact assessments (Clause 6.1.4 and Control A.5.2)

The second way in which both privacy governance and AI governance intersect in ISO 42001 is regarding impact assessments. Clause 6.1.4 of ISO 42001 notes how AI system impact assessments focused on privacy (such as data protection impact assessments) may need to be integrated into the organization's broader risk management program, specifically when it comes to AI systems where privacy is of utmost importance.

This is buttressed by Implementation Guidance B.5.2 which repeats what was clearly stated in Clause 6.1.4 about performing privacy-specific impact assessments as part of the organization's overall risk management program.

One interpretation of these clauses and controls is that when it comes to privacy, a separate AI system impact assessment may not be necessary. Where an AI system impact assessment may contribute is in identifying and addressing risks linked to the privacy risks addressed by the data protection impact assessment.

The underlying purpose of a discipline-specific impact assessment, as provided for under ISO 42001, is to support a unified risk management framework at the organizational level. This may enable a more effective treatment of AI risks related to privacy. In this context, organizations can choose between embedding the AI system impact assessment within the data protection impact assessment or conducting the AI system impact assessment concurrently with it, bearing in mind that privacy risks are already taken into account for organization-wide risk management strategies. Such data protection impact assessments delve deeper than AI system impact assessments, examining the purpose of data collection, the method of data processing, the scope of data processing, the sensitivity of the data, the data subjects affected, the context of the processing, and the extent of individual participation provided. Hence, this more specialized impact assessment, which is discipline-specific, should be taken into account under ISO 42001.

3. Privacy by design

The third way in which privacy governance and AI governance intersect is in the design and development of AI systems.

Control A.6.1.3, which provides for the responsible design and development of AI systems, does not explicitly mention privacy by design. Privacy by design involves embedding privacy into the system itself from the outset. In this context, the responsible design and development of AI systems, including consideration of privacy at various stages of the AI system's life cycle, would be a more proactive approach to addressing privacy concerns. Privacy by design is not conducted at the end of the process but is a process in itself, interwoven with the software development life cycle. Data protection concerns are considered throughout this life cycle. Methods in which privacy by design can be incorporated into the design and development of AI systems include adding privacy controls to existing AI control catalogs.

CHAPTER 6　PRIVACY

Further, this could include the incorporation of privacy-enhancing technologies (Figure 6-2). Several shall be listed here:

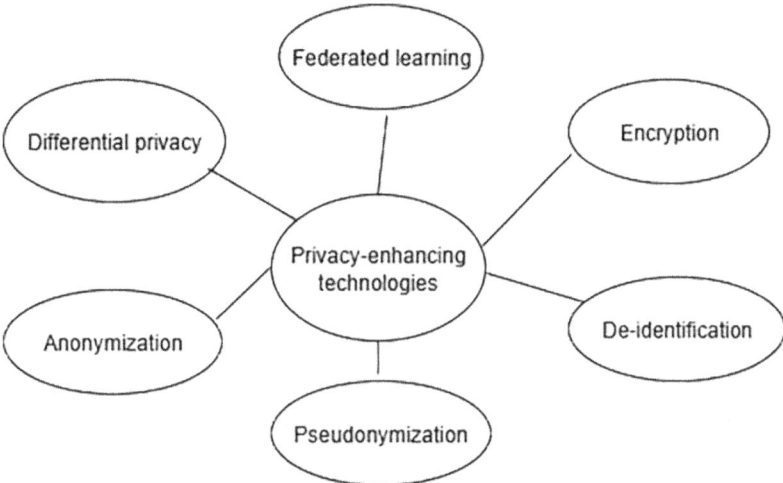

Figure 6-2. *Privacy-enhancing technologies*

   a. Use of synthetic data to replicate the statistical properties of training data. AI models generate it and are subsequently used to train and test these models, particularly when data from the real world is limited. Even if adversarial attacks are to occur such that the AI model leaks some training data, that would not threaten privacy because it is not, in a sense, "real" data.

   b. Anonymization, which removes personal identifiers

   c. Pseudonymization, which changes personal identifiers, including names, to some other name; and de-identification, which removes some but not all of the personal identifiers. These three methods constitute data masking, where sensitive data is altered to provide little value to malicious actors.

   d. Encryption to ensure that the data is never exposed, requiring a key to encrypt and decrypt the data, preventing adversarial actors who intercept the data from reading the actual content.

e. Differential privacy adds noise to the data, thereby obfuscating it such that malicious actors seeking to reverse-engineer data outputs cannot effectively re-identify individual data.

f. A last form of privacy-enhancing technology is federated learning. This addresses the issue that aggregating data from multiple parties increases the risk of privacy breaches and creates a single point of failure if such data were to be breached. Federated learning allows organizations to train a shared model without combining their data. No private data is aggregated into a single place with a single point of failure.

(2) Data governance

Data acquisition and quality (Controls A.7.3 and A.7.4)

We start with the acquisition and selection of the data. Under Control A.7.3, your organization should establish precisely where the data has been obtained from, by establishing a data inventory. This enables better compliance with the privacy requirements outlined in Implementation Guidance B.7.3. Implementation Guidance B.7.3 states that the details for the acquisition and selection of the data used in this AI system can include

- prior handling of the data, such as previous users of this data
- compliance with privacy requirements
- data rights related to personally identifiable information.

Each of these elements shall be examined in turn.

Regarding the details of prior handling of the data and the previous uses of this data, this is related to the concern of secondary use mentioned in Section A (Principles) of this chapter. The reuse of data provided by data subjects may violate the principle of use limitation if it is used to train an AI system without the data subject's consent. Therefore, this control requires your organization to consider whether such secondary use is in compliance with relevant privacy requirements, such as those under applicable data protection laws.

Also, regarding the mention of personally identifiable information in Implementation Guidance B.7.3, what is required of your organization is to clearly classify data accordingly and note that specific privacy legal requirements attach to such personally identifiable information, where data subjects have specific data rights in this regard.

Furthermore, in conducting an inventory of its data, your organization should also determine whether any privacy-enhancing technologies have already been applied to the dataset. Such information can be captured in data sheets. Documents such as privacy impact assessments or data protection impact assessments of the data that has been acquired and selected can also be included.

Overall, understanding how the data has been collected helps an organization properly assess the integrity and quality of the data, which relates to Control A.7.4 concerning data quality for AI systems, where organizations should define and document data quality requirements to ensure that data used for the development of AI systems meets those requirements.

Data management processes (Control A.7.2)

Having covered the data itself, the processes of managing data are the subject of Control A.7.2, which requires organizations to define, document, and implement data management processes regarding the development of AI systems.

These data management processes can include privacy implications arising from the use of data, especially personally identifiable information. In this regard, measures such as the anonymization of personally identifiable information should be incorporated into your organization's data management processes and implemented to protect the privacy of data subjects. Other techniques include encryption and access controls. Data sharing, which is also related to access controls, also ensures that only relevant parties will have permission to access data - and this should be included in your organization's data management processes under Control A.7.2.

Data resources and preparation (Controls A.4.3 and A.7.6)

Further, under Control A.4.3 (the control on documentation of data resources), your organization should also document exactly how it intends to use the data, how it will retain and dispose of the data. Once again, Control A.4.3 requires your organization to categorize the data, distinguishing between personally identifiable information and other types of data used by your organization in the AI system. Control A.4.3 singles out the intended use of the data as a topic that your organization should document. This relates to the purpose specification principle mentioned in Section A (Principles) of this chapter, and is necessary for your organization to avoid violating the principle of use limitation.

Control A.4.3 also states that your organization should include documentation regarding data retention and disposal. They both relate to the collection limitation principle discussed in Section A (Principles) of this chapter. Bearing in mind that the risks of data breaches increase with the amount of data created and stored by an organization, a data retention policy is required to address these risks.

And regarding the disposal of data when it is no longer needed, the retention policy must specify how long your organization retains the data and when it will delete such information. It would also be helpful for your organization to state how the data is removed from the AI system.

Finally, for Control A.4.3, your organization should consider how the data has been prepared, and this relates to Control A.7.6 on data preparation. This would include information on the steps taken by your organization, such as the anonymization of personally identifiable information.

(3) Transparency and accountability

I shall conclude this chapter by examining the transparency and accountability measures related to privacy in ISO 42001. Here, transparency entails both communication and documentation.

Incident reporting (Control A.8.4)

Regarding communication, Control A.8.4 states that your organization should determine and document a plan for communicating incidents to system users. Such incidents can be related not only to the AI system itself, but also to privacy issues such as data breaches. This control further notes that organization can integrate reporting activities for AI into its broader organizational incident management processes, but should be aware of the unique requirements related not only to AI systems but also to unique components of AI systems. Implementation Guidance B.8.4 explains this with the example of a data breach concerning personally identifiable information (for which different reporting requirements may apply). Finally, Implementation Guidance B.8.4

refers to ISO 27701 for providing additional details on incident management related to privacy. Therefore, even for this transparency obligation, the standard provides for the integration of incident response, as well as for communication regarding incidents, and for the communication of incidents themselves. This standard also integrates privacy governance and data governance.

Communication of information to interested parties (Control A.8.5)

And in this regard, data protection authorities would constitute an interested party under Control A.8.5, which states that organizations should determine their obligations regarding the reporting of information to AI systems. This would cover incidents such as data breaches. Implementation Guidance B.8.5 states that in some cases the organization may be legally bound to provide necessary information to regulators. Information can be reported to interested parties, such as regulatory authorities, within the appropriate timeframe. Your organization should understand the legal obligations in this respect and ensure that the proper information is shared with the correct authorities. Control A.8.4 only mentions the communication of incidents to system users, and is hence a subset of Control A.8.5.

Intended use (Control A.9.4)

As for documentation, Implementation Guidance B.9.4 mentions that the organization should maintain event logs or other documentation related to the deployment and operation of the AI system, and goes on further to indicate that the time period during which event logs and other documentation are kept depends not only on the intended use of the AI system, but also on your organization's data retention policies and relevant legal requirements for data retention. Once again, there is the integration between AI governance and privacy governance. With this specific AI governance measure, Control A.9.4 must be consistent with your organization's data retention policies.

Allocation of roles and responsibilities within the organization (Control A.3.2)

Regarding accountability measures related to privacy, Control A.3.2 states that organizations should define the roles and responsibilities for AI according to their needs. Additionally, privacy is identified as an area requiring defined roles and responsibilities in Implementation Guidance B.3.2. Here, the existing privacy-related roles and existing privacy compliance programs enable an organization to satisfy this control. The structure is already in place to be leveraged for AI governance. Privacy officers often are well-placed within organizations to address privacy-related issues arising from AI systems. In this context, if your organization has individuals and teams responsible for privacy, they should ensure alignment between the existing privacy management processes and AI management processes. Again, in this context, AI governance and privacy governance intersect.

Allocation of responsibilities with third parties and customers (Control A.10.2)

Another aspect of accountability related to privacy is the allocation of responsibilities, as discussed under Control A.10.2, where your organization should ensure that responsibilities within the life cycle of the AI system are allocated among your organization, its partners, suppliers, customers, and third parties. The objective of this control is to ensure that risks and responsibilities are appropriately apportioned where third parties are involved. Implementation Guidance B.10.2 states that when processed data includes personally identifiable information, both the processors and controllers of such personally identifiable information usually bear responsibilities. The ISO 27701 controls should be considered depending on your organization's and AI systems' data processing activities concerning personally identifiable information, as well as your organization's role in applying and developing the AI system throughout its life cycle. Your organization itself can take on the role of a controller, joint controller, processor, or both, and should determine whether it is a controller, processor, or both, depending on the data processing arrangement.

In agreements with third parties, your organization should obtain information on the presence of personally identifiable information in the training data, or whether any privacy-enhancing technologies were used in the preparation of data.

External reporting (Control A.8.3)

Finally, external reporting, as provided for under Control A.8.3, allows users to report feedback on the AI system when it misuses data, thereby contributing to the accountability of the AI system regarding privacy and upholding the principle of individual participation, as discussed in Section A (Principles) of this chapter.

Summary and key takeaways

1. Integrate AI-specific privacy measures with your organization's overall approach to privacy by aligning the AI policy with your organization's privacy policy, specifically by updating the privacy policy to take into account AI-related issues and/or reproducing its language in the AI policies, and clarifying whether existing privacy-related roles will be leveraged to address AI governance issues [Controls A.2.3 and A.3.2].

2. Adopt a unified approach towards privacy risks either by embedding the AI system impact assessment within your organization's data protection impact assessment, or by conducting the AI system impact assessment alongside it concurrently [Clause 6.1.4 and Control A.5.2].

3. Design the AI system with privacy considerations in mind as part of an overall privacy-by-design approach, specifically by considering whether and how any of the various privacy-enhancing technologies (encryption, differential privacy, federated learning, anonymization, pseudonymization, de-identification, synthetic data) can be interwoven with the various stages of the AI life cycle. [Control A.6.1.3]

4. Conduct a comprehensive inventory and classification of the training data (including data obtained from third parties), pay special attention to personally identifiable information, and document the legal requirements attaching to such sensitive information and measures (such as privacy-enhancing technologies) in place to handle such sensitive information and avoid unauthorized access. [Controls A.4.3, A.7.2 and A.7.3]

5. Draft and negotiate agreements with third parties (including suppliers and other partners) stipulating the roles of data processor, controller and joint controller (if applicable) regarding personally identifiable information, throughout the entire AI life cycle. {Control A.10.2]

The next chapter will examine the principles, provisions, and practices related to fairness.

CHAPTER 7

FAIRNESS

This chapter on fairness starts with a discussion of the principle of fairness and several related concepts, examines the applicable regulations, and analyzes the relevant ISO 42001 clauses and controls.

A. Principles

In this section, I examine both concepts of fairness and bias.

(1) Fairness

ISO 42001 Annex C paragraph C.2.5 lists fairness as an objective, noting how decisions made by automatic AI systems may affect both individuals and groups unfairly. So the definition of fairness entails equal treatment of individuals and of groups.

Individual fairness requires that individuals in similar positions be accorded equal treatment. However, there are limits to this principle of individual fairness because not all individuals are placed at the same starting point. For example, should socioeconomic factors be taken into account when colleges make decisions about admissions into specific programs? Here, it can be challenging to agree on what constitutes likeness, especially in the context of AI algorithms. Developers would have to determine the relevant factors in deciding how to treat individuals fairly.

Group fairness focuses on whether and how groups differ statistically. In the context of AI, the question is whether there are specific groups that are disadvantaged by the AI system's algorithm. There are three distinct concepts when it comes to group fairness (Figure 7-1):

CHAPTER 7   FAIRNESS

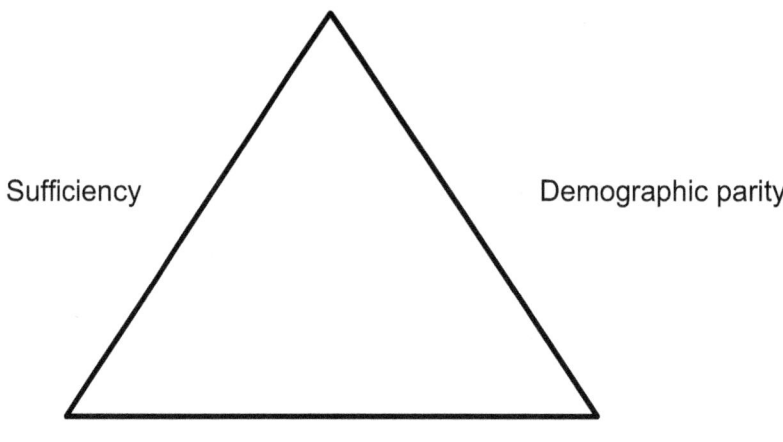

Figure 7-1. *Group fairness concepts*

1. Demographic parity: whether the likelihood of a positive prediction is similar across various groups
   Demographic parity is concerned with whether the distribution of predictions is the same across various groups. This could mean the proportion of granted loans is the same across groups. Outcomes must be equally distributed. Here, the accuracy of predictions is not the primary concern. This makes demographic parity somewhat inadequate as a measure of fairness. For example, demographic parity is satisfied even if all predictions regarding a specific subset of the population are wrong.

   Demographic parity is satisfied so long as the proportion of positive predictions is similar across various groups. The quality of predictions is not taken into account for demographic parity. This can be an issue in specific contexts, like the medical context, where the quality of prediction matters greatly. Therefore, the cost of false positives is high in these contexts, making the accuracy of predictions crucial and rendering demographic parity an insufficient measure of fairness.

2. Sufficiency: whether the likelihood of an accurate positive prediction is similar across various groups

   In contrast, sufficiency requires that all groups would have the same proportion of individuals correctly identified as positive as compared to those the AI model has predicted to be positive. The key point here is to minimize differences in terms of the proportion of false negatives and false positives across various groups. However, sufficiency does not account for base rate differences across various groups. Base rate refers to the frequency with which something occurs within a population. There may be different levels of poverty among different age groups or between different genders. If these base rates are significantly different, then achieving sufficiency becomes challenging and can impact the AI system's performance.

3. Equal opportunity: whether the likelihood of being positive when predicted to be positive is equal across multiple groups

   The third concept is equal opportunity, which requires that individuals from all groups share the same likelihood of being accurately identified as positive. Here, the true positive rate refers to the scenario where equal opportunity is applied, meaning that different demographic groups have the same chance of being correctly identified as positive. This measure of fairness ensures that the same proportion of individuals with a specific medical condition are correctly identified as such.
   Hence, when assessing fairness, decision-makers and organizations must determine precisely which measure of fairness is being applied, based on the AI system's intended objectives. Only then can bias be accurately tested, for what fairness means differs depending on the context. Deciding on the specific measure of fairness is crucial when developing an AI system, particularly due to various trade-offs that prevent all three notions of fairness from being satisfied simultaneously. The use case of the AI system will help organizations determine the appropriate concept of fairness.

CHAPTER 7   FAIRNESS

(2) Bias

Now, when it comes to bias, the definition of bias is an inclination that is opposed to fairness and impartiality. Here, the focus is on algorithmic bias, which is distinguished from the term "bias" used in other disciplines. Algorithmic bias occurs in the form of a systematic deviation resulting from an error in the algorithm. This deviation is measured by reference to a specific baseline standard, and this error results in certain groups being either privileged or overlooked repeatedly. This deviation from the algorithm's intended function is what makes the algorithm biased. If the algorithm of an AI system is intended to select the best university applicants and it does so based on unrelated features such as their religion, then this algorithm is deviating from its intended function to pick the best students and is therefore biased.

Algorithmic bias is distinct from the way bias is used in other disciplines. In data science and statistics, bias refers to systematic errors in prediction and measurement. In psychology, bias is a systematic error in human judgment. So the automation bias referred to in Chapter 5 (Security and Safety) is a good example of bias in the context of psychology.

Algorithmic bias extends beyond systematic errors to consider the unfair outcomes faced by subsets of a population. This is connected to a distinct form of bias known as societal bias, where one group is favored or discriminated against in comparison to another group.

When assessing algorithmic bias, it is crucial to acknowledge that not all biases are inherently problematic from an ethical standpoint. The point is that in AI systems, biases resulting in specific individuals or groups being disadvantaged for inappropriate reasons are what create the moral concern. It is hence crucial for AI systems to avoid ethically unacceptable biases. This is a relevant consideration when an AI system is being developed, and when the values of the AI system are determined by its developers and embedded in the AI system's design.

Algorithmic bias can specifically affect even the most well-designed AI systems, which aim to reflect ethical AI values, in several ways in which algorithmic bias can enter an AI system. The four distinct ways in which algorithmic bias affects AI systems are the following: a. Deciding the objectives, b. Data, c. Development, d. Deployment. I shall examine each of these stages in turn.

(a) Deciding the objectives

If the AI system's objectives engender specific issues such as subconscious bias, then the algorithm would contain that bias from the very beginning. The specific social and cultural lenses of the developers designing the AI system are key, considering that their implicit biases can influence the AI system through the manner in which they frame the problem the AI system is intended to address. In such cases, biases are often implicit and unintended. To address bias at this stage, examine and modify the AI system's objectives accordingly.

(b) Data

The second way bias affects the AI system is through data. Here, I examine various ways in which bias affects the data collection and data preparation stages. Training data which does not accurately reflect the statistical distribution of traits within the population fails to accurately represent the target population. Overrepresenting or underrepresenting specific social segments of a population leads to algorithmic decisions being biased and less accurate, resulting in increased disparities within the population. Such AI systems, using these datasets, would not perform as accurately in identifying the affected subsets of the population. Here, sampling bias is an issue when the data sample is not random. It is not easy to generalize the population trends to another population. Another way bias affects the data collection stage is when the methods of measuring data are inconsistent across the sample, leading to data being biased in favor of specific subsets of the population. A third way in which bias can affect the AI system at the data collection stage is when historical data is used as training data. Outdated data containing biases leads to the algorithm learning and perpetuating these biases, such that it no longer accurately reflects current trends. This, in turn, reinforces historical biases within a society, perpetuating societal biases.

(c) Development

Apart from bias being introduced into the AI system at the data collection and preparation stages, such biases can emerge during the development of the AI systems, including at the training, modelling, and validation phases. Designers of the AI system may program the algorithm to prefer certain groups of a population over others, and the algorithm may reinforce the bias present in the training data during the training process.

(d) Deployment

Finally, biases can emerge at the deployment stage. AI algorithms learn from their output, reflecting certain biases and thereby perpetuating those biases in a self-reinforcing feedback loop. And while the over-reliance on AI output is in itself a form of automation bias, human oversight, which seeks to address the issue of automation bias, may result in the biases of the humans monitoring and controlling the system's output affecting the output that the AI system learns from, thus reinforcing those human biases.

All of the above ways in which bias enters the AI system are compounded by the inscrutability of AI systems, algorithms, and models, where the input and output may be clear, but the opaqueness of the decision-making process makes it challenging to trace biases in the algorithm. As such, biases in the training data may be hidden and therefore difficult to remove.

Algorithmic bias constitutes discrimination in a legal sense when individuals and groups are disadvantaged based on specific characteristics that are legally protected. This may occur in various contexts, ranging from civil rights to economic opportunities, including social and insurance benefits, the criminal justice system, healthcare, and other aspects of life. Algorithms that determine different levels of access to these benefits across various sectors may lead to discrimination affecting certain groups. If algorithmic bias is not addressed correctly, it can, more broadly, deepen societal divides on multiple grounds, such as race, gender, and income level. Such discriminatory outcomes, perpetuated by algorithmic bias, contribute to societal inequalities.

B. Provisions

This sub-section covers legal provisions concerning fairness and bias in the laws of the EU, the US, and China.

EU   A. **EU AI Act:**

- The EU AI Act defines "diversity, non-discrimination and fairness" in the AI context as the development and use of AI systems "in a way that includes diverse actors and promotes equal access, gender equality and cultural diversity, while avoiding discriminatory impacts and unfair biases that are prohibited by Union or national law", and calls for consideration of the European Commission's Ethics Guidelines for Trustworthy AI (Recital 27).

- Datasets for AI training, validation and testing must be "sufficiently representative," and this entails the "appropriate statistical properties" regarding "the persons or groups of persons" relevant to the high-risk AI system's intended use (Article 10(3)).

- Providers must examine training, validation and testing data sets for possible biases likely to affect personal health and safety and fundamental rights or result in discrimination prohibited under EU law "especially where data outputs influence inputs for future operations" (Article 10(2)(f)), and take "appropriate measures to detect, prevent and mitigate" these possible biases (Article 10(2)(g)).

- Providers must eliminate or reduce the risk of biases emanating from feedback loops in high-risk AI systems after these systems have been put on the market or into service (Article 15(4)).

- Finally, the EU AI Act prohibits the following AI practices:

    - Exploitation of the vulnerabilities of individuals or groups based on their age, disability, socio-economic situation, with the aim or effect of "materially distorting" their behavior in a way that actually causes or is likely to cause significant harm to them or others (Article 5(1)(b)).

    - Social evaluation, classification, and scoring practices concerning individuals or groups based on their behaviors and personality, leading to the "detrimental or unfavourable treatment" of such individuals or groups (i) in unrelated social contexts, or/and (ii) which is either unjustified or disproportionate to their behavior (Article 5(1)(c)).

- Categorization of individuals based on their biometric data to deduce or infer their race and ethnicity, political opinions, religious and philosophical beliefs, trade union membership, genetic and biometric data, health data, and sexuality and sexual orientation (Article 5(1)(g)).

B. **Digital Services Act**: This regulation briefly takes into consideration the issue of bias, whereby providers of very large online platforms and of very large online search engines, when assessing and addressing risks, should assess and, if necessary, adjust their recommender systems' design, for example by taking measures preventing or minimizing biases leading to the discrimination of persons in vulnerable situations (Recital 94).

US:

The US adopts a more piecemeal approach to tackling the issue of bias in AI at both the federal and state levels:

At the federal level:

- **Americans with Disabilities Act** requires employers to provide "reasonable accommodations" (Section 12112(a)(5)) and prohibits them from screening out individuals with disabilities (Section 12112(a)(6)) and making disability-related inquiries and conducting disability-related medical examinations (Section 12112(d)).

- **Title VII of the Civil Rights Act of 1964** prohibits employment discrimination based on "discrimination based on race, color, religion, sex, or national origin" (Section 2000e-16(a)) and assigns enforcement powers to the Equal Employment Opportunity Commission (Section 2000e-16(b)).

- Section 1557(a) of the **Affordable Care Act** prohibits discrimination in health programs or activities.

At the state and local level:

A. **Colorado SB 205**

- Both developers and deployers must "use reasonable care to protect consumers from any known or reasonably foreseeable risks of algorithmic discrimination" (Sections 6-1-1702(1) and 6-1-1703(1).

- There is a "rebuttable presumption" that they used reasonable care if they complied with their duties under these two legal provisions - which Chapters 4 (Accountability), 6 (Privacy) and 7 (Fairness) of this book have fleshed out.

B. **Texas Responsible AI Governance Act**

- Individuals must not develop or deploy AI systems to discriminate on grounds of race, color, national origin, sex, age, religion, or disability in violation of federal or state law (though "a disparate impact is not sufficient by itself to demonstrate an intent to discriminate") (Section 552.056(b)), or to restrict one's communication on grounds of their political opinion (Section 552.005(a)(1)).

- Governmental entities must not use AI systems for social scoring of persons or groups based on their behavior or personal characteristics, which may lead to their "detrimental or unfavorable treatment" which is either unrelated to the context of, or "unjustified or disproportionate" to, their behavior or personal characteristics (Section 552.053(1)-(2)).

C. **New York City Local Law 144**

- Employers and employment agencies that use automated employment decision-making tools to screen employees and candidates must obtain a bias audit for the tool within a year prior to its use (§ 20-871(a)).

- An independent auditor will have to conduct an impartial evaluation of the tool for "disparate impact on persons of the race/ethnicity, gender and job categories listed in the EEO-1 Component 1 Report (§ 20-870).

China:

A. **Generative AI Interim Measures**

- This law prohibits content "promoting ethnic hatred and ethnic discrimination" (Article 4(1)).

- During the selection of training data, model generation, and optimization during processes such as algorithm design, and the provision of services, service providers must take effective measures to "prevent the creation of discrimination such as by race, ethnicity, faith, nationality, region, sex, age, profession, or health" (Article 4(2)).

B. **Algorithm Recommendation Provisions**: Service providers that sell goods and services to consumers are prohibited from using algorithms to unreasonably differentiate prices and other transaction terms based on consumer preferences, trading habits, or "other traits" (Article 21).

C. Practices

The starting point for fairness in ISO 42001 is Control A.6.1.2, which requires organizations to identify and document objectives regarding the responsible development of AI systems. What is crucial to note here is Implementation Guidance B.6.1.2, which clearly states that if the organization defines fairness as one objective, it should be incorporated into the requirements specification, data acquisition, data conditioning, model training, verification, and validation. Your organization should provide requirements and guidelines as necessary to ensure that measures are integrated into the various stages. For example, the requirement to use a specific testing tool or method to address unfairness or unwanted bias to achieve such objectives. Bearing that in mind, there are four parts in this section: 1. Team diversity. 2. Data governance. 3. Assurance measures. 4. Transparency and accountability.

(1) Team diversity

To ensure fairness in AI systems, it is essential to promote diversity and inclusivity in teams working on AI systems throughout their entire life cycle. Control A.4.6 on human resources states that, as part of resource identification, the organization should document information about the human resources and their competencies utilized for the development, deployment, operation, change management, maintenance, transfer, and decommissioning of the AI system, as well as the verification and integration of the AI system. It is the entire AI system that is the subject of concern, and Implementation Guidance B.4.6 requires your organization to consider the need for expertise and include the type of roles necessary for the system. It provides the example of an organization, including specific demographic groups related to data sets used to train machine learning models, if their inclusion is a necessary component of the system design. This control ensures a cross-functional, diverse group that participates throughout the entire AI life cycle, including planning, design, development, and deployment of AI. This acknowledges that the diversity of background and perspective helps avoid cognitive biases, which can affect the AI system's operations. This is a crucial measure to prevent an AI system from creating biased output.

(2) Data governance

Here, ISO 42001 focuses on the representativeness of training data to ensure that the AI system avoids bias. Several controls support this:

Data management processes (Control A.7.2)

Regarding data for the development and enhancement of AI systems, Control A.7.2 requires your organization to define, document, and implement data management processes related to the development of AI systems. Implementation Guidance B.7.2 states that data management can entail comparing the training data's representativeness to the AI system's operational domain.

Data acquisition (Control A.7.3)

Implementation Guidance B.7.3 provides that details of data acquisition can include data subject demographics and characteristics, including known or potential biases or other systematic errors. Checking for such issues at the acquisition stage allows the company to acquire more representative samples of data, or the company can also pre-process the data to make it less biased and more balanced.

Data resources (Control A.4.3)

This is supported by Control A.4.3 on data resources, which requires your organization to document information about the data resources used for the AI system. Implementation Guidance B.4.3 provides that such documentation should include known or potential bias issues in the data. Identification of biases is a crucial factor in addressing the lack of representativeness in the dataset. However, balancing the dataset entails increasing the proportion of the less represented subset of the demographic in a dataset. This can result in challenges, especially in domains where relevant cases cannot be found. Knowing exactly which groups to pay special attention to so as to balance a dataset can also be tricky. Such groups may include individuals sharing a characteristic protected under the law. There are no simple solutions to the question of how datasets can be balanced, and the values informing this decision would be determined by the team members responsible for designing the AI system.

In summary, paying attention to the representativeness of the dataset at the data acquisition stage is crucial to ensure the absence of bias in the data.

Data quality (Control A.7.4)

This balancing of the dataset to address the issue of bias is also dealt with in Control A.7.4 on the quality of data for AI systems, where the control states that the organization should define and document requirements for data quality and ensure that data used to develop and operate the AI system meets those requirements. Implementation Guidance B.7.4 requires your organization to consider the impact of bias on system performance and system fairness and make such adjustments as necessary to the model and data used to improve performance and fairness so they are acceptable for the use case. Bias in the data affects the system's performance and is a quality concern.

Balancing the data set with more representative samples is one such adjustment that can be made to the data. Another method could be adjusting the model to account for imbalance. Moreover, just as bias can affect the quality of data, poor data quality can also introduce bias, particularly in cases where data is missing. In such cases, the data is not entirely representative, which affects the effectiveness of the AI algorithms. Additionally, data containing cognitive biases constitutes weaker quality data, which in turn affects the system's performance and results in unfair outcomes. A third possibility is to use synthetic data, as discussed in Chapter 6 (Privacy). Synthetic data can be easily designed to exclude biases.

(3) Assurance measures

There are several assurance measures relevant to the principle of fairness in ISO 42001.

Risk assessment (Clause 6.1.2) and impact assessment (Clause 6.1.4)

The first is the risk assessment under Clause 6.1.2. One risk source listed in Annex C paragraph C.3.3 is the level of automation, which can have an impact on various areas of concern, such as fairness. In the risk assessment, your organization should consider whether the training data lacks diversity, which could affect technologies such as facial recognition, leading to biased outcomes, with greater accuracy for some subsets rather than others. If AI-driven recruitment system models are trained on historical data containing biases, they may screen out candidates from specific subsets of the population, leading to unfair outcomes.

Linked to the risk assessment in Clause 6.1.2 is the AI system impact assessment in Clause 6.1.4, which requires the organization responsible for the AI system to assess the consequences on various groups of individuals in society, taking into consideration the possibility that some groups may be treated unfairly compared to others by the AI system. More broadly, your organization should also consider the impact of the AI system on society as a whole, and whether the algorithms in the AI system may even perpetuate existing biases in society itself.

Internal audits (Clause 9.2)

Apart from risk and impact assessments, algorithmic audits are another assurance measure. Clause 9.2 provides for internal audits. Algorithmic auditing involves a fresh examination of algorithms to determine whether the system is exhibiting biases.

Algorithmic audits are distinct from risk assessments. Risk assessments examine the socio-technical environment in which the AI is deployed, whereas algorithmic assessments inspect the inner functioning of the algorithm. Testing the system for bias involves using personal information, as provided for under the EU AI Act. The point is to use data to determine whether the system contains any biases.

(4) Transparency and accountability measures in relation to fairness

Providing system documentation and information to users (Control A.8.2)

Control A.8.2 requires your organization to determine and provide the necessary information to system users. Implementation Guidance B.8.2 further states that this information can include relevant details from the impact assessment, such as potential benefits and harms, particularly if applicable to specific demographic groups. Here, model cards help reveal the potential biases of an AI system.

External reporting (Control A.8.3)

As for accountability measures, Control A.8.3 pertains to external reporting by interested parties to the organization regarding the impacts of the system. Implementation Guidance B.8.3 requires your organization to provide capabilities for users or other external parties to report adverse impacts, and includes the example of unfairness. This is crucial because users may notice biases in the AI system's output. Such biases may amount to discrimination based on protected characteristics. It is essential for organizations to be aware of this, and the feedback mechanism in A.8.3 is helpful in this regard.

Supplier relationships (Control A.10.3)

Furthermore, regarding agreements with third parties, as outlined in Control A.10.3, organizations should determine how third-party suppliers address the issue of bias, whether their AI systems exhibit bias, and how they handle unfair outcomes. Organizations can require bias reports from independent assessors regarding the performance of third-party AI systems.

Summary and key takeaways:

1. Determine which measure of fairness is to be applied (demographic parity, sufficiency, equal opportunity) based on your organization's AI system's use case, bearing in mind that fairness is context-dependent and the measure chosen affects the accuracy of bias testing.

2. Ensure that your organization has cross-functional and well-represented teams providing a diversity of perspectives while working on the AI system throughout its life cycle. [Control A.4.6]

3. Check for, identify, and document known or potential bias issues and lack of representativeness in the dataset at the data acquisition stage. [Controls A.4.3, A.7.2, and A.7.3]

4. Determine how to correct imbalances in the dataset by including more representative samples, adjusting the model, or including synthetic data. [Control A.7.4]

5. Conduct regular algorithmic audits with personal data (in compliance with existing privacy laws) to test AI systems for bias. [Clause 9.2]

The next chapter will examine the principles, provisions, and practices related to transparency and explainability.

CHAPTER 8

TRANSPARENCY AND EXPLAINABILITY

This chapter on transparency and explainability starts with a discussion of the principles and several related concepts, examines the applicable regulations, and analyzes the relevant ISO 42001 clauses and controls.

A. Principles

This subsection starts by examining 1. the black box problem, followed by 2. transparency and 3. explainability, and 4. the impact of (not) having both.

(1) The black box problem

Transparency and explainability are principles aimed at addressing what is known as the black box problem in AI. The black box problem operates at several levels, which I will examine before discussing the definitions of transparency and explainability.

At the most basic level, an individual subjected to an AI system's algorithm may not even be aware of this fact. They may not even be aware of the algorithm's existence, let alone the fact that they are subject to its decision-making process. This is particularly the case for private companies, which may not be subject to the same level of scrutiny as public institutions.

The bigger issue in the black box problem relates to the difficulties we have in understanding how AI systems arrive at decisions and how we can ascertain the accuracy of predictions. Even if individuals are aware that they are subject to algorithmic decision-making, they may not have access to how algorithms work or the reasoning behind their specific outcomes.

There are several reasons behind this inscrutability of AI systems:

a. Opacity: Specifically in the case of neural networks which have several layers of reasoning and large amounts of data, it is challenging to find an explanation as to how they reach their predictions. In contrast to decision trees which can be interpreted in a manner that is more easily understood by human beings, neural networks are black boxes. Experts may know the input and output, but do not fully understand the specific decision-making process.

b. High knowledge barrier: Specialized knowledge is often necessary to fully comprehend an algorithm. Without that, even with access to training data and source codes, algorithms, especially neural networks, can be too complicated to understand.

c. Confidentiality: The algorithm's workings are kept confidential for two reasons.

   i. Intellectual property protection. These algorithms constitute proprietary interests and trade secrets of the algorithm's owners, which safeguard and maintain their competitive advantage.

   ii. Security: Making the details of an algorithm public increases the likelihood of cyberattacks by malicious actors and other risks, such as scams, spam, and fraud.

This inscrutability is precisely what the principles of transparency and explainability are intended to address.

(2) Transparency

ISO 42001 Annex C paragraph C.2.11 lists transparency as an objective for both AI systems and the entities operating them. Transparency refers to the extent to which an organization clearly communicates its policies and provides information on its AI systems, which may include both technical and non-technical documentation.

Transparency does not necessarily mean that users will be aware of everything about how an AI system or model works. Transparency involves helping users understand the training data, its capabilities, limitations, and algorithms, and keeping users informed about when an AI system is interacting with them, or when content they are exposed to is AI-generated. It means that the organization makes available information regarding the system (taking into account the limitations of the AI system) and it informs users and other stakeholders what the organization knows and does not know about the AI system. Transparency is related to but distinct from explainability.

(3) Explainability

ISO 42001 Annex C paragraph C.2.11 lists explainability as an objective, which entails helping one understand the reasoning behind the outcomes of the AI system. Explainability helps promote transparency. Ensuring that AI systems remain transparent and explainable is a key aspect of maintaining trust.

At the same time, providing access to code or training datasets, especially in the open source world, will increase transparency. It will not contribute to explainability. Explainability entails expressing the key aspects of an AI system's decision and the reasoning behind it in a way that the average user can understand. This is often after the AI system has made its decision.

Explainability operates at several levels. Understanding the decision of an AI system is at one level of complexity. Another is understanding how an AI system operates in various contexts. However, explainability is limited in the case of deep neural network models. Any explanation regarding such black box models may not be entirely correct, given that full explainability is not possible in this scenario.

Interpretability is the alternative. There are several differences between interpretability and explainability. Interpretability seeks to ensure that the model's architecture is built so as to ensure that the reasoning process is comprehensible. Rather than relying on black boxes such as neural network models, interpretability is also about the ability to explain the AI model's reasoning. But unlike explainability, which explains why a decision was made after the fact, interpretability is applied before that. It provides an understanding of the reasoning process, which is inherent in the system's design. Interpretable models are usually used in domain-specific applications.

(4) Consequences

ISO 42001 Annex C paragraph C.3.2 lists the lack of transparency and explainability as a risk source, where the organization's credibility can be impacted by its inability to provide suitable information to relevant entities. Explaining and interpreting the decision-making process of an AI system is crucial to mitigating the risks associated with AI systems, ensuring that they adhere to ethical standards and comply with relevant requirements.

The two primary consequences of a lack of transparency and explainability are:

a. Erosion of trust

The lack of confidence by customers, users, and other stakeholders stems from the difficulty in understanding the decisions made by AI systems, such as black boxes and neural networks, and, more broadly, understanding how AI works in the first place. This is especially true when decisions made by AI systems have a significant impact on individuals or groups. In such cases, the inability to explain decisions made by AI systems results in a loss of trust. Explainability increases trust by making AI systems appear more predictable.

b. Corresponding lack of accountability

Bearing in mind that AI systems' decisions can significantly affect the lives of individuals and groups, promoting explainability of such systems enables the creators of such AI systems to be held accountable to these individuals and groups, for example, by addressing biased decisions reached by these AI systems. Without such explainability, the creators of such AI systems may not adhere to legal and ethical rules.

B. Provisions

This sub-section covers approaches to the issue of transparency and explainability in the laws of the EU, the US, and China.

    EU

        A. **EU AI Act**

            Specific obligations regarding transparency attach to different categories of organizations, depending on the level of risk in their AI systems:

Table 8-1. *Transparency obligations for various categories of organizations under the EU AI Act*

Organization category	Transparency requirements
Level 1: Providers <u>and</u> deployers of "certain" AI systems, including: — Those engaging in direct human interaction (chatbots and digital assistants — content generation systems (e.g. ChatGPT, Dall-E) — other systems that can generate deepfakes and biometric systems (e.g. those engaged in emotion and facial recognition)	— Informing users that they are interacting with an AI — Implementing machine-readable watermarks so that users know the content is AI-generated (Article 50)

(*continued*)

Table 8-1. (*continued*)

Organization category	Transparency requirements
Level 2: Providers of high-risk AI systems	A. Documentation: • Technical documentation (Article 11) • Record-keeping (Article 12) • Documentation related to system design, development processes, and data used for training, testing, and validation (Article 18) • Automatically generated logs (Article 19) B. Disclosure: Alert the relevant stakeholders (the market surveillance authorities, in particular) if • a high-risk AI system that they have placed on the market or put into service is not in conformity with this Regulation (Article 20) • any serious incident has occurred (Article 73). Overall, the high-risk AI system must be "designed and developed in such a way as to ensure that their operation is "sufficiently transparent to enable deployers to interpret a system's output and use it appropriately" (Article 13(1)).
Level 3: Providers of general-purpose AI systems (both with and without "systemic risks")	• More extensive documentation requirements (Articles 53 and 55) • Information listed in Section 1 of Annex XI • Information listed in Annex XII for the benefit of downstream providers integrating the general-purpose AI mode into their system
Level 4: Providers of general-purpose AI systems with "systemic risks"	• Additional information listed in Section 2 of Annex XI

B. **GDPR:** The data controller must provide "meaningful information" to the data subject about the logic underpinning any automated decision, and the significance and envisaged consequences of the data processing for the data subject - in both instances where:

   a. Personal data has been obtained from the data subject (Article 13(2)(f))

   b. Personal data has not been obtained from the data subject (Article 14(2)(g)).

C. **Digital Services Act**

   a. Recommender systems: Providers must explain to viewers "in plain and intelligible language" the main parameters used in recommender systems, including the "why" behind the information shown to viewers (Article 27(1)-(2))

   b. Online advertising: Very large online platforms or very large online search engines must explain in a repository the parameters for online advertisements intended to be presented specifically to – or excluded from – "particular groups" (Article 39(2)(e)).

US

Various US state laws impose transparency obligations on organizations that develop or deploy AI.

A. **California** has three regulations concerning transparency:

   I. **California Artificial Intelligence Training Data Transparency Act**: Developers must post on their website detailed documentation regarding the training datasets of the generative AI system or service (whether paid or free) prior to its release for public use or its "substantial modification" (Section 3111).

   II. **California AI Transparency Act**: Organizations that produce generative AI systems with over one million monthly users or visitors must include:

   - A "latent" disclosure regarding the details of the generative AI system (Section 22757.3(b))

CHAPTER 8   TRANSPARENCY AND EXPLAINABILITY

- The option by the user or visitor for the generative AI system to also include a "manifest" (easily recognized) disclosure clearly identifies the content as AI-generated (Section 22757.3(a))
- Free AI detection tools (Section 22757.2(a))

III. **The California Bot Act**: Both commercial and political communications require disclosure of the use of automated online accounts (Section 17941(a)), and such disclosure must be "clear, conspicuous, and reasonably designed to inform persons with whom the bot communicates or interacts that it is a bot" (Section 17941(b)).

B. **Colorado SB 205** imposes extensive transparency obligations on both developers and deployers:

- Public disclosure: Both developers and deployers must include on their website (or, in the developer's case, a public use case inventory) a statement disclosing how they manage the reasonably foreseeable risks of the algorithmic discrimination of the high-risk AI system (Sections 6-1-1702(4)(a) and 6-1-1703(5)(a)).

- Disclosure to the Attorney-General: The Attorney-General may also require from the developer a copy of the standard documentation it has provided to deployers, and from the deployer a copy of the risk management and impact assessment documentation (Sections 6-1-1702(7) and 6-1-1703(9)) – all of which have been covered in Chapter 4 (Accountability). The deployer must also notify the Attorney-General of any instances of algorithmic discrimination caused by the high-risk AI system (Section 6-1-1703(7)).

- Developer-deployer disclosure: Aside from the documentation developers must provide to deployers as covered in Chapter 4 (Accountability), they must inform all of their deployers (and other developers if relevant) of any known or reasonably foreseeable risks of algorithmic discrimination which they were alerted to either by their own testing or from a "credible report" of one of their deployers that the AI system "has caused algorithmic discrimination" (Section 6-1-1702(5)).

- Deployer-consumer disclosure: As for the transparency obligations owed by the deployer to the consumer:

    – Where the deployer uses the high-risk AI system to make or substantially contribute to a "consequential decision" concerning the consumer, the deployer must inform the consumer of the AI system's purpose and the nature of the decision (Section 6-1-1703(4)(a)).

    – Where such a "consequential decision" is "adverse" to the consumer, the deployer must further disclose how the high-risk AI system contributed to the decision, and the details of the data the decision was based upon (Section 6-1-1703(4)(b).

    – Where it is not "obvious to a reasonable person that the person is interacting with an artificial intelligence system", the deployer must "ensure" disclosure to consumers that they are interacting with an AI system (Section 6-1-1704)

In contrast with the disclosure to consumers by deployers required under Colorado SB 205,

C. **Texas Responsible AI Governance Act**

- Governmental agencies (Section 552.051(b)) and healthcare service providers (Section 552.051(e)(2)) must disclose to consumers that they are interacting with an AI system "regardless of whether it would be obvious to a reasonable consumer that the consumer is interacting with an artificial intelligence system" (Section 552.051(c)).

- Such disclosure is required "before or at the time of the interaction" (Section 552.051(d)) and must satisfy all 3 conditions:

1. It must be clear and conspicuous

2. It must be written in plain language

3. It must not use a dark pattern" - defined as "a user interface designed or manipulated with the effect of substantially subverting or impairing user autonomy, decision-making, or choice" (Section 541.001(10) (Business and Commerce Code)).

D. **Utah's AI Policy Act**

- Those in "regulated occupations" (requiring a license or state certification to practice) must "prominently disclose" that a consumer is interacting with generative AI (Section 13-2-12(4)(a)), both verbally at the start of an oral exchange and via electronic messaging prior to a written exchange (Section 13-2-12(5)(a)-(b)).

- Outside of "regulated occupations", those using, prompting or causing generative AI to interact with a person must, "if asked or prompted by the person," "clearly and conspicuously disclose" that the person is interacting with generative AI and not a human (Section 13-2-12 (3)).

E. **New York City Local Law 144**

- Employers and employment agencies must provide notice to employees and candidates concerning any use of automated employment decision tools in assessing and evaluating them for positions (§ 20-871(b)(1), including the job qualifications and characteristics used by the tool (§ 20-871(b)(2)).

- The employer or employment agency must provide such information at least 10 business days in advance and allow the employee or candidate to request an alternative selection process or accommodation (§ 20-871(b)(1)).

- They must also publish on their website the summary of the results of the tool's most recent bias audit (§ 20-871(a)(2)).

China:

A. **Generative AI Interim Measures**: Generative AI service providers must "clarify and disclose" to users "the user groups, occasions, and uses of their services" (Article 10).

B. **Algorithm Recommendation Provisions**: Service providers must "inform users in a conspicuous fashion" of the algorithmic recommendation service's circumstances, "basic principles, intended purposes, main operation mechanisms", displayed to users "in an appropriate manner" (Article 16).

C. **Deep Synthesis Provisions**: Service providers must label deep synthetic content conspicuously and "prominently" and "in a reasonable position or location" if such content may confuse or mislead the public (Article 17), provided that such labels do not interfere with the use of such services by users (Article 16).

D. **Synthetic Content Labeling Measures**: Service providers must add

   – Explicit labels to the synthetic content, including via text and voice notifications (Article 4).

   – "Implicit labels" in the form of digital watermarks - not only to the AI-generated synthetic content but also to the files' metadata (Article 5).

C. Practices

This section is divided into three parts: (1) Data governance, (2) Documentation, and (3) Disclosure.

(1) Data governance

Data management processes (Control A.7.2)

Transparency and explainability are essential concerns in data management. Control A.7.2, regarding data for development and enhancement of AI system, requires your organization to define, document, and implement data management processes related to the AI system's development. Implementation Guidance B.7.2 states that data management can include transparency and explainability aspects, including data provenance and the ability to provide an explanation of how data is used for determining an AI system's output if the system requires transparency and explainability. Data provenance is repeated in three other controls:

Data resources (Control A.4.3)

Control A.4.3 on data resources states that, as part of resource identification, your organization should document information about the data resources used for the AI system. Implementation Guidance B.4.3 specifies that documentation on data should include the provenance of the data. This contributes to the transparency of the system because it allows stakeholders to understand the origin of the data, how it was collected, and how it was processed.

Data provenance (Control A.7.5)

This is a control that focuses solely on data provenance: Control A.7.5 requires your organization to define and document a process for recording the provenance of data used in its AI systems over the life cycles of the data and the AI system. Bringing all this together, data provenance is crucial for the transparency of the system because knowing the origin of the data — where it came from, how it was processed, and who handled it — increases the trust of stakeholders and users in the AI system.

Data acquisition (Control A.7.3)

Data provenance is also referred to in Implementation Guidance B.7.3 concerning acquisition of data. There, Implementation Guidance B.7.3 states that the details for data acquisition can include data provenance.

In addition, Implementation Guidance B.7.3 states that such details of data acquisition can include associated metadata, such as details of data labeling. Data labels explain the processes for using specific data and the rationale behind such use, as well as how the data has been utilized in the training, design, development, and deployment of the AI system. This serves to increase the transparency of the AI system. It requires organizations to disclose how the data has been collected and used to train AI models.

(2) Documentation

This includes both technical documentation and non-technical documentation.

(a) Technical documentation

AI system technical documentation (Control A.6.2.7)

This is included in Control A.6.2.7, where your organization is to determine what AI system technical documentation is needed for each relevant category of interested parties, including users, partners, supervisory bodies, and to provide the technical documentation to them in the appropriate form. Implementation Guidance B.6.2.7 states that such documentation can include a general description of the AI system, including its intended purpose, usage instructions, technical assumptions about the AI system's deployment and operation, the AI system's technical limitations as they relate to accuracy, robustness, reliability, and also the AI system's monitoring capabilities and functions which allow users or operators to influence the system operation. This control also entails documenting the technical information related to the AI system's responsible operation and the roles of the responsible team members, indicating the team members accountable for monitoring the system.

(b) Non-technical documentation

Providing system documentation and information to users (Control A.8.2)

Specifically, regarding information for users of the AI system, there is an additional control: A.8.2. This goes beyond technical documentation, technical details, and instructions which your organization should provide to users if necessary, to also include general notifications to users that they are interacting with an AI system, depending on the context. This is clearly stated in Implementation Guidance B.8.2. Such information can include both information regarding the system itself and the system's output, such as informing the user that the output is AI-generated. Several examples are listed in Implementation Guidance B.8.2.

The information which can be provided to users include information concerning the purpose of the system, that the user is interacting with the AI system, how the user can interact with the AI system, how and when to override the system, information about the AI system's accuracy and performance, the technical requirements for the AI system's operation, including the computational resources needed and the limitations

CHAPTER 8　TRANSPARENCY AND EXPLAINABILITY

of the system as well as its expected lifetime, the AI system's need for human oversight, relevant information from the impact assessment of the AI system, including potential benefits and harms, especially if they are applicable in specific contexts or concern specific demographic groups, revisions to claims about the system's benefits, updates and changes in how the system works, as well as any necessary maintenance measures, including the frequency, contact information of your organization, and educational materials for system use.

The above is a broad range of information that can be provided to users. This section now elaborates on several formats in which the above information can be effectively communicated to users of the AI system, in the spirit of transparency and explainability.

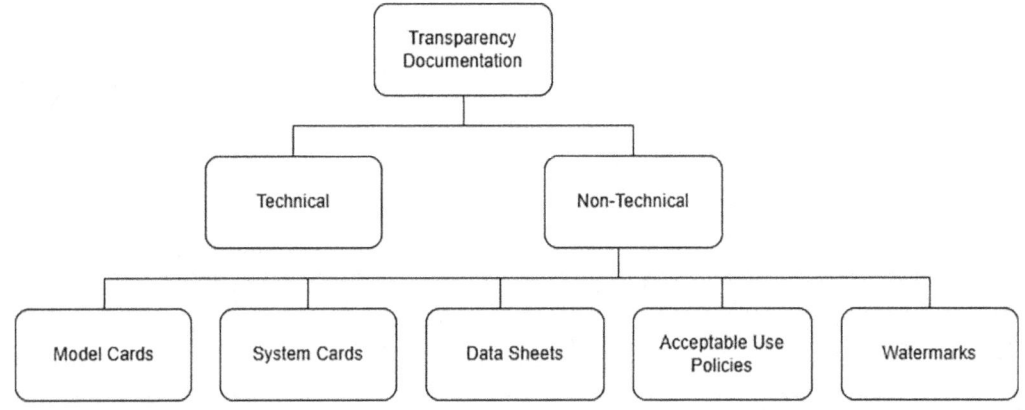

Figure 8-1. *Transparency documentation*

(a) The first format is that of model cards which usually come with the AI model and provide information about the model's training, the data on which the model has been trained, tested, and validated, and on the intended use of the AI model, thereby discouraging the use of models outside their intended purpose. They may reveal biases and errors in the AI model, hence increasing the credibility of the model. They provide information on benchmarks and the AI model's performance in relation to those benchmarks, which are tests that evaluate the AI model's performance. The purpose of the model card is to standardize the information provided to a broad demographic, and it is restricted to the AI model itself, notwithstanding that AI models often form part of a larger group of models.

(b) System cards may be of utility here by explaining how several AI models in a group function together. A model card is designed for a single AI model. A system card explains how machine learning models and other non-machine learning AI models, as well as non-AI technologies, operate together to achieve a specific goal. Similar to model cards, system cards are intended to provide standardized information serving a broad demographic. As such, both model cards and system cards may face accessibility challenges, given that some portions of the demographic are more comfortable with technical concepts than others. Both system cards and model cards may contribute to the risks of adversarial attacks and other security risks, given that malicious actors can use the information in model cards and system cards to the AI system developers' disadvantage.

(c) Another format in which information can be communicated to the user is the data sheet. Data sheets facilitate transparency by enhancing the communication between the AI system developer and the consumer. They help to track data provenance as discussed in the previous subsection. They clearly explain the details of the data on which the model has been trained.

(d) A fourth format is the acceptable use policy for the user. Not only do acceptable use policies provide information on exactly how the AI system is to be used, but also they outline how users can opt in or opt out of specific functions of the AI system. Finally, bear in mind that the information to be provided to the user not only includes information regarding the system, but also potential outputs of the system, including whether the output is AI-generated.

(e) A fifth format is that of watermarks. Watermarks label AI-generated content as such, hence enhancing transparency. While the naked human eye may not be able to see watermarks, they can be read by machines and detected by computers. Embedding unique identifiers in AI-generated outputs enables the effective verification of the AI-generated output's actual origin, making it clear that it is not created by humans but generated by a generative AI system. This leaves a digital fingerprint that can be verified, thus contributing to transparency.

(3) Disclosure

Communication of information to interested parties (Control A.8.5)

More broadly, Control A.8.5 entails providing information for interested parties. According to this control, your organization should determine and document its obligations to report information about the AI system to interested parties. Your organization would need to clarify exactly what information needs to be reported to satisfy this control. The interested parties listed in Implementation Guidance B.8.5 include not only customers but also regulatory authorities. Such information can include technical documentation (as discussed in the previous subsection), or system risks, or impact assessment results, or system logs and other records. The notice provided to these different interested parties would differ. And such notice would also depend on the exact type of product or service or industry, which are regulated differently even within the same jurisdiction.

Intended use (Control A.9.4)

As for Control A.9.4, your organization should ensure that the AI system is used according to the intended uses of the AI system and its accompanying documentation. Implementation Guidance B.9.4 goes further to state that where the correct deployment of the AI system (according to its associated instructions) causes concern regarding the impact on relevant interested parties or your organization's legal requirements, your organization should communicate its concerns to the appropriate personnel inside your organization as well as to any third-party suppliers of the AI system. Any output of the AI system that has unintended consequences for users should be communicated promptly to internal and external stakeholders, especially when it is third parties who have provided the AI system or have been involved in the design and development of the AI system.

Specifically, there are two controls concerning disclosure to system users. A.8.4 on communication of incidents, and A.10.4 concerning customers. Each will be examined in turn.

Incident reporting (Control A.8.4)

Incidents in Control A.8.4 refer not only to unexpected failures of an AI system, but also to issues concerning privacy and security. This is why Implementation Guidance B.8.4 states that ISO 27001 and ISO 27701 provide additional details on incident management for security and privacy, respectively. The primary purpose of incident communication is to promote transparency and maintain user trust, ensuring users are kept informed in a timely and responsible manner. So organizations would have to determine what constitutes an incident. Is it unauthorized access to data? Is it a system malfunction? Underpinning this control is the need for your organization to build and maintain trust.

Customer relationships (Control A.10.4)

Finally, Control A.10.4 requires your organization to ensure that its responsible approach to development and use of AI systems considers the customer's expectations and needs. Implementation Guidance B.10.4 goes even further to mention that, for example, the organization can identify risks related to the use of its AI products and services by the customer, and can decide to treat identified risks by giving appropriate information to its customer so that the customer can then treat the corresponding risks. Implementation Guidance B.10.4 further includes an example of proper information, specifically that when an AI system is valid for a specific domain of use, the limits of this domain should be communicated to the customer. According to this control, it is essential to know what the customer prioritizes. Some may prioritize fairness over robustness, and this would indicate different risks that your organization should inform the customer of. This can be complicated by the fact that an organization may serve two distinct customer groups with vastly different priorities.

CHAPTER 8 TRANSPARENCY AND EXPLAINABILITY

Summary and key takeaways

1. Keep detailed records of the training data's provenance: where it was collected from, whether it has been labeled, how it was collected and processed, how it is used throughout the AI life cycle, and who handles the data at the various stages. [Controls A.4.3, A.7.2, A.7.3, and A.7.5]

2. Define and provide the necessary technical documentation to various stakeholders: users, third parties (suppliers and other partners, supervisory bodies) [Control A.6.2.7]

3. Draft model cards, system cards, data sheets, and acceptable use policies in language understandable to the user, and consider adopting watermarking technology for content generated by your organization's AI system. [A.8.2.]

4. List your organization's disclosure requirements (especially the reporting of incidents) according to legal regulations and contracts, including details of the interested parties (users, third parties like suppliers and other partners, supervisory bodies), timelines, conditions, and content of such disclosure. [Controls A.8.4, A.8.5, and A.9.4]

5. Provide information concerning the risks and limitations of AI systems to users to ensure informed consent. [Control 10.4]

The next chapter will examine the principles, provisions, and practices related to robustness.

CHAPTER 9

ROBUSTNESS

This chapter on robustness starts with a discussion of the principles and several related concepts, examines the applicable regulations, and analyzes the relevant ISO 42001 clauses and controls.

A. Principles

Robustness is also referred to as reliability. We use the term robustness because that is how Annex C of ISO 42001 refers to it as an objective. ISO 42001 mentions reliability several times throughout the standard, but not in the list of objectives in Annex C. There are two aspects to this principle of robustness/reliability. The first is accuracy, and the second is consistency.

(1) Accuracy

Regarding accuracy, it is essential to note that generative AI and large language models are not based on objective truth. Generative AI is what we call a probabilistic system. Some differentiation between deterministic systems and probabilistic systems is necessary here. Deterministic systems are those that follow a pre-established set of rules, abide by fixed algorithms, have outputs specified by the system's parameters, and produce consistent results. However, probabilistic systems involve much more uncertainty. Therefore, their decision-making process may yield very different outputs despite having similar inputs. Probabilistic systems assign different probabilities or weights to potential outcomes when processing the output, and as new data emerges, these systems adapt and transform accordingly. Generative AI systems, such as large language models, make statistical inferences and probabilistic guesses in response to prompts.

These responses are not necessarily truthful; however, they sound plausible and convincing. It is essential to note the existence of risks such as misinformation and hallucinations. Hallucinations are generative AI content that appears to be true but is actually false.

Bearing this in mind, accuracy focuses on how correct the data is, whether it is based on real-world insights, and in turn, the quality of data. The quality of data that the AI is based on, trained on, and tested on impacts the quality of the outputs. Therefore, the data needs to be of high quality to ensure the system's accuracy.

(2) Consistency

The second aspect of robustness is consistency, which is especially relevant for deterministic systems that aim to produce consistent, repeatable results. Certain types of AI, particularly neural networks with hidden layers, often yield unpredictable and variable outcomes.

Unpredictability and variability are key concerns of AI. Such systems, including AI systems, can yield surprising results and errors, posing risks to individuals and organizations that utilize these AI systems. Here, the robustness principle, specifically its consistency aspect, is about reducing variability and unpredictability to produce consistent results, even in the face of environmental changes.

Additionally, robustness and consistency require the system to produce consistent output regardless of new data. ISO 42001 Annex C paragraph C.2.8 lists robustness as an objective whereby the AI system operates similarly when new data is introduced, as compared to its standard operating and training data. Hence, robustness entails the system behaving as expected, especially with unseen data. It must perform well not only with the training data, but also in the real world with new data.

The opposite of this is overfitting. This is one of the various ways in which the robustness of an AI system can be compromised (Figure 9-1):

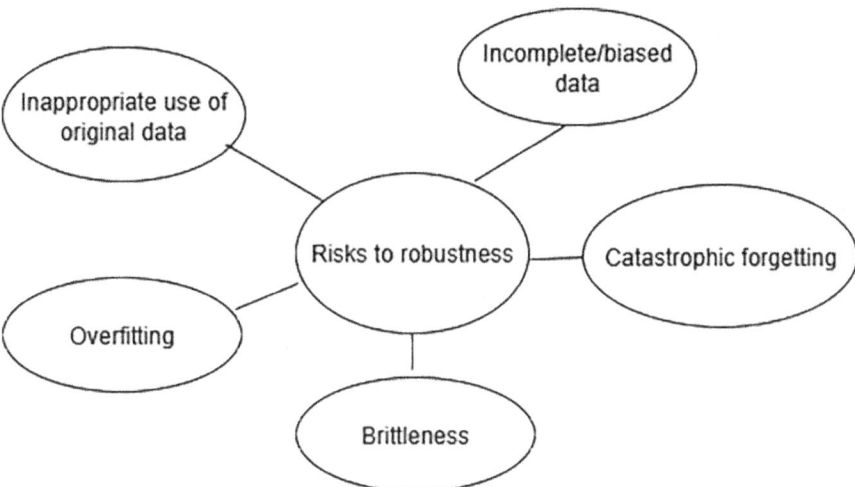

Figure 9-1. *Risks to robustness*

- Overfitting occurs when the system performs as expected with training data, but when presented with data it has not seen before, the system performs poorly.

- Other risks include the risks associated with introducing new data. One risk is that of brittleness. Brittleness occurs when multiple changes are made to the input data, which subsequently negatively affect the model's performance.

- Another risk is that of catastrophic forgetting, where newly introduced data weakens or even overrides the weights in a large language model.

- Further, there may be issues with the original data that affect the robustness of an AI system. An example of this is where the original input data is incomplete, allowing gaps and ambiguity in the data to impact the system's performance. If the input data contains embedded bias, it can affect the system's output and lead to harmful outcomes.

- A last risk is where the input data is being used in an inappropriate manner. Data is collected for specific purposes. If the system is used for a different purpose for which the data is not a good fit, this can affect the AI system's outcomes and predictions.

CHAPTER 9   ROBUSTNESS

B. Provisions

EU: EU AI Act

- The general principle is that high-risk AI systems must be "designed and developed in such a way that they achieve an appropriate level of accuracy, robustness", and that they "perform consistently in those respects throughout their life cycle." (Article 15(1))

Regarding accuracy:

- The quality of training, validation, and testing data, requiring that datasets for training, validation, and testing must be "relevant, sufficiently representative, and, to the best extent possible, free of errors, and complete in view of the intended purpose" (Article 10(3)). Datasets must also possess the "appropriate statistical properties" regarding "the persons or groups of persons" relevant to the high-risk AI system's intended use. (Article 10(3)).

- Providers must declare the levels of accuracy and relevant accuracy metrics of these high-risk AI systems in the instructions of use accompanying the AI system (Article 15(3)). This transparency requirement indirectly encourages greater accuracy in high-risk AI systems, as providers of such systems will now pay closer attention to accuracy metrics.

Regarding consistency:

- High-risk AI systems must "be as resilient as possible against errors, faults, or inconsistencies that may occur within the system or the environment in which the system operates, particularly due to their interaction with natural persons or other systems" (Article 15(4)).

The EU AI Act proposes measures to enhance the robustness of AI systems.

Accuracy: The European Commission shall develop benchmarks and measurement methodologies in consultation with relevant stakeholders to address the technical aspects of measurement (Article 15(2)).

Consistency: Technical and organizational measures must be taken to support the resilience of high-risk AI systems, such as technical redundancy solutions which include back-up or fail-safe plans (Article 15(4)).

China: Generative AI Interim Measures

- Generative AI service providers must "take effective measures to improve" the accuracy and reliability of AI-generated content, specifically in terms of data quality (Article 4(5)).

- They must employ effective measures to increase the quality of training data and increase the truth, accuracy, objectivity, and diversity of training data (Article 7(4)).

- And if manual tagging is conducted during the development of generative AI technology, the providers must carry out assessments of the quality of data tagging and conduct spot checks to verify the accuracy of the data tagging content (Article 8).

C. Practices

In this subsection, I discuss four aspects of ISO 42001 implementation related to robustness: 1. Data governance. 2. Computing infrastructure. 3. Operational safeguards. 4. Accountability and transparency measures as they relate to robustness.

(1) Data governance
Clause 6.1.2

In the risk assessment, as outlined in Clause 6.1.2 of the standard, one of the resources that should be considered for the risk assessment is the quality of data used for machine learning. And another risk source is the process used to collect data. Both of these can be sources of risk as they can impact objectives such as safety and robustness due to issues in data quality. This was clearly stated in Annex C paragraph C.3.4. Therefore, I shall examine both data quality and the processes related to data.

CHAPTER 9   ROBUSTNESS

a. Data quality

Data quality and resources (Controls A.7.4 and A.4.3)

Under data quality, the relevant controls are A.7.4, combined with A.4.3. Control A.7.4, which pertains to the quality of data for an AI system, requires your organization to define and document the requirements for data quality to ensure that the data used to develop and operate the AI system meets those requirements. This is to be read in conjunction with Control A.4.3 which requires your organization to document information about data resources, including the topic of data quality.

Moving on to the topic of data quality, this is crucial for accuracy and, more broadly, for the performance of AI systems. Implementation Guidance B.7.4 states that data quality has a potentially significant impact on the validity of the system's output. Therefore, for AI systems utilizing supervised or semi-supervised machine learning, the quality of training data, validation data, testing data, and production data must be defined, measured, and continually improved as much as possible. And your organization should also ensure that the data is suitable for its intended purpose. Part of ensuring data quality would be establishing the necessary criteria for assessing it. These criteria include accuracy, completeness, consistency, relevance, and timeliness. Applying these criteria ensures that the data used in such AI systems yields reliable output and reduces the variability and unpredictability of the results.

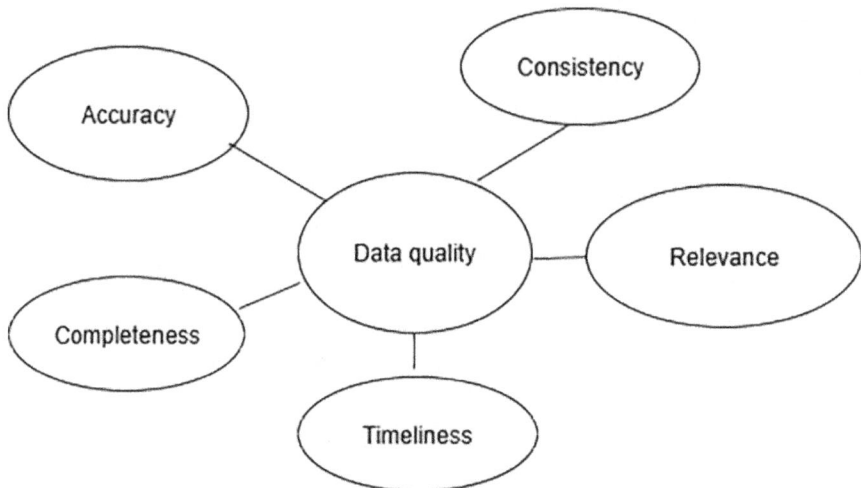

Figure 9-2. Criteria for assessing data quality

132

To elaborate on these five criteria: accuracy refers to the correctness of the data, ensuring it is free from errors and inaccuracies that could lead to incorrect conclusions or predictions by the AI models.

The second criterion is completeness, which refers to the extent to which all necessary information is included in the set of data. This includes all the required fields, attributes, and variables. Missing data can reduce the effectiveness of the AI system.

The third criterion is consistency, meaning the data should be free of inconsistencies, and exhibit consistent formats, definitions, and patterns to ensure coherence and uniformity. Inconsistent data is likely to lead to errors and misinterpretations stemming from the output of the data.

The fourth criterion is relevance, which refers to the extent to which the data is valuable and applicable to the analysis objectives intended by the AI system. The data should be relevant to the AI system's use case and provide meaningful features, resulting in an AI model and system that are more effective. Irrelevant data reduces the signal-to-noise ratio, making the AI system less useful.

The fifth criterion is timeliness, which assesses the currentness of the data. If the data is not updated, it will not accurately reflect the current reality, resulting in suboptimal output from AI systems.

By attempting to meet these five criteria for data quality, your organization can enhance the reliability and robustness of your AI system, ultimately benefiting more from it.

b. Data governance processes

Data management processes (Control A.7.2)

After covering data quality, I now discuss processes in data governance. The relevant control is A.7.2. The control requires your organization to define, document, and implement data management processes regarding the AI system's development. This data management can include topics such as the accuracy and integrity of the data, as well as the representativeness of the training data in comparison to the operational domain of use.

There are three components of data management processes that I will examine in turn.

The first is data labeling, the second is data acquisition, provenance, and metadata, and the third is data wrangling and cleaning.

CHAPTER 9   ROBUSTNESS

Data quality and resources (Controls A.7.4 and A.4.3)

Implementation Guidance B.4.3 includes data labeling processes in its list of what documentation on data should consist of. Implementation Guidance B.7.4 refers explicitly to AI systems using supervised or semi-supervised machine learning. For both of these systems, data labeling is particularly relevant compared to unsupervised machine learning. For supervised or semi-supervised machine learning, data labeling has a significant impact on the quality of the data. Data labeling involves assigning tags and annotations to the data, helping supervised or semi-supervised models recognize patterns. Your organization should establish protocols accurately or annotate delays. This could include automated labeling tools or manual annotation by humans. Your organization needs a quality assurance process that verifies and confirms the validity of the data labeling process, ensuring the consistency and reliability of the data used.

Data acquisition and provenance and resources (A.7.3 and A.7.5 and A.4.3)

Given that one of the sources of risk is the method of data collection, it is necessary to take into account data acquisition, data provenance, and the metadata. These involve the collection of data, including the source of the data. The relevant controls are A.7.3, A.7.5, and A.4.3.

A.7.3 requires your organization to determine and document details about how the data used in AI systems is acquired and selected. Your organization may require data from various sources in different categories. Such information for the acquisition of data can include the provenance of the data and the associated metadata, such as the details of the data labeling and enhancement.

Control A.7.5 states that your organization should define and document the process for recording the data provenance. Data provenance can include information about how the data is created, updated, transcribed, abstracted, validated, and how the control of the data has been transferred. Part of this process involves organizations considering how to verify data provenance, depending on the data source, the data's content, and the data's use context.

Regarding the reference to metadata in Control A.7.3, a key reason for documenting data provenance is to ensure the quality and accuracy of the data. Organizations provide the reliability of the data by identifying and resolving any inconsistencies that may arise. Implementation Guidance B.4.3 also includes the provenance of the data under the list of topics that the documentation on data should consist of. According to Implementation Guidance B.7.3, data acquisition details may include associated metadata, including the details of data labeling and enhancement. And according to Implementation Guidance B.4.3, documentation on data may include the date on which the data was last updated or modified, and the date tag in the metadata. Metadata provides additional information about the data, including its format, quality, timestamp, and source. It supports data provenance, helps assess the data's reliability, and ensures that the data is high-quality, accurate, and consistent. Robust metadata management is a key aspect of data provenance, contributing to the robustness of an AI system.

Data preparation and resources (Controls A.7.6 and A.4.3)

The third process is that of data wrangling and cleaning. Here, the relevant control is A.7.6, where your organization should define and document its criteria for selecting data preparation methods to be used. Data preparation is crucial in the AI life cycle because raw data is rarely directly used in AI systems. Without data preparation, AI system errors are likely to occur, affecting the reliability and performance of the AI system. Hence, selecting and using the appropriate data preparation technique is necessary to ensure data quality. Data cleaning is often a crucial aspect of data preparation. This could include removing inaccurate and irrelevant data, as well as standardizing the data to ensure consistency and accuracy. This is the most time-consuming aspect of the entire AI project. Raw data that is unusable is converted into a format that can be used and processed by the model. According to Implementation Guidance B.7.6, correcting entries and addressing missing entries are examples of data cleaning. Data cleaning and, more broadly, data preparation are pivotal to ensuring the reliability of the AI system. Implementation Guidance B.4.3 also includes data preparation as one of the topics that documentation on data should cover. When selecting a data preparation technique, your organization should document its decision, justifying how this technique helps maintain the system's reliability.

(2) Computing infrastructure

Resources (Clause 7.1) - including documentation (Control A.4.2) and system and computing resources (Control A.4.5)

I now examine the computing infrastructure and its impact on the robustness of the AI system. The starting point for this is Clause 7.1 which requires your organization to determine and provide the resources needed for establishing, implementing, maintaining, and continually improving the AI management system. And here the relevant controls are A.4.2 and A.4.5.

System and computing resources are explicitly referred to in Implementation Guidance B.4.2, which states that your organization should identify and document, at relevant AI system life cycle stages, system and computing resources that can include, but are not limited to, hardware for developing and running AI models, storage for data, and tooling resources. Implementation Guidance B.4.5 reiterates the above point and requires your organization to document information about the system and computing resources utilized for the AI system, which can include, but are not limited to, processing resources, including network and storage, and the impact of the hardware used to run the AI system workloads. An example given is the cost of using the hardware. In this section, I examine hardware, storage, and network components as key elements of a system's infrastructure, focusing on their impact on robustness.

Focusing on hardware, Annex C paragraph C.3.5 lists system hardware issues as a risk source, entailing both hardware defects and errors resulting from the inter-system transfer of trained machine learning models. Hence, this risk source should be taken into consideration for the risk assessment. AI systems rely on hardware components, including memory modules, networking equipment, and GPUs, all of which are potential failure points. Even minor hardware failures can lead to significant performance issues if they disrupt critical services. The ability of AI systems to produce accurate output is inextricably linked to the hardware used and the capacity to process large volumes of data, which is in turn related to the AI system's processing power.

Related to that is storage capacity. Machine learning algorithms produce more accurate output when the dataset is larger. When a machine learning model has access to more data, its accuracy level is significantly increased. Hence, storage capacity is a relevant consideration in an AI system's computing infrastructure.

Networking infrastructure also impacts an AI system's output accuracy and consistency. The network infrastructure affects the time required for AI systems to respond to inputs, which in turn impacts the reliability of the AI system.

To summarize, these three components — hardware, storage capacity, and network infrastructure — demonstrate how computing infrastructure plays a crucial role in an AI system's robustness.

(3) Operational safeguards

I now examine operational safeguards within an AI system, specifically during its life cycle.

a. Testing

System verification and validation (Control A.6.2.4)

The first safeguard is testing. Here, the relevant control is A.6.2.4, which pertains to the verification and validation of an AI system. The control requires your organization to define and document verification and validation measures and specify criteria for their use. Such verification and validation measures, according to Implementation Guidance B.6.2.4, can include testing methodologies and tools, selection of test data, and their representation of the intended domain of use and release criteria requirements. The criteria for evaluating the AI system's components can be based on reliability requirements of the AI system, such as acceptable error rates for the AI system's performance. Testing is critical to the robustness of an AI system because, once the model is trained, it must be explicitly tested on unseen data for your organization to understand how the AI model will perform in an operational setting.

Regarding the evaluation criteria, one key criterion to consider is repeatability, which is defined as the ability to obtain the same results with the same input using the same system. A repeatability assessment is what validates the consistency of a system's output.

Control A.6.2.4 also includes release criteria requirements, which are necessary for verification and validation activities to be successfully concluded. Accuracy rates set the benchmark for an AI system to meet before its deployment in an operational setting.

b. Monitoring

System operation and monitoring (Clause 9.1 and Control A.6.2.6)

After testing is concluded and the AI system has been deployed, monitoring is another crucial aspect of the AI life cycle that impacts the system's robustness. Here, the relevant control is A.6.2.6 on operation and monitoring, where your organization should define and document necessary elements for the AI system's ongoing operation, which should include system and performance monitoring, repairs, updates, and support.

Monitoring, even after deployment, is crucial in ensuring the model's accuracy and consistency. This entails regularly evaluating both the AI model's input and output. The AI model is to be assessed against benchmarks, ensuring that the AI model is performing appropriately. This entails tracking the behavior of the AI system in the operational environment to verify whether it performs as expected. The benchmarks to be used in monitoring the AI system could include error rates and reference data defined as ground truth. Ground truth serves as an objective measure of the AI system's performance, evaluating its accuracy and consistency to ensure that the system is producing the expected outputs.

In some cases, continuous learning may occur when the AI model updates itself with new live data. In such a situation, your organization should set up controls to monitor the performance of the AI system. However, even if AI systems do not experience continuous learning, their performance can still change, typically due to data drift in the production data, as outlined in Implementation Guidance B.6.2.6. Data drift occurs when the characteristics of the input data shift relative to those of the training data. This includes changes in the statistical attributes of input and output, resulting in the AI model producing deviations and irregular results.

To address the issue of data drift, which is particularly relevant to AI models compared to traditional models, Implementation Guidance B.6.2.6 suggests that monitoring will identify the need for retraining to ensure the AI system continues to meet its design goals and operates on production data as intended. Hence, your organization will need to detect these shifts in the data and address the question of when retraining the data is necessary. This may also include increasing the frequency of monitoring, which enables the detection of performance degradation or drift more effectively, allowing for timely intervention to maintain the accuracy of the model's output. This may also include automated alerts for detecting anomalies in the output stemming from data drift. A key part of monitoring involves examining the input data specifically to address the issue of data drift.

Intended use (Control A.9.4)

Apart from data drift, the second scenario to consider is that of intended use. Here, the relevant control is A.9.4, requiring your organization to ensure that the AI system is used according to the intended uses of the AI system as documented. Implementation Guidance B.9.4 further notes that the data used by the AI system should align with the documentation associated with the AI system to ensure accuracy in the AI system's performance. In other words, your organization should ensure that the data used by your AI system is similar to the data your system has been trained and tested on. This is necessary to maintain the performance and reliability of your AI system's output. Monitoring the AI system ensures that it functions as intended and remains within its intended boundaries of use. This entails reference to benchmarks such as accuracy rates, error rates, and user feedback, to which I now turn.

(4) Accountability and transparency measures
External reporting (Control A.8.3)

External reporting is a measure of accountability relevant to the robustness of an AI system. Here, the relevant control, A.8.3, enables users to provide feedback on inaccuracies or performance degradation. If the AI system produces inaccurate results, user feedback helps ensure the AI system's reliability and accuracy. Where the AI system's performance has declined over time, external reporting helps improve the system's efficiency by pointing out issues for your organization to address, ultimately contributing to the AI system's robustness.

Supplier relationships (Control A.10.3)

The second accountability measure relevant to robustness of the AI system is vendor risk management, provided for under Control A.10.3. When contracting with third parties such as suppliers, your organization should know the results of validation and testing, accuracy and reliability measurements, performance benchmarks, technical specifications, and the system's architecture and design.

Apart from the above two accountability measures relating to the robustness of the AI system, transparency measures are also pertinent to the AI system's robustness. The relevant controls are Control A.6.2.7 on AI system technical documentation and Control A.8.2 on system documentation and information for users.

AI system technical documentation (Control A.6.2.7)

Control A.6.7 requires your organization to determine the AI system technical documentation needed for various stakeholders, users, partners, supervisory authorities, and provide the technical documentation to them in the appropriate form. Implementation Guidance B.6.2.7 states that such technical documentation can include technical limitations, such as acceptable error rates, accuracy, reliability, and robustness, and that this documentation should be up-to-date and accurate.

Providing system documentation and information to users (Control A.8.2)

This is supported by Control A.8.2, which focuses specifically on the users and requires your organization to communicate the necessary information to them regarding the AI system. Implementation Guidance B.8.2 states that such information can include details about the AI system's accuracy and performance. It should ensure that the information provided to these users is complete, up-to-date, and accurate.

Summary and key takeaways

1. Assess the quality of data regularly using the criteria of accuracy, completeness, consistency, relevance and timeliness. [Control A.7.4]

2. Evaluate the processes for labeling the data, including the metadata, and cleaning the data, specifically looking out for inconsistencies which may affect the system's reliability. [Controls A.7.2; A.4.3 and A.7.4; A.7.3, A.7.5, and A.7.6]

3. Test the AI system on unseen data prior to deployment based on clearly defined evaluation metrics such as accuracy and repeatability, and conclude the verification and validation only after the release criteria have been satisfied. [Control A.6.2.4]

4. Monitor the AI system for performance degradation evidenced by anomalies in the output due to data drift [Control A.6.2.6], and also to ensure it stays within its intended boundaries of use [Control A.9.4].

5. Establish a solid two-way communication channel with users to both provide them with the most up-to-date information and solicit feedback from them regarding the AI system's performance. [Controls A.8.2 and A.8.3]

The next chapter will conclude by summarizing the relationships between the principles and between ISO 42001 and the law.

CHAPTER 10

CONCLUSION

In this study of what a principled implementation of an AI management system would look like, one thing becomes clear: Your organization needs to select its core principles based on its specific use cases. Controls A.6.1.3 and A.9.3 on the responsible development and use of AI systems respectively refer to the objectives listed in Annex C, which include the six principles discussed in this book. Not all principles or objectives will apply equally to the AI system(s) developed or used by your organization, and your partners and customers will also value some principles over others.

It would be helpful to gain a better understanding of the relationship between the different principles covered in this book. These principles may either support or conflict with each other, and understanding this is crucial for your organization to make informed choices.

Supportive relationships between the principles include:

1. **Security and privacy.** Data is a component of the AI system, and the security of the data component directly impacts the system's overall privacy. Hence, security safeguards are one of the Fair Information Principles underpinning most data protection laws today.

2. **Transparency, explainability, and accountability.** Transparency entails communication and disclosure, providing information to other parties. Accountability entails contestability and feedback, having a mechanism to receive critical information that would improve your system. This is a two-way communication, with both principles working together. Moreover, explainability provides the means for subjects, individuals, and groups affected by an AI system to challenge it by better understanding how the system operates and the outcomes it produces. Decisions made by AI systems in sectors such as healthcare, criminal justice,

and finance have a significant impact on the lives of individuals and groups. By ensuring the explainability of these AI systems, organizations responsible for them can be held accountable. We see this most clearly in data provenance, where the explainability of a system enables us to trace issues through the model and hold AI system developers accountable. Traceability is what connects explainability to accountability.

3. **Explainability, fairness and robustness**. Given that the explainability of an AI system leads to more effective identification and rectification of bias, explainability can also contribute to fairness and robustness.

4. **Fairness and robustness**. Biases in data can distort the output of an AI system, affecting its outcomes.

5. **Security and robustness**. Adversarial attacks that cause models to malfunction affect the reliability and consistency of the AI system's performance.

6. **Transparency, explainability, and fairness**. The transparency and explainability of a system enable a more effective identification and rectification of biases in the system's output. Where transparency challenges exist, particularly in black-box systems, it can be difficult to identify biases in the algorithm.

7. **Transparency and privacy**. Openness is one of the fundamental Fair Information Principles, which underpin privacy laws today. Transparency obligations imposed on data controllers are crucial for data subjects to exercise their individual participation rights, such as access and amendment.

8. **Security and accountability**. Human-in-the-loop approaches to AI systems entail oversight, which makes the detection of incidents, such as adversarial attacks, much more efficient.

As for principles that may conflict with each other:

1. **Privacy and fairness**. While enabling an organization to determine if the objective of fairness has been met, bias testing requires particularly sensitive information. By adhering to the collection limitation principle, which is one of the eight Fair Information Principles, it can be challenging to obtain data to mitigate biases in AI systems. Hence, there may be a trade-off between fairness and privacy. However, there are solutions around this tension between the two principles, such as the use of synthetic data. Both principles may not necessarily be in conflict if consent is obtained from data subjects before collecting such data for bias testing. With such fully informed consent where the purpose of bias testing has been effectively disclosed to data subjects, this upholds both the individual's participation rights and the principle of openness, both of which are fundamental Fair Information Principles.

2. **Accountability and fairness**. Human-in-the-loop approaches may introduce biases of human operators who monitor the AI system, potentially influencing the AI system's algorithm, particularly since this involves human operators' judgments regarding the AI output.

3. **Privacy and robustness**. Anonymizing data sets reduces the risk of privacy breaches, but it also negatively impacts the data's usefulness, making it less accurate.

4. **Security and transparency**. Open-source models and AI models that rely on open-source components are more susceptible to adversarial attacks, regardless of the fact that they address the black-box challenge. Providing too much information about an algorithm's workings increases the possibility of cyberattacks. As such, organizations should be cautious about the volume of information revealed in their system cards and model cards.

CHAPTER 10   CONCLUSION

Having covered the relationship between the various principles discussed in this book, we return to the relationship between law and ISO 42001. Apart from Colorado SB 205's inclusion of the "safe harbor" provision discussed as an exception at the beginning of this book, the relationship between AI law and ISO 42001 is more indirect:

1. Implementing ISO 42001 does not mean that the organization is compliant with the relevant regulations. For example, ISO 42001 implementation or certification does not lead to a presumption of conformity with the EU AI Act. Unlike the harmonized standards (Article 40) which, at the time of writing, have yet to be finalized, ISO 42001 focuses on the organization. In contrast, the EU AI Act focuses on the product or system.

2. Furthermore, the ISO clauses and controls do not always align neatly with legal provisions. A good example is how the AI impact assessment in ISO 42001 is significantly broader than the EU AI Act fundamental rights impact assessment, both in terms of scope where the AI impact assessment concerns impacts beyond fundamental rights to include security and harm to the environment, for example, and also in terms of the parties involved with the fundamental rights impact assessment being restricted to select categories of deployers.

Nonetheless, as this book has sought to demonstrate, understanding the principles underlying both the legal provisions and the technical standards clause or control will significantly enable your organization to better prepare to fulfill its compliance obligations. If your organization is bound by the EU AI Act, completing the preparatory work for certification under ISO 42001 will significantly assist your organization in meeting the harmonized standards and conformity assessment requirements. More broadly, with US officials recently rejecting a global AI governance regime at the UN Security Council which suggests increased fragmentation and multipolarity in AI governance, and with the fate of the NIST AI Risk Management hanging in the balance after the White House's release of the AI Action Plan calling for references to misinformation, "DEI" (diversity, equity, and inclusion), and climate change to be removed from the framework, ISO 42001 will become even more important and valuable as a truly global standard in helping multi-national organizations navigate various AI regulatory regimes.

APPENDIX

EU Artificial Intelligence Act Recital (27):

While the risk-based approach is the basis for a proportionate and effective set of binding rules, it is important to recall the 2019 Ethics guidelines for trustworthy AI developed by the independent AI HLEG appointed by the Commission. In those guidelines, the AI HLEG developed seven non-binding ethical principles for AI which are intended to help ensure that AI is trustworthy and ethically sound. The seven principles include human agency and oversight; technical robustness and safety; privacy and data governance; transparency; diversity, non-discrimination and fairness; societal and environmental well-being and accountability. Without prejudice to the legally binding requirements of this Regulation and any other applicable Union law, those guidelines contribute to the design of coherent, trustworthy and human-centric AI, in line with the Charter and with the values on which the Union is founded. According to the guidelines of the AI HLEG, human agency and oversight means that AI systems are developed and used as a tool that serves people, respects human dignity and personal autonomy, and that is functioning in a way that can be appropriately controlled and overseen by humans. Technical robustness and safety means that AI systems are developed and used in a way that allows robustness in the case of problems and resilience against attempts to alter the use or performance of the AI system so as to allow unlawful use by third parties, and minimise unintended harm. Privacy and data governance means that AI systems are developed and used in accordance with privacy and data protection rules, while processing data that meets high standards in terms of quality and integrity. Transparency means that AI systems are developed and used in a way that allows appropriate traceability and explainability, while making humans aware that they communicate or interact with an AI system, as well as duly informing deployers of the capabilities and limitations of that AI system and affected persons about their rights. Diversity, non-discrimination and fairness means that AI systems are developed and used in a way that includes diverse actors and promotes equal access, gender equality and cultural diversity, while avoiding discriminatory impacts and unfair biases that are prohibited by Union or national law. Social and environmental well-being means that AI systems are developed and used in a sustainable and environmentally friendly manner as well as in a way to benefit all human beings, while monitoring and assessing the long-term impacts on the individual, society and democracy. The application of those principles should be translated, when possible, in the design and use of AI models. They should in any case serve as a basis for the drafting of codes of conduct under this Regulation. All stakeholders, including industry, academia, civil society and standardisation organisations, are encouraged to take into account, as appropriate, the ethical principles for the development of voluntary best practices and standards.

Recital (106): Providers that place general-purpose AI models on the Union market should ensure compliance with the relevant obligations in this Regulation. To that end, providers of general-purpose AI models should put in place a policy to comply with Union law on copyright and related rights, in particular to identify and comply with the reservation of rights expressed by rightsholders pursuant to Article 4(3) of Directive (EU) 2019/790. Any provider placing a general-purpose AI model on the Union market should comply with this obligation, regardless of the jurisdiction in which the copyright-relevant acts underpinning the training of those general-purpose AI models take place. This is necessary to ensure a level playing field among providers of general-purpose AI models where no provider should be able to gain a competitive advantage in the Union market by applying lower copyright standards than those provided in the Union.

Recital (108): With regard to the obligations imposed on providers of general-purpose AI models to put in place a policy to comply with Union copyright law and make publicly available a summary of the content used for the training, the AI Office should monitor whether the provider has fulfilled those obligations without verifying or proceeding to a work-by-work assessment of the training data in terms of copyright compliance. This Regulation does not affect the enforcement of copyright rules as provided for under Union law

Recital (110): General-purpose AI models could pose systemic risks which include, but are not limited to, any actual or reasonably foreseeable negative effects in relation to major accidents, disruptions of critical sectors and serious consequences to public health and safety; any actual or reasonably foreseeable negative effects on democratic processes, public and economic security; the dissemination of illegal, false, or discriminatory content. Systemic risks should be understood to increase with model capabilities and model reach, can arise along the entire lifecycle of the model, and are influenced by conditions of misuse, model reliability, model fairness and model security, the level of autonomy of the model, its access to tools, novel or combined modalities, release and distribution strategies, the potential to remove guardrails and other factors. In particular, international approaches have so far identified the need to pay attention to risks from potential intentional misuse or unintended issues of control relating to alignment with human intent; chemical, biological, radiological, and nuclear risks, such as the ways in which barriers to entry can be lowered, including for weapons development, design acquisition, or use; offensive cyber capabilities, such as the ways in vulnerability discovery, exploitation, or operational use can be enabled; the effects of interaction and tool use, including for example the capacity to control physical systems and interfere with critical infrastructure; risks from models of making copies of themselves or 'self-replicating' or training other models; the ways in which models can give rise to harmful bias and discrimination with risks to individuals, communities or societies; the facilitation of disinformation or harming privacy with threats to democratic values and human rights; risk that a particular event could lead to a chain reaction with considerable negative effects that could affect up to an entire city, an entire domain activity or an entire community.

Recital (123): In order to ensure a high level of trustworthiness of high-risk AI systems, those systems should be subject to a conformity assessment prior to their placing on the market or putting into service.

Article 3: Definitions

For the purposes of this Regulation, the following definitions apply:

(20) 'conformity assessment' means the process of demonstrating whether the requirements set out in Chapter III, Section 2 relating to a high-risk AI system have been fulfilled;

Chapter II: Prohibited AI Practices

Article 5: Prohibited AI Practices

1. The following AI practices shall be prohibited:

   (a) the placing on the market, the putting into service or the use of an AI system that deploys subliminal techniques beyond a person's consciousness or purposefully manipulative or deceptive techniques, with the objective, or the effect of materially distorting the behaviour of a person or a group of persons by appreciably impairing their ability to make an informed decision, thereby causing them to take a decision that they would not have otherwise taken in a manner that causes or is reasonably likely to cause that person, another person or group of persons significant harm;

Chapter III: High-Risk AI System

Section 2: Requirements for High-risk AI Systems

Article 8: Compliance with the Requirements

1. High-risk AI systems shall comply with the requirements laid down in this Section, taking into account their intended purpose as well as the generally acknowledged state of the art on AI and AI-related technologies. The risk management system referred to in Article 9 shall be taken into account when ensuring compliance with those requirements.

2. Where a product contains an AI system, to which the requirements of this Regulation as well as requirements of the Union harmonisation legislation listed in Section A of Annex I apply, providers shall be responsible for ensuring that their product is fully compliant with all applicable requirements under applicable Union harmonisation legislation. In ensuring the compliance of high-risk AI systems referred to in paragraph 1 with the requirements set out in this Section, and in order to ensure consistency, avoid duplication and minimise additional burdens, providers shall have a choice of integrating, as appropriate, the necessary testing and reporting processes, information and documentation they provide with regard to their product into documentation and procedures that already exist and are required under the Union harmonisation legislation listed in Section A of Annex I.

Article 9: Risk Management System

1. A risk management system shall be established, implemented, documented and maintained in relation to high-risk AI systems.

2. The risk management system shall be understood as a continuous iterative process planned and run throughout the entire lifecycle of a high-risk AI system, requiring regular systematic review and updating. It shall comprise the following steps:

    (a) the identification and analysis of the known and the reasonably foreseeable risks that the high-risk AI system can pose to health, safety or fundamental rights when the high-risk AI system is used in accordance with its intended purpose;

    (b) the estimation and evaluation of the risks that may emerge when the high-risk AI system is used in accordance with its intended purpose, and under conditions of reasonably foreseeable misuse;

    (c) the evaluation of other risks possibly arising, based on the analysis of data gathered from the post-market monitoring system referred to in Article 72;

    (d) the adoption of appropriate and targeted risk management measures designed to address the risks identified pursuant to point (a).

3. The risks referred to in this Article shall concern only those which may be reasonably mitigated or eliminated through the development or design of the high-risk AI system, or the provision of adequate technical information.

4. The risk management measures referred to in paragraph 2, point (d), shall give due consideration to the effects and possible interaction resulting from the combined application of the requirements set out in this Section, with a view to minimising risks more effectively while achieving an appropriate balance in implementing the measures to fulfil those requirements.

5. The risk management measures referred to in paragraph 2, point (d), shall be such that the relevant residual risk associated with each hazard, as well as the overall residual risk of the high-risk AI systems is judged to be acceptable.

APPENDIX

In identifying the most appropriate risk management measures, the following shall be ensured:

(a) elimination or reduction of risks identified and evaluated pursuant to paragraph 2 in as far as technically feasible through adequate design and development of the high-risk AI system;

(b) where appropriate, implementation of adequate mitigation and control measures addressing risks that cannot be eliminated;

(c) provision of information required pursuant to Article 13 and, where appropriate, training to deployers.

With a view to eliminating or reducing risks related to the use of the high-risk AI system, due consideration shall be given to the technical knowledge, experience, education, the training to be expected by the deployer, and the presumable context in which the system is intended to be used.

6. High-risk AI systems shall be tested for the purpose of identifying the most appropriate and targeted risk management measures. Testing shall ensure that high-risk AI systems perform consistently for their intended purpose and that they are in compliance with the requirements set out in this Section.

7. Testing procedures may include testing in real-world conditions in accordance with Article 60.

8. The testing of high-risk AI systems shall be performed, as appropriate, at any time throughout the development process, and, in any event, prior to their being placed on the market or put into service. Testing shall be carried out against prior defined metrics and probabilistic thresholds that are appropriate to the intended purpose of the high-risk AI system.

9. When implementing the risk management system as provided for in paragraphs 1 to 7, providers shall give consideration to whether in view of its intended purpose the high-risk AI system is likely to have an adverse impact on persons under the age of 18 and, as appropriate, other vulnerable groups.

10. For providers of high-risk AI systems that are subject to requirements regarding internal risk management processes under other relevant provisions of Union law, the aspects provided in paragraphs 1 to 9 may be part of, or combined with, the risk management procedures established pursuant to that law.

Article 10: Data and data Governance

1. High-risk AI systems which make use of techniques involving the training of AI models with data shall be developed on the basis of training, validation and testing data sets that meet the quality criteria referred to in paragraphs 2 to 5 whenever such data sets are used.

2. Training, validation and testing data sets shall be subject to data governance and management practices appropriate for the intended purpose of the high-risk AI system. Those practices shall concern in particular:

   (a) the relevant design choices;

   (b) data collection processes and the origin of data, and in the case of personal data, the original purpose of the data collection;

   (c) relevant data-preparation processing operations, such as annotation, labelling, cleaning, updating, enrichment and aggregation;

   (d) the formulation of assumptions, in particular with respect to the information that the data are supposed to measure and represent;

   (e) an assessment of the availability, quantity and suitability of the data sets that are needed;

   (f) examination in view of possible biases that are likely to affect the health and safety of persons, have a negative impact on fundamental rights or lead to discrimination prohibited under Union law, especially where data outputs influence inputs for future operations;

   (g) appropriate measures to detect, prevent and mitigate possible biases identified according to point (f);

APPENDIX

(h) the identification of relevant data gaps or shortcomings that prevent compliance with this Regulation, and how those gaps and shortcomings can be addressed.

3. Training, validation and testing data sets shall be relevant, sufficiently representative, and to the best extent possible, free of errors and complete in view of the intended purpose. They shall have the appropriate statistical properties, including, where applicable, as regards the persons or groups of persons in relation to whom the high-risk AI system is intended to be used. Those characteristics of the data sets may be met at the level of individual data sets or at the level of a combination thereof.

4. Data sets shall take into account, to the extent required by the intended purpose, the characteristics or elements that are particular to the specific geographical, contextual, behavioural or functional setting within which the high-risk AI system is intended to be used.

5. To the extent that it is strictly necessary for the purpose of ensuring bias detection and correction in relation to the high-risk AI systems in accordance with paragraph (2), points (f) and (g) of this Article, the providers of such systems may exceptionally process special categories of personal data, subject to appropriate safeguards for the fundamental rights and freedoms of natural persons. In addition to the provisions set out in Regulations (EU) 2016/679 and (EU) 2018/1725 and Directive (EU) 2016/680, all the following conditions must be met in order for such processing to occur:

(a) the bias detection and correction cannot be effectively fulfilled by processing other data, including synthetic or anonymised data;

(b) the special categories of personal data are subject to technical limitations on the re-use of the personal data, and state-of-the-art security and privacy-preserving measures, including pseudonymisation;

(c) the special categories of personal data are subject to measures to ensure that the personal data processed are secured, protected, subject to suitable safeguards, including strict controls and documentation of the access, to avoid misuse and ensure that only authorised persons have access to those personal data with appropriate confidentiality obligations;

(d) the special categories of personal data are not to be transmitted, transferred or otherwise accessed by other parties;

(e) the special categories of personal data are deleted once the bias has been corrected or the personal data has reached the end of its retention period, whichever comes first;

(f) the records of processing activities pursuant to Regulations (EU) 2016/679 and (EU) 2018/1725 and Directive (EU) 2016/680 include the reasons why the processing of special categories of personal data was strictly necessary to detect and correct biases, and why that objective could not be achieved by processing other data.

6. For the development of high-risk AI systems not using techniques involving the training of AI models, paragraphs 2 to 5 apply only to the testing data sets.

Article 11: Technical Documentation

1. The technical documentation of a high-risk AI system shall be drawn up before that system is placed on the market or put into service and shall be kept up-to date.

   The technical documentation shall be drawn up in such a way as to demonstrate that the high-risk AI system complies with the requirements set out in this Section and to provide national competent authorities and notified bodies with the necessary information in a clear and comprehensive form to assess the compliance of the AI system with those requirements. It shall contain, at a minimum, the elements set out in Annex IV. SMEs, including start-ups, may provide the elements of the technical documentation specified in Annex IV in a simplified manner. To that end, the Commission shall establish a simplified

APPENDIX

technical documentation form targeted at the needs of small and microenterprises. Where an SME, including a start-up, opts to provide the information required in Annex IV in a simplified manner, it shall use the form referred to in this paragraph. Notified bodies shall accept the form for the purposes of the conformity assessment.

2. Where a high-risk AI system related to a product covered by the Union harmonisation legislation listed in Section A of Annex I is placed on the market or put into service, a single set of technical documentation shall be drawn up containing all the information set out in paragraph 1, as well as the information required under those legal acts.

3. The Commission is empowered to adopt delegated acts in accordance with Article 97 in order to amend Annex IV, where necessary, to ensure that, in light of technical progress, the technical documentation provides all the information necessary to assess the compliance of the system with the requirements set out in this Section.

Article 12: Record-keeping

1. High-risk AI systems shall technically allow for the automatic recording of events (logs) over the lifetime of the system.

2. In order to ensure a level of traceability of the functioning of a high-risk AI system that is appropriate to the intended purpose of the system, logging capabilities shall enable the recording of events relevant for:

    (a) identifying situations that may result in the high-risk AI system presenting a risk within the meaning of Article 79(1) or in a substantial modification;

    (b) facilitating the post-market monitoring referred to in Article 72; and

    (c) monitoring the operation of high-risk AI systems referred to in Article 26(5).

3. For high-risk AI systems referred to in point 1 (a), of Annex III, the logging capabilities shall provide, at a minimum:

   (a) recording of the period of each use of the system (start date and time and end date and time of each use);

   (b) the reference database against which input data has been checked by the system;

   (c) the input data for which the search has led to a match;

   (d) the identification of the natural persons involved in the verification of the results, as referred to in Article 14(5).

Article 13: Transparency and provision of information to deployers

1. High-risk AI systems shall be designed and developed in such a way as to ensure that their operation is sufficiently transparent to enable deployers to interpret a system's output and use it appropriately. An appropriate type and degree of transparency shall be ensured with a view to achieving compliance with the relevant obligations of the provider and deployer set out in Section 3.

2. High-risk AI systems shall be accompanied by instructions for use in an appropriate digital format or otherwise that include concise, complete, correct and clear information that is relevant, accessible and comprehensible to deployers.

3. The instructions for use shall contain at least the following information:

   (a) the identity and the contact details of the provider and, where applicable, of its authorised representative;

   (b) the characteristics, capabilities and limitations of performance of the high-risk AI system, including:

      (i) its intended purpose;

(ii) the level of accuracy, including its metrics, robustness and cybersecurity referred to in Article 15 against which the high-risk AI system has been tested and validated and which can be expected, and any known and foreseeable circumstances that may have an impact on that expected level of accuracy, robustness and cybersecurity;

(iii) any known or foreseeable circumstance, related to the use of the high-risk AI system in accordance with its intended purpose or under conditions of reasonably foreseeable misuse, which may lead to risks to the health and safety or fundamental rights referred to in Article 9(2);

(iv) where applicable, the technical capabilities and characteristics of the high-risk AI system to provide information that is relevant to explain its output;

(v) when appropriate, its performance regarding specific persons or groups of persons on which the system is intended to be used;

(vi) when appropriate, specifications for the input data, or any other relevant information in terms of the training, validation and testing data sets used, taking into account the intended purpose of the high-risk AI system;

(vii) where applicable, information to enable deployers to interpret the output of the high-risk AI system and use it appropriately;

(c) the changes to the high-risk AI system and its performance which have been pre-determined by the provider at the moment of the initial conformity assessment, if any;

(d) the human oversight measures referred to in Article 14, including the technical measures put in place to facilitate the interpretation of the outputs of the high-risk AI systems by the deployers;

(e) the computational and hardware resources needed, the expected lifetime of the high-risk AI system and any necessary maintenance and care measures, including their frequency, to ensure the proper functioning of that AI system, including as regards software updates;

(f) where relevant, a description of the mechanisms included within the high-risk AI system that allows deployers to properly collect, store and interpret the logs in accordance with Article 12.

Article 14: Human oversight

1. High-risk AI systems shall be designed and developed in such a way, including with appropriate human-machine interface tools, that they can be effectively overseen by natural persons during the period in which they are in use.

2. Human oversight shall aim to prevent or minimise the risks to health, safety or fundamental rights that may emerge when a high-risk AI system is used in accordance with its intended purpose or under conditions of reasonably foreseeable misuse, in particular where such risks persist despite the application of other requirements set out in this Section.

3. The oversight measures shall be commensurate with the risks, level of autonomy and context of use of the high-risk AI system, and shall be ensured through either one or both of the following types of measures:

    (a) measures identified and built, when technically feasible, into the high-risk AI system by the provider before it is placed on the market or put into service;

    (b) measures identified by the provider before placing the high-risk AI system on the market or putting it into service and that are appropriate to be implemented by the deployer.

4. For the purpose of implementing paragraphs 1, 2 and 3, the high-risk AI system shall be provided to the deployer in such a way that natural persons to whom human oversight is assigned are enabled, as appropriate and proportionate:

(a) to properly understand the relevant capacities and limitations of the high-risk AI system and be able to duly monitor its operation, including in view of detecting and addressing anomalies, dysfunctions and unexpected performance;

(b) to remain aware of the possible tendency of automatically relying or over-relying on the output produced by a high-risk AI system (automation bias), in particular for high-risk AI systems used to provide information or recommendations for decisions to be taken by natural persons;

(c) to correctly interpret the high-risk AI system's output, taking into account, for example, the interpretation tools and methods available;

(d) to decide, in any particular situation, not to use the high-risk AI system or to otherwise disregard, override or reverse the output of the high-risk AI system;

(e) to intervene in the operation of the high-risk AI system or interrupt the system through a 'stop' button or a similar procedure that allows the system to come to a halt in a safe state.

5. For high-risk AI systems referred to in point 1(a) of Annex III, the measures referred to in paragraph 3 of this Article shall be such as to ensure that, in addition, no action or decision is taken by the deployer on the basis of the identification resulting from the system unless that identification has been separately verified and confirmed by at least two natural persons with the necessary competence, training and authority.

The requirement for a separate verification by at least two natural persons shall not apply to high-risk AI systems used for the purposes of law enforcement, migration, border control or asylum, where Union or national law considers the application of this requirement to be disproportionate.

Article 15: Accuracy, robustness and cybersecurity

1. High-risk AI systems shall be designed and developed in such a way that they achieve an appropriate level of accuracy, robustness, and cybersecurity, and that they perform consistently in those respects throughout their lifecycle.

2. To address the technical aspects of how to measure the appropriate levels of accuracy and robustness set out in paragraph 1 and any other relevant performance metrics, the Commission shall, in cooperation with relevant stakeholders and organisations such as metrology and benchmarking authorities, encourage, as appropriate, the development of benchmarks and measurement methodologies.

3. The levels of accuracy and the relevant accuracy metrics of high-risk AI systems shall be declared in the accompanying instructions of use.

4. High-risk AI systems shall be as resilient as possible regarding errors, faults or inconsistencies that may occur within the system or the environment in which the system operates, in particular due to their interaction with natural persons or other systems. Technical and organisational measures shall be taken in this regard.

    The robustness of high-risk AI systems may be achieved through technical redundancy solutions, which may include backup or fail-safe plans.

    High-risk AI systems that continue to learn after being placed on the market or put into service shall be developed in such a way as to eliminate or reduce as far as possible the risk of possibly biased outputs influencing input for future operations (feedback loops), and as to ensure that any such feedback loops are duly addressed with appropriate mitigation measures.

5. High-risk AI systems shall be resilient against attempts by unauthorised third parties to alter their use, outputs or performance by exploiting system vulnerabilities.

The technical solutions aiming to ensure the cybersecurity of high-risk AI systems shall be appropriate to the relevant circumstances and the risks.

The technical solutions to address AI specific vulnerabilities shall include, where appropriate, measures to prevent, detect, respond to, resolve and control for attacks trying to manipulate the training data set (data poisoning), or pre-trained components used in training (model poisoning), inputs designed to cause the AI model to make a mistake (adversarial examples or model evasion), confidentiality attacks or model flaws.

Section 3: Obligations of Providers and Deployers of High-risk AI Systems and other Parties

Article 16: Obligations of Providers of High-risk AI Systems

Providers of high-risk AI systems shall:

(a) ensure that their high-risk AI systems are compliant with the requirements set out in Section 2;

(b) indicate on the high-risk AI system or, where that is not possible, on its packaging or its accompanying documentation, as applicable, their name, registered trade name or registered trade mark, the address at which they can be contacted;

(c) have a quality management system in place which complies with Article 17;

(d) keep the documentation referred to in Article 18;

(e) when under their control, keep the logs automatically generated by their high-risk AI systems as referred to in Article 19;

(f) ensure that the high-risk AI system undergoes the relevant conformity assessment procedure as referred to in Article 43, prior to its being placed on the market or put into service;

(g) draw up an EU declaration of conformity in accordance with Article 47;

(h) affix the CE marking to the high-risk AI system or, where that is not possible, on its packaging or its accompanying documentation, to indicate conformity with this Regulation, in accordance with Article 48;

(i) comply with the registration obligations referred to in Article 49(1);

(j) take the necessary corrective actions and provide information as required in Article 20;

(k) upon a reasoned request of a national competent authority, demonstrate the conformity of the high-risk AI system with the requirements set out in Section 2;

(l) ensure that the high-risk AI system complies with accessibility requirements in accordance with Directives (EU) 2016/2102 and (EU) 2019/882.

Article 18: Documentation keeping

1. The provider shall, for a period ending 10 years after the high-risk AI system has been placed on the market or put into service, keep at the disposal of the national competent authorities:

   (a) the technical documentation referred to in Article 11;

   (b) the documentation concerning the quality management system referred to in Article 17;

   (c) the documentation concerning the changes approved by notified bodies, where applicable;

   (d) the decisions and other documents issued by the notified bodies, where applicable;

   (e) the EU declaration of conformity referred to in Article 47.

2. Each Member State shall determine conditions under which the documentation referred to in paragraph 1 remains at the disposal of the national competent authorities for the period indicated in that paragraph for the cases when a provider or its authorised representative established on its territory goes bankrupt or ceases its activity prior to the end of that period.

3. Providers that are financial institutions subject to requirements regarding their internal governance, arrangements or processes under Union financial services law shall maintain the technical documentation as part of the documentation kept under the relevant Union financial services law.

Article 19: Automatically generated logs

1. Providers of high-risk AI systems shall keep the logs referred to in Article 12(1), automatically generated by their high-risk AI systems, to the extent such logs are under their control. Without prejudice to applicable Union or national law, the logs shall be kept for a period appropriate to the intended purpose of the high-risk AI system, of at least six months, unless provided otherwise in the applicable Union or national law, in particular in Union law on the protection of personal data.

2. Providers that are financial institutions subject to requirements regarding their internal governance, arrangements or processes under Union financial services law shall maintain the logs automatically generated by their high-risk AI systems as part of the documentation kept under the relevant financial services law.

Article 20: Corrective actions and duty of information

1. Providers of high-risk AI systems which consider or have reason to consider that a high-risk AI system that they have placed on the market or put into service is not in conformity with this Regulation shall immediately take the necessary corrective actions to bring

that system into conformity, to withdraw it, to disable it, or to recall it, as appropriate. They shall inform the distributors of the high-risk AI system concerned and, where applicable, the deployers, the authorised representative and importers accordingly.

2. Where the high-risk AI system presents a risk within the meaning of Article 79(1) and the provider becomes aware of that risk, it shall immediately investigate the causes, in collaboration with the reporting deployer, where applicable, and inform the market surveillance authorities competent for the high-risk AI system concerned and, where applicable, the notified body that issued a certificate for that high-risk AI system in accordance with Article 44, in particular, of the nature of the non-compliance and of any relevant corrective action taken.

Article 26: Obligations of deployers of high-risk AI systems

1. Deployers of high-risk AI systems shall take appropriate technical and organisational measures to ensure they use such systems in accordance with the instructions for use accompanying the systems, pursuant to paragraphs 3 and 6.

2. Deployers shall assign human oversight to natural persons who have the necessary competence, training and authority, as well as the necessary support.

3. The obligations set out in paragraphs 1 and 2, are without prejudice to other deployer obligations under Union or national law and to the deployer's freedom to organise its own resources and activities for the purpose of implementing the human oversight measures indicated by the provider.

4. Without prejudice to paragraphs 1 and 2, to the extent the deployer exercises control over the input data, that deployer shall ensure that input data is relevant and sufficiently representative in view of the intended purpose of the high-risk AI system.

APPENDIX

5. Deployers shall monitor the operation of the high-risk AI system on the basis of the instructions for use and, where relevant, inform providers in accordance with Article 72. Where deployers have reason to consider that the use of the high-risk AI system in accordance with the instructions may result in that AI system presenting a risk within the meaning of Article 79(1), they shall, without undue delay, inform the provider or distributor and the relevant market surveillance authority, and shall suspend the use of that system. Where deployers have identified a serious incident, they shall also immediately inform first the provider, and then the importer or distributor and the relevant market surveillance authorities of that incident. If the deployer is not able to reach the provider, Article 73 shall apply *mutatis mutandis*. This obligation shall not cover sensitive operational data of deployers of AI systems which are law enforcement authorities.

   For deployers that are financial institutions subject to requirements regarding their internal governance, arrangements or processes under Union financial services law, the monitoring obligation set out in the first subparagraph shall be deemed to be fulfilled by complying with the rules on internal governance arrangements, processes and mechanisms pursuant to the relevant financial service law.

6. Deployers of high-risk AI systems shall keep the logs automatically generated by that high-risk AI system to the extent such logs are under their control, for a period appropriate to the intended purpose of the high-risk AI system, of at least six months, unless provided otherwise in applicable Union or national law, in particular in Union law on the protection of personal data.

   Deployers that are financial institutions subject to requirements regarding their internal governance, arrangements or processes under Union financial services law shall maintain the logs as part of the documentation kept pursuant to the relevant Union financial service law.

APPENDIX

7. Before putting into service or using a high-risk AI system at the workplace, deployers who are employers shall inform workers' representatives and the affected workers that they will be subject to the use of the high-risk AI system. This information shall be provided, where applicable, in accordance with the rules and procedures laid down in Union and national law and practice on information of workers and their representatives.

8. Deployers of high-risk AI systems that are public authorities, or Union institutions, bodies, offices or agencies shall comply with the registration obligations referred to in Article 49. When such deployers find that the high-risk AI system that they envisage using has not been registered in the EU database referred to in Article 71, they shall not use that system and shall inform the provider or the distributor.

9. Where applicable, deployers of high-risk AI systems shall use the information provided under Article 13 of this Regulation to comply with their obligation to carry out a data protection impact assessment under Article 35 of Regulation (EU) 2016/679 or Article 27 of Directive (EU) 2016/680.

10. Without prejudice to Directive (EU) 2016/680, in the framework of an investigation for the targeted search of a person suspected or convicted of having committed a criminal offence, the deployer of a high-risk AI system for post-remote biometric identification shall request an authorisation, *ex ante*, or without undue delay and no later than 48 hours, by a judicial authority or an administrative authority whose decision is binding and subject to judicial review, for the use of that system, except when it is used for the initial identification of a potential suspect based on objective and verifiable facts directly linked to the offence. Each use shall be limited to what is strictly necessary for the investigation of a specific criminal offence.

    If the authorisation requested pursuant to the first subparagraph is rejected, the use of the post-remote biometric identification system linked to that requested authorisation shall be stopped with immediate effect and the personal data linked to the use of the high-risk AI system for which the authorisation was requested shall be deleted.

APPENDIX

In no case shall such high-risk AI system for post-remote biometric identification be used for law enforcement purposes in an untargeted way, without any link to a criminal offence, a criminal proceeding, a genuine and present or genuine and foreseeable threat of a criminal offence, or the search for a specific missing person. It shall be ensured that no decision that produces an adverse legal effect on a person may be taken by the law enforcement authorities based solely on the output of such post-remote biometric identification systems.

This paragraph is without prejudice to Article 9 of Regulation (EU) 2016/679 and Article 10 of Directive (EU) 2016/680 for the processing of biometric data.

Regardless of the purpose or deployer, each use of such high-risk AI systems shall be documented in the relevant police file and shall be made available to the relevant market surveillance authority and the national data protection authority upon request, excluding the disclosure of sensitive operational data related to law enforcement. This subparagraph shall be without prejudice to the powers conferred by Directive (EU) 2016/680 on supervisory authorities.

Deployers shall submit annual reports to the relevant market surveillance and national data protection authorities on their use of post-remote biometric identification systems, excluding the disclosure of sensitive operational data related to law enforcement. The reports may be aggregated to cover more than one deployment.

Member States may introduce, in accordance with Union law, more restrictive laws on the use of post-remote biometric identification systems.

11. Without prejudice to Article 50 of this Regulation, deployers of high-risk AI systems referred to in Annex III that make decisions

or assist in making decisions related to natural persons shall inform the natural persons that they are subject to the use of the high-risk AI system. For high-risk AI systems used for law enforcement purposes Article 13 of Directive (EU) 2016/680 shall apply.

12. Deployers shall cooperate with the relevant competent authorities in any action those authorities take in relation to the high-risk AI system in order to implement this Regulation.

Article 27: Fundamental rights impact assessment for high-risk AI systems

1. Prior to deploying a high-risk AI system referred to in Article 6(2), with the exception of high-risk AI systems intended to be used in the area listed in point 2 of Annex III, deployers that are bodies governed by public law, or are private entities providing public services, and deployers of high-risk AI systems referred to in points 5 (b) and (c) of Annex III, shall perform an assessment of the impact on fundamental rights that the use of such system may produce. For that purpose, deployers shall perform an assessment consisting of:

    (a) a description of the deployer's processes in which the high-risk AI system will be used in line with its intended purpose;

    (b) a description of the period of time within which, and the frequency with which, each high-risk AI system is intended to be used;

    (c) the categories of natural persons and groups likely to be affected by its use in the specific context;

    (d) the specific risks of harm likely to have an impact on the categories of natural persons or groups of persons identified pursuant to point (c) of this paragraph, taking into account the information given by the provider pursuant to Article 13;

    (e) a description of the implementation of human oversight measures, according to the instructions for use;

APPENDIX

(f) the measures to be taken in the case of the materialisation of those risks, including the arrangements for internal governance and complaint mechanisms.

2. The obligation laid down in paragraph 1 applies to the first use of the high-risk AI system. The deployer may, in similar cases, rely on previously conducted fundamental rights impact assessments or existing impact assessments carried out by provider. If, during the use of the high-risk AI system, the deployer considers that any of the elements listed in paragraph 1 has changed or is no longer up to date, the deployer shall take the necessary steps to update the information.

3. Once the assessment referred to in paragraph 1 of this Article has been performed, the deployer shall notify the market surveillance authority of its results, submitting the filled-out template referred to in paragraph 5 of this Article as part of the notification. In the case referred to in Article 46(1), deployers may be exempt from that obligation to notify.

4. If any of the obligations laid down in this Article is already met through the data protection impact assessment conducted pursuant to Article 35 of Regulation (EU) 2016/679 or Article 27 of Directive (EU) 2016/680, the fundamental rights impact assessment referred to in paragraph 1 of this Article shall complement that data protection impact assessment.

5. The AI Office shall develop a template for a questionnaire, including through an automated tool, to facilitate deployers in complying with their obligations under this Article in a simplified manner.

Section 5: Standards, Conformity Assessment, Certificates, Registration

Article 40: Harmonised Standards and Standardisation Deliverables

1. High-risk AI systems or general-purpose AI models which are in conformity with harmonised standards or parts thereof the references of which have been published in the *Official Journal of the European Union* in accordance with Regulation (EU) No 1025/2012 shall be presumed to be in conformity with the requirements set out in Section 2 of this Chapter or, as applicable, with the obligations set out in of Chapter V, Sections 2 and 3, of this Regulation, to the extent that those standards cover those requirements or obligations.

2. In accordance with Article 10 of Regulation (EU) No 1025/2012, the Commission shall issue, without undue delay, standardisation requests covering all requirements set out in Section 2 of this Chapter and, as applicable, standardisation requests covering obligations set out in Chapter V, Sections 2 and 3, of this Regulation. The standardisation request shall also ask for deliverables on reporting and documentation processes to improve AI systems' resource performance, such as reducing the high-risk AI system's consumption of energy and of other resources during its lifecycle, and on the energy-efficient development of general-purpose AI models. When preparing a standardisation request, the Commission shall consult the Board and relevant stakeholders, including the advisory forum.

   When issuing a standardisation request to European standardisation organisations, the Commission shall specify that standards have to be clear, consistent, including with the standards developed in the various sectors for products covered by the existing Union harmonisation legislation listed in Annex I, and aiming to ensure that high-risk AI systems or general-purpose AI models placed on the market or put into service in the Union meet the relevant requirements or obligations laid down in this Regulation.

The Commission shall request the European standardisation organisations to provide evidence of their best efforts to fulfil the objectives referred to in the first and the second subparagraph of this paragraph in accordance with Article 24 of Regulation (EU) No 1025/2012.

3. The participants in the standardisation process shall seek to promote investment and innovation in AI, including through increasing legal certainty, as well as the competitiveness and growth of the Union market, to contribute to strengthening global cooperation on standardisation and taking into account existing international standards in the field of AI that are consistent with Union values, fundamental rights and interests, and to enhance multi-stakeholder governance ensuring a balanced representation of interests and the effective participation of all relevant stakeholders in accordance with Articles 5, 6, and 7 of Regulation (EU) No 1025/2012.

Article 41: Common Specifications

1. The Commission may adopt, implementing acts establishing common specifications for the requirements set out in Section 2 of this Chapter or, as applicable, for the obligations set out in Sections 2 and 3 of Chapter V where the following conditions have been fulfilled:

    (a) the Commission has requested, pursuant to Article 10(1) of Regulation (EU) No 1025/2012, one or more European standardisation organisations to draft a harmonised standard for the requirements set out in Section 2 of this Chapter, or, as applicable, for the obligations set out in Sections 2 and 3 of Chapter V, and:

    (i) the request has not been accepted by any of the European standardisation organisations; or

    (ii) the harmonised standards addressing that request are not delivered within the deadline set in accordance with Article 10(1) of Regulation (EU) No 1025/2012; or

APPENDIX

      (iii) the relevant harmonised standards insufficiently address fundamental rights concerns; or

      (iv) the harmonised standards do not comply with the request; and

  (b) no reference to harmonised standards covering the requirements referred to in Section 2 of this Chapter or, as applicable, the obligations referred to in Sections 2 and 3 of Chapter V has been published in the *Official Journal of the European Union* in accordance with Regulation (EU) No 1025/2012, and no such reference is expected to be published within a reasonable period.

When drafting the common specifications, the Commission shall consult the advisory forum referred to in Article 67.

The implementing acts referred to in the first subparagraph of this paragraph shall be adopted in accordance with the examination procedure referred to in Article 98(2).

2. Before preparing a draft implementing act, the Commission shall inform the committee referred to in Article 22 of Regulation (EU) No 1025/2012 that it considers the conditions laid down in paragraph 1 of this Article to be fulfilled.

3. High-risk AI systems or general-purpose AI models which are in conformity with the common specifications referred to in paragraph 1, or parts of those specifications, shall be presumed to be in conformity with the requirements set out in Section 2 of this Chapter or, as applicable, to comply with the obligations referred to in Sections 2 and 3 of Chapter V, to the extent those common specifications cover those requirements or those obligations.

4. Where a harmonised standard is adopted by a European standardisation organisation and proposed to the Commission for the publication of its reference in the *Official Journal of the European Union*, the Commission shall assess the harmonised standard in accordance with Regulation (EU) No 1025/2012. When reference to a harmonised standard is published in the *Official Journal of the European Union*, the Commission shall

repeal the implementing acts referred to in paragraph 1, or parts thereof which cover the same requirements set out in Section 2 of this Chapter or, as applicable, the same obligations set out in Sections 2 and 3 of Chapter V.

5. Where providers of high-risk AI systems or general-purpose AI models do not comply with the common specifications referred to in paragraph 1, they shall duly justify that they have adopted technical solutions that meet the requirements referred to in Section 2 of this Chapter or, as applicable, comply with the obligations set out in Sections 2 and 3 of Chapter V to a level at least equivalent thereto.

6. Where a Member State considers that a common specification does not entirely meet the requirements set out in Section 2 or, as applicable, comply with obligations set out in Sections 2 and 3 of Chapter V, it shall inform the Commission thereof with a detailed explanation. The Commission shall assess that information and, if appropriate, amend the implementing act establishing the common specification concerned.

Article 42: Presumption of Conformity with certain Requirements

1. High-risk AI systems that have been trained and tested on data reflecting the specific geographical, behavioural, contextual or functional setting within which they are intended to be used shall be presumed to comply with the relevant requirements laid down in Article 10(4).

2. High-risk AI systems that have been certified or for which a statement of conformity has been issued under a cybersecurity scheme pursuant to Regulation (EU) 2019/881 and the references of which have been published in the *Official Journal of the European Union* shall be presumed to comply with the cybersecurity requirements set out in Article 15 of this Regulation in so far as the cybersecurity certificate or statement of conformity or parts thereof cover those requirements.

Article 43: Conformity Assessment

1. For high-risk AI systems listed in point 1 of Annex III, where, in demonstrating the compliance of a high-risk AI system with the requirements set out in Section 2, the provider has applied harmonised standards referred to in Article 40, or, where applicable, common specifications referred to in Article 41, the provider shall opt for one of the following conformity assessment procedures based on:

   a) the internal control referred to in Annex VI; or

   b) the assessment of the quality management system and the assessment of the technical documentation, with the involvement of a notified body, referred to in Annex VII.

   In demonstrating the compliance of a high-risk AI system with the requirements set out in Section 2, the provider shall follow the conformity assessment procedure set out in Annex VII where:

   a) harmonised standards referred to in Article 40 do not exist, and common specifications referred to in Article 41 are not available;

   b) the provider has not applied, or has applied only part of, the harmonised standard;

   c) the common specifications referred to in point (a) exist, but the provider has not applied them;

   d) one or more of the harmonised standards referred to in point (a) has been published with a restriction, and only on the part of the standard that was restricted.

   For the purposes of the conformity assessment procedure referred to in Annex VII, the provider may choose any of the notified bodies. However, where the high-risk AI system is intended to be put into service by law enforcement, immigration or asylum authorities or by Union institutions, bodies, offices or agencies, the market surveillance authority referred to in Article 74(8) or (9), as applicable, shall act as a notified body.

APPENDIX

2. For high-risk AI systems referred to in points 2 to 8 of Annex III, providers shall follow the conformity assessment procedure based on internal control as referred to in Annex VI, which does not provide for the involvement of a notified body.

3. For high-risk AI systems covered by the Union harmonisation legislation listed in Section A of Annex I, the provider shall follow the relevant conformity assessment procedure as required under those legal acts. The requirements set out in Section 2 of this Chapter shall apply to those high-risk AI systems and shall be part of that assessment. Points 4.3., 4.4., 4.5. and the fifth paragraph of point 4.6 of Annex VII shall also apply.

   For the purposes of that assessment, notified bodies which have been notified under those legal acts shall be entitled to control the conformity of the high-risk AI systems with the requirements set out in Section 2, provided that the compliance of those notified bodies with requirements laid down in Article 31(4), (5), (10) and (11) has been assessed in the context of the notification procedure under those legal acts.

   Where a legal act listed in Section A of Annex I enables the product manufacturer to opt out from a third-party conformity assessment, provided that that manufacturer has applied all harmonised standards covering all the relevant requirements, that manufacturer may use that option only if it has also applied harmonised standards or, where applicable, common specifications referred to in Article 41, covering all requirements set out in Section 2 of this Chapter.

4. High-risk AI systems that have already been subject to a conformity assessment procedure shall undergo a new conformity assessment procedure in the event of a substantial modification, regardless of whether the modified system is intended to be further distributed or continues to be used by the current deployer.

For high-risk AI systems that continue to learn after being placed on the market or put into service, changes to the high-risk AI system and its performance that have been pre-determined by the provider at the moment of the initial conformity assessment and are part of the information contained in the technical documentation referred to in point 2(f) of Annex IV, shall not constitute a substantial modification.

5. The Commission is empowered to adopt delegated acts in accordance with Article 97 in order to amend Annexes VI and VII by updating them in light of technical progress.

6. The Commission is empowered to adopt delegated acts in accordance with Article 97 in order to amend paragraphs 1 and 2 of this Article in order to subject high-risk AI systems referred to in points 2 to 8 of Annex III to the conformity assessment procedure referred to in Annex VII or parts thereof. The Commission shall adopt such delegated acts taking into account the effectiveness of the conformity assessment procedure based on internal control referred to in Annex VI in preventing or minimising the risks to health and safety and protection of fundamental rights posed by such systems, as well as the availability of adequate capacities and resources among notified bodies.

Article 44: Certificates

1. Certificates issued by notified bodies in accordance with Annex VII shall be drawn-up in a language which can be easily understood by the relevant authorities in the Member State in which the notified body is established.

2. Certificates shall be valid for the period they indicate, which shall not exceed five years for AI systems covered by Annex I, and four years for AI systems covered by Annex III. At the request of the provider, the validity of a certificate may be extended for further periods, each not exceeding five years for AI systems covered by Annex I, and four years for AI systems covered by Annex III, based

on a re-assessment in accordance with the applicable conformity assessment procedures. Any supplement to a certificate shall remain valid, provided that the certificate which it supplements is valid.

3. Where a notified body finds that an AI system no longer meets the requirements set out in Section 2, it shall, taking account of the principle of proportionality, suspend or withdraw the certificate issued or impose restrictions on it, unless compliance with those requirements is ensured by appropriate corrective action taken by the provider of the system within an appropriate deadline set by the notified body. The notified body shall give reasons for its decision.

An appeal procedure against decisions of the notified bodies, including on conformity certificates issued, shall be available.

Article 45: Information Obligations of Notified Bodies

1. Notified bodies shall inform the notifying authority of the following:

    (a) any Union technical documentation assessment certificates, any supplements to those certificates, and any quality management system approvals issued in accordance with the requirements of Annex VII;

    (b) any refusal, restriction, suspension or withdrawal of a Union technical documentation assessment certificate or a quality management system approval issued in accordance with the requirements of Annex VII;

    (c) any circumstances affecting the scope of or conditions for notification;

    (d) any request for information which they have received from market surveillance authorities regarding conformity assessment activities;

    (e) on request, conformity assessment activities performed within the scope of their notification and any other activity performed, including cross-border activities and subcontracting.

2. Each notified body shall inform the other notified bodies of:

    (a) quality management system approvals which it has refused, suspended or withdrawn, and, upon request, of quality system approvals which it has issued;

    (b) Union technical documentation assessment certificates or any supplements thereto which it has refused, withdrawn, suspended or otherwise restricted, and, upon request, of the certificates and/or supplements thereto which it has issued.

3. Each notified body shall provide the other notified bodies carrying out similar conformity assessment activities covering the same types of AI systems with relevant information on issues relating to negative and, on request, positive conformity assessment results.

4. Notified bodies shall safeguard the confidentiality of the information that they obtain, in accordance with Article 78.

Article 46: Derogation From Conformity Assessment Procedure

1. By way of derogation from Article 43 and upon a duly justified request, any market surveillance authority may authorise the placing on the market or the putting into service of specific high-risk AI systems within the territory of the Member State concerned, for exceptional reasons of public security or the protection of life and health of persons, environmental protection or the protection of key industrial and infrastructural assets. That authorisation shall be for a limited period while the necessary conformity assessment procedures are being carried out, taking into account the exceptional reasons justifying the derogation. The completion of those procedures shall be undertaken without undue delay.

2. In a duly justified situation of urgency for exceptional reasons of public security or in the case of specific, substantial and imminent threat to the life or physical safety of natural persons, law-enforcement authorities or civil protection authorities may put a specific high-risk

APPENDIX

AI system into service without the authorisation referred to in paragraph 1, provided that such authorisation is requested during or after the use without undue delay. If the authorisation referred to in paragraph 1 is refused, the use of the high-risk AI system shall be stopped with immediate effect and all the results and outputs of such use shall be immediately discarded.

3. The authorisation referred to in paragraph 1 shall be issued only if the market surveillance authority concludes that the high-risk AI system complies with the requirements of Section 2. The market surveillance authority shall inform the Commission and the other Member States of any authorisation issued pursuant to paragraphs 1 and 2. This obligation shall not cover sensitive operational data in relation to the activities of law-enforcement authorities.

4. Where, within 15 calendar days of receipt of the information referred to in paragraph 3, no objection has been raised by either a Member State or the Commission in respect of an authorisation issued by a market surveillance authority of a Member State in accordance with paragraph 1, that authorisation shall be deemed justified.

5. Where, within 15 calendar days of receipt of the notification referred to in paragraph 3, objections are raised by a Member State against an authorisation issued by a market surveillance authority of another Member State, or where the Commission considers the authorisation to be contrary to Union law, or the conclusion of the Member States regarding the compliance of the system as referred to in paragraph 3 to be unfounded, the Commission shall, without delay, enter into consultations with the relevant Member State. The operators concerned shall be consulted and have the possibility to present their views. Having regard thereto, the Commission shall decide whether the authorisation is justified. The Commission shall address its decision to the Member State concerned and to the relevant operators.

6. Where the Commission considers the authorisation unjustified, it shall be withdrawn by the market surveillance authority of the Member State concerned.

7. For high-risk AI systems related to products covered by Union harmonisation legislation listed in Section A of Annex I, only the derogations from the conformity assessment established in that Union harmonisation legislation shall apply.

Article 47: EU Declaration of Conformity

1. The provider shall draw up a written machine readable, physical or electronically signed EU declaration of conformity for each high-risk AI system, and keep it at the disposal of the national competent authorities for 10 years after the high-risk AI system has been placed on the market or put into service. The EU declaration of conformity shall identify the high-risk AI system for which it has been drawn up. A copy of the EU declaration of conformity shall be submitted to the relevant national competent authorities upon request.

2. The EU declaration of conformity shall state that the high-risk AI system concerned meets the requirements set out in Section 2. The EU declaration of conformity shall contain the information set out in Annex V, and shall be translated into a language that can be easily understood by the national competent authorities of the Member States in which the high-risk AI system is placed on the market or made available.

3. Where high-risk AI systems are subject to other Union harmonisation legislation which also requires an EU declaration of conformity, a single EU declaration of conformity shall be drawn up in respect of all Union law applicable to the high-risk AI system. The declaration shall contain all the information required to identify the Union harmonisation legislation to which the declaration relates.

4. By drawing up the EU declaration of conformity, the provider shall assume responsibility for compliance with the requirements set out in Section 2. The provider shall keep the EU declaration of conformity up-to-date as appropriate.

5. The Commission is empowered to adopt delegated acts in accordance with Article 97 in order to amend Annex V by updating the content of the EU declaration of conformity set out in that Annex, in order to introduce elements that become necessary in light of technical progress.

Article 48: CE Marking

1. The CE marking shall be subject to the general principles set out in Article 30 of Regulation (EC) No 765/2008.

2. For high-risk AI systems provided digitally, a digital CE marking shall be used, only if it can easily be accessed via the interface from which that system is accessed or via an easily accessible machine-readable code or other electronic means.

3. The CE marking shall be affixed visibly, legibly and indelibly for high-risk AI systems. Where that is not possible or not warranted on account of the nature of the high-risk AI system, it shall be affixed to the packaging or to the accompanying documentation, as appropriate.

4. Where applicable, the CE marking shall be followed by the identification number of the notified body responsible for the conformity assessment procedures set out in Article 43. The identification number of the notified body shall be affixed by the body itself or, under its instructions, by the provider or by the provider's authorised representative. The identification number shall also be indicated in any promotional material which mentions that the high-risk AI system fulfils the requirements for CE marking.

5. Where high-risk AI systems are subject to other Union law which also provides for the affixing of the CE marking, the CE marking shall indicate that the high-risk AI system also fulfil the requirements of that other law.

Article 49: Registration

1. Before placing on the market or putting into service a high-risk AI system listed in Annex III, with the exception of high-risk AI systems referred to in point 2 of Annex III, the provider or, where applicable, the authorised representative shall register themselves and their system in the EU database referred to in Article 71.

2. Before placing on the market or putting into service an AI system for which the provider has concluded that it is not high-risk according to Article 6(3), that provider or, where applicable, the authorised representative shall register themselves and that system in the EU database referred to in Article 71.

3. Before putting into service or using a high-risk AI system listed in Annex III, with the exception of high-risk AI systems listed in point 2 of Annex III, deployers that are public authorities, Union institutions, bodies, offices or agencies or persons acting on their behalf shall register themselves, select the system and register its use in the EU database referred to in Article 71.

4. For high-risk AI systems referred to in points 1, 6 and 7 of Annex III, in the areas of law enforcement, migration, asylum and border control management, the registration referred to in paragraphs 1, 2 and 3 of this Article shall be in a secure non-public section of the EU database referred to in Article 71 and shall include only the following information, as applicable, referred to in:

    (a) Section A, points 1 to 10, of Annex VIII, with the exception of points 6, 8 and 9;

    (b) Section B, points 1 to 5, and points 8 and 9 of Annex VIII;

    (c) Section C, points 1 to 3, of Annex VIII;

    (d) points 1, 2, 3 and 5, of Annex IX.

    Only the Commission and national authorities referred to in Article 74(8) shall have access to the respective restricted sections of the EU database listed in the first subparagraph of this paragraph.

5. High-risk AI systems referred to in point 2 of Annex III shall be registered at national level.

Chapter IV: Transparency Obligations for Providers and Deployers of Certain AI Systems

Article 50: Transparency Obligations for Providers and Deployers of Certain AI Systems

1. Providers shall ensure that AI systems intended to interact directly with natural persons are designed and developed in such a way that the natural persons concerned are informed that they are interacting with an AI system, unless this is obvious from the point of view of a natural person who is reasonably well-informed, observant and circumspect, taking into account the circumstances and the context of use. This obligation shall not apply to AI systems authorised by law to detect, prevent, investigate or prosecute criminal offences, subject to appropriate safeguards for the rights and freedoms of third parties, unless those systems are available for the public to report a criminal offence.

2. Providers of AI systems, including general-purpose AI systems, generating synthetic audio, image, video or text content, shall ensure that the outputs of the AI system are marked in a machine-readable format and detectable as artificially generated or manipulated. Providers shall ensure their technical solutions are effective, interoperable, robust and reliable as far as this is technically feasible, taking into account the specificities and limitations of various types of content, the costs of implementation and the generally acknowledged state of the art, as may be reflected in relevant technical standards. This obligation shall not apply to the extent the AI systems perform an assistive function for standard editing or do not substantially

alter the input data provided by the deployer or the semantics thereof, or where authorised by law to detect, prevent, investigate or prosecute criminal offences.

3. Deployers of an emotion recognition system or a biometric categorisation system shall inform the natural persons exposed thereto of the operation of the system, and shall process the personal data in accordance with Regulations (EU) 2016/679 and (EU) 2018/1725 and Directive (EU) 2016/680, as applicable. This obligation shall not apply to AI systems used for biometric categorisation and emotion recognition, which are permitted by law to detect, prevent or investigate criminal offences, subject to appropriate safeguards for the rights and freedoms of third parties, and in accordance with Union law.

4. Deployers of an AI system that generates or manipulates image, audio or video content constituting a deep fake, shall disclose that the content has been artificially generated or manipulated. This obligation shall not apply where the use is authorised by law to detect, prevent, investigate or prosecute criminal offence. Where the content forms part of an evidently artistic, creative, satirical, fictional or analogous work or programme, the transparency obligations set out in this paragraph are limited to disclosure of the existence of such generated or manipulated content in an appropriate manner that does not hamper the display or enjoyment of the work.

Deployers of an AI system that generates or manipulates text which is published with the purpose of informing the public on matters of public interest shall disclose that the text has been artificially generated or manipulated. This obligation shall not apply where the use is authorised by law to detect, prevent, investigate or prosecute criminal offences or where the AI-generated content has undergone a process of human review or editorial control and where a natural or legal person holds editorial responsibility for the publication of the content.

APPENDIX

5. The information referred to in paragraphs 1 to 4 shall be provided to the natural persons concerned in a clear and distinguishable manner at the latest at the time of the first interaction or exposure. The information shall conform to the applicable accessibility requirements.

6. Paragraphs 1 to 4 shall not affect the requirements and obligations set out in Chapter III, and shall be without prejudice to other transparency obligations laid down in Union or national law for deployers of AI systems.

7. The AI Office shall encourage and facilitate the drawing up of codes of practice at Union level to facilitate the effective implementation of the obligations regarding the detection and labelling of artificially generated or manipulated content. The Commission may adopt implementing acts to approve those codes of practice in accordance with the procedure laid down in Article 56 (6). If it deems the code is not adequate, the Commission may adopt an implementing act specifying common rules for the implementation of those obligations in accordance with the examination procedure laid down in Article 98(2).

Chapter V: General-Purpose AI Models

Section 2: Obligations for Providers of General-Purpose AI Models

Article 53 : Obligations for Providers of General-Purpose AI Models

1. Providers of general-purpose AI models shall:

    (a) draw up and keep up-to-date the technical documentation of the model, including its training and testing process and the results of its evaluation, which shall contain, at a minimum, the information set out in Annex XI for the purpose of providing it, upon request, to the AI Office and the national competent authorities;

(b) draw up, keep up-to-date and make available information and documentation to providers of AI systems who intend to integrate the general-purpose AI model into their AI systems. Without prejudice to the need to observe and protect intellectual property rights and confidential business information or trade secrets in accordance with Union and national law, the information and documentation shall:

   (i) enable providers of AI systems to have a good understanding of the capabilities and limitations of the general-purpose AI model and to comply with their obligations pursuant to this Regulation; and

   (ii) contain, at a minimum, the elements set out in Annex XII;

(c) put in place a policy to comply with Union law on copyright and related rights, and in particular to identify and comply with, including through state-of-the-art technologies, a reservation of rights expressed pursuant to Article 4(3) of Directive (EU) 2019/790;

(d) draw up and make publicly available a sufficiently detailed summary about the content used for training of the general-purpose AI model, according to a template provided by the AI Office.

2. The obligations set out in paragraph 1, points (a) and (b), shall not apply to providers of AI models that are released under a free and open-source licence that allows for the access, usage, modification, and distribution of the model, and whose parameters, including the weights, the information on the model architecture, and the information on model usage, are made publicly available. This exception shall not apply to general-purpose AI models with systemic risks.

3. Providers of general-purpose AI models shall cooperate as necessary with the Commission and the national competent authorities in the exercise of their competences and powers pursuant to this Regulation.

APPENDIX

4. Providers of general-purpose AI models may rely on codes of practice within the meaning of Article 56 to demonstrate compliance with the obligations set out in paragraph 1 of this Article, until a harmonised standard is published. Compliance with European harmonised standards grants providers the presumption of conformity to the extent that those standards cover those obligations. Providers of general-purpose AI models who do not adhere to an approved code of practice or do not comply with a European harmonised standard shall demonstrate alternative adequate means of compliance for assessment by the Commission.

5. For the purpose of facilitating compliance with Annex XI, in particular points 2 (d) and (e) thereof, the Commission is empowered to adopt delegated acts in accordance with Article 97 to detail measurement and calculation methodologies with a view to allowing for comparable and verifiable documentation.

6. The Commission is empowered to adopt delegated acts in accordance with Article 97(2) to amend Annexes XI and XII in light of evolving technological developments.

7. Any information or documentation obtained pursuant to this Article, including trade secrets, shall be treated in accordance with the confidentiality obligations set out in Article 78.

Section 3: Obligations of Providers of General-Purpose AI Models with Systemic Risk

Article 55: Obligations of Providers of General-Purpose AI Models with Systemic Risk

1. In addition to the obligations listed in Articles 53 and 54, providers of general-purpose AI models with systemic risk shall:

(a) perform model evaluation in accordance with standardised protocols and tools reflecting the state of the art, including conducting and documenting adversarial testing of the model with a view to identifying and mitigating systemic risks;

(b) assess and mitigate possible systemic risks at Union level, including their sources, that may stem from the development, the placing on the market, or the use of general-purpose AI models with systemic risk;

(c) keep track of, document, and report, without undue delay, to the AI Office and, as appropriate, to national competent authorities, relevant information about serious incidents and possible corrective measures to address them;

(d) ensure an adequate level of cybersecurity protection for the general-purpose AI model with systemic risk and the physical infrastructure of the model.

2. Providers of general-purpose AI models with systemic risk may rely on codes of practice within the meaning of Article 56 to demonstrate compliance with the obligations set out in paragraph 1 of this Article, until a harmonised standard is published. Compliance with European harmonised standards grants providers the presumption of conformity to the extent that those standards cover those obligations. Providers of general-purpose AI models with systemic risks who do not adhere to an approved code of practice or do not comply with a European harmonised standard shall demonstrate alternative adequate means of compliance for assessment by the Commission.

3. Any information or documentation obtained pursuant to this Article, including trade secrets, shall be treated in accordance with the confidentiality obligations set out in Article 78.

APPENDIX

Chapter IX: Post-Market Monitoring, Information Sharing and Market Surveillance

Section 1: Post-market Monitoring

Article 72: Post-market Monitoring by Providers and Post-market Monitoring Plan for High-risk AI Systems

1. Providers shall establish and document a post-market monitoring system in a manner that is proportionate to the nature of the AI technologies and the risks of the high-risk AI system.

2. The post-market monitoring system shall actively and systematically collect, document and analyse relevant data which may be provided by deployers or which may be collected through other sources on the performance of high-risk AI systems throughout their lifetime, and which allow the provider to evaluate the continuous compliance of AI systems with the requirements set out in Chapter III, Section 2. Where relevant, post-market monitoring shall include an analysis of the interaction with other AI systems. This obligation shall not cover sensitive operational data of deployers which are law-enforcement authorities.

3. The post-market monitoring system shall be based on a post-market monitoring plan. The post-market monitoring plan shall be part of the technical documentation referred to in Annex IV. The Commission shall adopt an implementing act laying down detailed provisions establishing a template for the post-market monitoring plan and the list of elements to be included in the plan by 2 February 2026. That implementing act shall be adopted in accordance with the examination procedure referred to in Article 98(2).

4. For high-risk AI systems covered by the Union harmonisation legislation listed in Section A of Annex I, where a post-market monitoring system and plan are already established under that legislation, in order to ensure consistency, avoid duplications

and minimise additional burdens, providers shall have a choice of integrating, as appropriate, the necessary elements described in paragraphs 1, 2 and 3 using the template referred in paragraph 3 into systems and plans already existing under that legislation, provided that it achieves an equivalent level of protection.

The first subparagraph of this paragraph shall also apply to high-risk AI systems referred to in point 5 of Annex III placed on the market or put into service by financial institutions that are subject to requirements under Union financial services law regarding their internal governance, arrangements or processes.

Section 2: Sharing of Information on Serious Incidents

Article 73: Reporting of serious incidents

1. Providers of high-risk AI systems placed on the Union market shall report any serious incident to the market surveillance authorities of the Member States where that incident occurred.

2. The report referred to in paragraph 1 shall be made immediately after the provider has established a causal link between the AI system and the serious incident or the reasonable likelihood of such a link, and, in any event, not later than 15 days after the provider or, where applicable, the deployer, becomes aware of the serious incident.

   The period for the reporting referred to in the first subparagraph shall take account of the severity of the serious incident.

3. Notwithstanding paragraph 2 of this Article, in the event of a widespread infringement or a serious incident as defined in Article 3, point (49)(b), the report referred to in paragraph 1 of this Article shall be provided immediately, and not later than two days after the provider or, where applicable, the deployer becomes aware of that incident.

APPENDIX

4. Notwithstanding paragraph 2, in the event of the death of a person, the report shall be provided immediately after the provider or the deployer has established, or as soon as it suspects, a causal relationship between the high-risk AI system and the serious incident, but not later than 10 days after the date on which the provider or, where applicable, the deployer becomes aware of the serious incident.

5. Where necessary to ensure timely reporting, the provider or, where applicable, the deployer, may submit an initial report that is incomplete, followed by a complete report.

6. Following the reporting of a serious incident pursuant to paragraph 1, the provider shall, without delay, perform the necessary investigations in relation to the serious incident and the AI system concerned. This shall include a risk assessment of the incident, and corrective action.

   The provider shall cooperate with the competent authorities, and where relevant with the notified body concerned, during the investigations referred to in the first subparagraph, and shall not perform any investigation which involves altering the AI system concerned in a way which may affect any subsequent evaluation of the causes of the incident, prior to informing the competent authorities of such action.

7. Upon receiving a notification related to a serious incident referred to in Article 3, point (49)(c), the relevant market surveillance authority shall inform the national public authorities or bodies referred to in Article 77(1). The Commission shall develop dedicated guidance to facilitate compliance with the obligations set out in paragraph 1 of this Article. That guidance shall be issued by 2 August 2025, and shall be assessed regularly.

8. The market surveillance authority shall take appropriate measures, as provided for in Article 19 of Regulation (EU) 2019/1020, within seven days from the date it received the notification referred to in paragraph 1 of this Article, and shall follow the notification procedures as provided in that Regulation.

9. For high-risk AI systems referred to in Annex III that are placed on the market or put into service by providers that are subject to Union legislative instruments laying down reporting obligations equivalent to those set out in this Regulation, the notification of serious incidents shall be limited to those referred to in Article 3, point (49)(c).

10. For high-risk AI systems which are safety components of devices, or are themselves devices, covered by Regulations (EU) 2017/745 and (EU) 2017/746, the notification of serious incidents shall be limited to those referred to in Article 3, point (49)(c) of this Regulation, and shall be made to the national competent authority chosen for that purpose by the Member States where the incident occurred.

11. National competent authorities shall immediately notify the Commission of any serious incident, whether or not they have taken action on it, in accordance with Article 20 of Regulation (EU) 2019/1020.

Section 4: Remedies
Article 86: Right to Explanation of Individual Decision-making

1. Any affected person subject to a decision which is taken by the deployer on the basis of the output from a high-risk AI system listed in Annex III, with the exception of systems listed under point 2 thereof, and which produces legal effects or similarly significantly affects that person in a way that they consider to have an adverse impact on their health, safety or fundamental rights shall have the right to obtain from the deployer clear and meaningful explanations of the role of the AI system in the decision-making procedure and the main elements of the decision taken.

2. Paragraph 1 shall not apply to the use of AI systems for which exceptions from, or restrictions to, the obligation under that paragraph follow from Union or national law in compliance with Union law.

3. This Article shall apply only to the extent that the right referred to in paragraph 1 is not otherwise provided for under Union law.

Annex XI: Technical documentation referred to in Article 53(1), Point (a) — Technical Documentation for Providers of General-purpose AI Models

Section 1: Information to be Provided by all Providers of General-Purpose AI Models

The technical documentation referred to in Article 53(1), point (a) shall contain at least the following information as appropriate to the size and risk profile of the model:

1. A general description of the general-purpose AI model including:

    (a) the tasks that the model is intended to perform and the type and nature of AI systems in which it can be integrated;

    (b) the acceptable use policies applicable;

    (c) the date of release and methods of distribution;

    (d) the architecture and number of parameters;

    (e) the modality (e.g. text, image) and format of inputs and outputs;

    (f) the licence.

2. A detailed description of the elements of the model referred to in point 1, and relevant information of the process for the development, including the following elements:

APPENDIX

(a) the technical means (e.g. instructions of use, infrastructure, tools) required for the general-purpose AI model to be integrated in AI systems;

(b) the design specifications of the model and training process, including training methodologies and techniques, the key design choices including the rationale and assumptions made; what the model is designed to optimise for and the relevance of the different parameters, as applicable;

(c) information on the data used for training, testing and validation, where applicable, including the type and provenance of data and curation methodologies (e.g. cleaning, filtering, etc.), the number of data points, their scope and main characteristics; how the data was obtained and selected as well as all other measures to detect the unsuitability of data sources and methods to detect identifiable biases, where applicable;

(d) the computational resources used to train the model (e.g. number of floating point operations), training time, and other relevant details related to the training;

(e) known or estimated energy consumption of the model.

With regard to point (e), where the energy consumption of the model is unknown, the energy consumption may be based on information about computational resources used.

Section 2: Additional Information to be Provided by Providers of General-Purpose AI Models with Systemic Risk

1. A detailed description of the evaluation strategies, including evaluation results, on the basis of available public evaluation protocols and tools or otherwise of other evaluation methodologies. Evaluation strategies shall include evaluation criteria, metrics and the methodology on the identification of limitations.

APPENDIX

2. Where applicable, a detailed description of the measures put in place for the purpose of conducting internal and/or external adversarial testing (e.g. red teaming), model adaptations, including alignment and fine-tuning.

3. Where applicable, a detailed description of the system architecture explaining how software components build or feed into each other and integrate into the overall processing.

Annex XII: Transparency Information Referred to in Article 53(1), point (b) — Technical Documentation for Providers of General-Purpose AI Models to downstream Providers that Integrate the Model into their AI System

The information referred to in Article 53(1), point (b) shall contain at least the following:

1. A general description of the general-purpose AI model including:

    (a) the tasks that the model is intended to perform and the type and nature of AI systems into which it can be integrated;

    (b) the acceptable use policies applicable;

    (c) the date of release and methods of distribution;

    (d) how the model interacts, or can be used to interact, with hardware or software that is not part of the model itself, where applicable;

    (e) the versions of relevant software related to the use of the general-purpose AI model, where applicable;

    (f) the architecture and number of parameters;

    (g) the modality (e.g. text, image) and format of inputs and outputs;

    (h) the licence for the model.

2. A description of the elements of the model and of the process for its development, including:

    (a) the technical means (e.g. instructions for use, infrastructure, tools) required for the general-purpose AI model to be integrated into AI systems;

    (b) the modality (e.g. text, image, etc.) and format of the inputs and outputs and their maximum size (e.g. context window length, etc.);

    (c) information on the data used for training, testing and validation, where applicable, including the type and provenance of data and curation methodologies.

General Data Protection Regulation

Recital (26): The principles of data protection should apply to any information concerning an identified or identifiable natural person. Personal data which have undergone pseudonymisation, which could be attributed to a natural person by the use of additional information should be considered to be information on an identifiable natural person. To determine whether a natural person is identifiable, account should be taken of all the means reasonably likely to be used, such as singling out, either by the controller or by another person to identify the natural person directly or indirectly. To ascertain whether means are reasonably likely to be used to identify the natural person, account should be taken of all objective factors, such as the costs of and the amount of time required for identification, taking into consideration the available technology at the time of the processing and technological developments. The principles of data protection should therefore not apply to anonymous information, namely information which does not relate to an identified or identifiable natural person or to personal data rendered anonymous in such a manner that the data subject is not or no longer identifiable. This Regulation does not therefore concern the processing of such anonymous information, including for statistical or research purposes.

Recital (71): The data subject should have the right not to be subject to a decision, which may include a measure, evaluating personal aspects relating to him or her which is based solely on automated processing and which produces legal effects concerning him or her or similarly significantly affects him or her, such as automatic refusal of an online credit application or e-recruiting practices without any human intervention. Such processing includes 'profiling' that consists of any form of automated processing of personal data evaluating the personal aspects relating to a natural person, in particular to analyse or predict aspects concerning the data subject's performance at work, economic situation, health, personal preferences or interests, reliability or behaviour, location or movements, where it produces legal effects concerning him or her or similarly significantly affects him or her. However, decision-making based on such processing, including profiling, should be allowed where expressly authorised by Union or Member State law to which the controller is subject, including for fraud and tax-evasion monitoring and prevention purposes conducted in accordance with the regulations, standards and recommendations of Union institutions or national oversight bodies and to ensure the security and reliability of a service provided by the controller, or necessary for the entering or performance of a contract between the data subject and a controller, or when the data subject has given his or her explicit consent. In any case, such processing should be subject to suitable safeguards, which should include specific information to the data subject and the right to obtain human intervention, to express his or her point of view, to obtain an explanation of the decision reached after such assessment and to challenge the decision. Such measure should not concern a child.

In order to ensure fair and transparent processing in respect of the data subject, taking into account the specific circumstances and context in which the personal data are processed, the controller should use appropriate mathematical or statistical procedures for the profiling, implement technical and organisational measures appropriate to ensure, in particular, that factors which result in inaccuracies in personal data are corrected and the risk of errors is minimised, secure personal data in a manner that takes account of the potential risks involved for the interests and rights of the data subject and that prevents, inter alia, discriminatory effects on natural persons on the basis of racial or ethnic origin, political opinion, religion or beliefs, trade union membership, genetic or health status or sexual orientation, or that result in measures having such an effect. Automated decision-making and profiling based on special categories of personal data should be allowed only under specific conditions.

Article 6:Lawfulness of Processing

1. Processing shall be lawful only if and to the extent that at least one of the following applies:

(a) the data subject has given consent to the processing of his or her personal data for one or more specific purposes;

(b) processing is necessary for the performance of a contract to which the data subject is party or in order to take steps at the request of the data subject prior to entering into a contract;

(c) processing is necessary for compliance with a legal obligation to which the controller is subject;

(d) processing is necessary in order to protect the vital interests of the data subject or of another natural person;

(e) processing is necessary for the performance of a task carried out in the public interest or in the exercise of official authority vested in the controller;

(f) processing is necessary for the purposes of the legitimate interests pursued by the controller or by a third party, except where such interests are overridden by the interests or fundamental rights and freedoms of the data subject which require protection of personal data, in particular where the data subject is a child.

Point (f) of the first subparagraph shall not apply to processing carried out by public authorities in the performance of their tasks.

2. Member States may maintain or introduce more specific provisions to adapt the application of the rules of this Regulation with regard to processing for compliance with points (c) and (e) of paragraph 1 by determining more precisely specific requirements for the processing and other measures to ensure lawful and fair processing including for other specific processing situations as provided for in Chapter IX.

3. The basis for the processing referred to in point (c) and (e) of paragraph 1 shall be laid down by:

(a) Union law; or

(b) Member State law to which the controller is subject.

The purpose of the processing shall be determined in that legal basis or, as regards the processing referred to in point (e) of paragraph 1, shall be necessary for the performance of a task carried out in the public interest or in the exercise of official authority vested in the controller. That legal basis may contain specific provisions to adapt the application of rules of this Regulation, inter alia: the general conditions governing the lawfulness of processing by the controller; the types of data which are subject to the processing; the data subjects concerned; the entities to, and the purposes for which, the personal data may be disclosed; the purpose limitation; storage periods; and processing operations and processing procedures, including measures to ensure lawful and fair processing such as those for other specific processing situations as provided for in Chapter IX. The Union or the Member State law shall meet an objective of public interest and be proportionate to the legitimate aim pursued.

4. Where the processing for a purpose other than that for which the personal data have been collected is not based on the data subject's consent or on a Union or Member State law which constitutes a necessary and proportionate measure in a democratic society to safeguard the objectives referred to in Article 23(1), the controller shall, in order to ascertain whether processing for another purpose is compatible with the purpose for which the personal data are initially collected, take into account, inter alia:

   (a) any link between the purposes for which the personal data have been collected and the purposes of the intended further processing;

   (b) the context in which the personal data have been collected, in particular regarding the relationship between data subjects and the controller;

   (c) the nature of the personal data, in particular whether special categories of personal data are processed, pursuant to Article 9, or whether personal data related to criminal convictions and offences are processed, pursuant to Article 10;

(d) the possible consequences of the intended further processing for data subjects;

(e) the existence of appropriate safeguards, which may include encryption or pseudonymisation.

Article 9: Processing of Special Categories of Personal Data

1. Processing of personal data revealing racial or ethnic origin, political opinions, religious or philosophical beliefs, or trade union membership, and the processing of genetic data, biometric data for the purpose of uniquely identifying a natural person, data concerning health or data concerning a natural person's sex life or sexual orientation shall be prohibited.

2. Paragraph 1 shall not apply if one of the following applies:

    (a) the data subject has given explicit consent to the processing of those personal data for one or more specified purposes, except where Union or Member State law provide that the prohibition referred to in paragraph 1 may not be lifted by the data subject;

    (b) processing is necessary for the purposes of carrying out the obligations and exercising specific rights of the controller or of the data subject in the field of employment and social security and social protection law in so far as it is authorised by Union or Member State law or a collective agreement pursuant to Member State law providing for appropriate safeguards for the fundamental rights and the interests of the data subject;

    (c) processing is necessary to protect the vital interests of the data subject or of another natural person where the data subject is physically or legally incapable of giving consent;

APPENDIX

(d) processing is carried out in the course of its legitimate activities with appropriate safeguards by a foundation, association or any other not-for-profit body with a political, philosophical, religious or trade union aim and on condition that the processing relates solely to the members or to former members of the body or to persons who have regular contact with it in connection with its purposes and that the personal data are not disclosed outside that body without the consent of the data subjects;

(e) processing relates to personal data which are manifestly made public by the data subject;

(f) processing is necessary for the establishment, exercise or defence of legal claims or whenever courts are acting in their judicial capacity;

(g) processing is necessary for reasons of substantial public interest, on the basis of Union or Member State law which shall be proportionate to the aim pursued, respect the essence of the right to data protection and provide for suitable and specific measures to safeguard the fundamental rights and the interests of the data subject;

(h) processing is necessary for the purposes of preventive or occupational medicine, for the assessment of the working capacity of the employee, medical diagnosis, the provision of health or social care or treatment or the management of health or social care systems and services on the basis of Union or Member State law or pursuant to contract with a health professional and subject to the conditions and safeguards referred to in paragraph 3;

(i) processing is necessary for reasons of public interest in the area of public health, such as protecting against serious cross-border threats to health or ensuring high standards of quality and safety of health care and of medicinal products or medical devices, on the basis of Union or Member State law which provides for suitable and specific measures to safeguard the rights and freedoms of the data subject, in particular professional secrecy;

(j) processing is necessary for archiving purposes in the public interest, scientific or historical research purposes or statistical purposes in accordance with Article 89(1) based on Union or Member State law which shall be proportionate to the aim pursued, respect the essence of the right to data protection and provide for suitable and specific measures to safeguard the fundamental rights and the interests of the data subject.

3. Personal data referred to in paragraph 1 may be processed for the purposes referred to in point (h) of paragraph 2 when those data are processed by or under the responsibility of a professional subject to the obligation of professional secrecy under Union or Member State law or rules established by national competent bodies or by another person also subject to an obligation of secrecy under Union or Member State law or rules established by national competent bodies.

4. Member States may maintain or introduce further conditions, including limitations, with regard to the processing of genetic data, biometric data or data concerning health.

Section 2: Information and Access to Personal Data
Article 13: Information to be Provided where Personal Data are Dollected From the Data Subject

2. In addition to the information referred to in paragraph 1, the controller shall, at the time when personal data are obtained, provide the data subject with the following further information necessary to ensure fair and transparent processing:

(f) the existence of automated decision-making, including profiling, referred to in Article 22(1) and (4) and, at least in those cases, meaningful information about the logic involved, as well as the significance and the envisaged consequences of such processing for the data subject.

APPENDIX

Article 14: Information to be Provided where Personal Data Have not Been Obtained from the Data Subject

2. In addition to the information referred to in paragraph 1, the controller shall provide the data subject with the following information necessary to ensure fair and transparent processing in respect of the data subject:

(g) the existence of automated decision-making, including profiling, referred to in Article 22(1) and (4) and, at least in those cases, meaningful information about the logic involved, as well as the significance and the envisaged consequences of such processing for the data subject.

Article 15: Right of Access by the Data Subject

1. The data subject shall have the right to obtain from the controller confirmation as to whether or not personal data concerning him or her are being processed, and, where that is the case, access to the personal data and the following information:

(h) the existence of automated decision-making, including profiling, referred to in Article 22(1) and (4) and, at least in those cases, meaningful information about the logic involved, as well as the significance and the envisaged consequences of such processing for the data subject.

Article 22: Automated Individual Decision-Making, Including Profiling

1. The data subject shall have the right not to be subject to a decision based solely on automated processing, including profiling, which produces legal effects concerning him or her or similarly significantly affects him or her.

2. Paragraph 1 shall not apply if the decision:

   (a) is necessary for entering into, or performance of, a contract between the data subject and a data controller;

   (b) is authorised by Union or Member State law to which the controller is subject and which also lays down suitable measures to safeguard the data subject's rights and freedoms and legitimate interests; or

   (c) is based on the data subject's explicit consent.

3. In the cases referred to in points (a) and (c) of paragraph 2, the data controller shall implement suitable measures to safeguard the data subject's rights and freedoms and legitimate interests, at least the right to obtain human intervention on the part of the controller, to express his or her point of view and to contest the decision.

4. Decisions referred to in paragraph 2 shall not be based on special categories of personal data referred to in Article 9(1), unless point (a) or (g) of Article 9(2) applies and suitable measures to safeguard the data subject's rights and freedoms and legitimate interests are in place.

Article 35: Data Protection Impact Assessment

1. Where a type of processing in particular using new technologies, and taking into account the nature, scope, context and purposes of the processing, is likely to result in a high risk to the rights and freedoms of natural persons, the controller shall, prior to the processing, carry out an assessment of the impact of the envisaged processing operations on the protection of personal data. A single assessment may address a set of similar processing operations that present similar high risks.

2. The controller shall seek the advice of the data protection officer, where designated, when carrying out a data protection impact assessment.

3. A data protection impact assessment referred to in paragraph 1 shall in particular be required in the case of:

   (a) a systematic and extensive evaluation of personal aspects relating to natural persons which is based on automated processing, including profiling, and on which decisions are based that produce legal effects concerning the natural person or similarly significantly affect the natural person;

   (b) processing on a large scale of special categories of data referred to in Article 9(1), or of personal data relating to criminal convictions and offences referred to in Article 10; or

   (c) a systematic monitoring of a publicly accessible area on a large scale.

4. The supervisory authority shall establish and make public a list of the kind of processing operations which are subject to the requirement for a data protection impact assessment pursuant to paragraph 1. The supervisory authority shall communicate those lists to the Board referred to in Article 68.

5. The supervisory authority may also establish and make public a list of the kind of processing operations for which no data protection impact assessment is required. The supervisory authority shall communicate those lists to the Board.

6. Prior to the adoption of the lists referred to in paragraphs 4 and 5, the competent supervisory authority shall apply the consistency mechanism referred to in Article 63 where such lists involve processing activities which are related to the offering of goods or services to data subjects or to the monitoring of their behaviour in several Member States, or may substantially affect the free movement of personal data within the Union.

7. The assessment shall contain at least:

   (a) a systematic description of the envisaged processing operations and the purposes of the processing, including, where applicable, the legitimate interest pursued by the controller;

(b) an assessment of the necessity and proportionality of the processing operations in relation to the purposes;

(c) an assessment of the risks to the rights and freedoms of data subjects referred to in paragraph 1; and

(d) the measures envisaged to address the risks, including safeguards, security measures and mechanisms to ensure the protection of personal data and to demonstrate compliance with this Regulation taking into account the rights and legitimate interests of data subjects and other persons concerned.

8. Compliance with approved codes of conduct referred to in Article 40 by the relevant controllers or processors shall be taken into due account in assessing the impact of the processing operations performed by such controllers or processors, in particular for the purposes of a data protection impact assessment.

9. Where appropriate, the controller shall seek the views of data subjects or their representatives on the intended processing, without prejudice to the protection of commercial or public interests or the security of processing operations.

10. Where processing pursuant to point (c) or (e) of Article 6(1) has a legal basis in Union law or in the law of the Member State to which the controller is subject, that law regulates the specific processing operation or set of operations in question, and a data protection impact assessment has already been carried out as part of a general impact assessment in the context of the adoption of that legal basis, paragraphs 1 to 7 shall not apply unless Member States deem it to be necessary to carry out such an assessment prior to processing activities.

11. Where necessary, the controller shall carry out a review to assess if processing is performed in accordance with the data protection impact assessment at least when there is a change of the risk represented by processing operations.

APPENDIX

Digital Services Act

Recital (94): The obligations on assessment and mitigation of risks should trigger, on a case-by-case basis, the need for providers of very large online platforms and of very large online search engines to assess and, where necessary, adjust the design of their recommender systems, for example by taking measures to prevent or minimise biases that lead to the discrimination of persons in vulnerable situations, in particular where such adjustment is in accordance with data protection law and when the information is personalised on the basis of special categories of personal data referred to in Article 9 of the Regulation (EU) 2016/679. In addition, and complementing the transparency obligations applicable to online platforms as regards their recommender systems, providers of very large online platforms and of very large online search engines should consistently ensure that recipients of their service enjoy alternative options which are not based on profiling, within the meaning of Regulation (EU) 2016/679, for the main parameters of their recommender systems. Such choices should be directly accessible from the online interface where the recommendations are presented.

Article 27: Recommender System Transparency

1. Providers of online platforms that use recommender systems shall set out in their terms and conditions, in plain and intelligible language, the main parameters used in their recommender systems, as well as any options for the recipients of the service to modify or influence those main parameters.

2. The main parameters referred to in paragraph 1 shall explain why certain information is suggested to the recipient of the service. They shall include, at least:

    (a) the criteria which are most significant in determining the information suggested to the recipient of the service;

    (b) the reasons for the relative importance of those parameters.

3. Where several options are available pursuant to paragraph 1 for recommender systems that determine the relative order of information presented to recipients of the service, providers of

online platforms shall also make available a functionality that allows the recipient of the service to select and to modify at any time their preferred option. That functionality shall be directly and easily accessible from the specific section of the online platform's online interface where the information is being prioritised.

Article 39: Additional Online Advertising Transparency

1. Providers of very large online platforms or of very large online search engines that present advertisements on their online interfaces shall compile and make publicly available in a specific section of their online interface, through a searchable and reliable tool that allows multicriteria queries and through application programming interfaces, a repository containing the information referred to in paragraph 2, for the entire period during which they present an advertisement and until one year after the advertisement was presented for the last time on their online interfaces. They shall ensure that the repository does not contain any personal data of the recipients of the service to whom the advertisement was or could have been presented, and shall make reasonable efforts to ensure that the information is accurate and complete.

2. The repository shall include at least all of the following information:

    The repository shall include at least all of the following information:

    (a) the content of the advertisement, including the name of the product, service or brand and the subject matter of the advertisement;

    (b) the natural or legal person on whose behalf the advertisement is presented;

(c) the natural or legal person who paid for the advertisement, if that person is different from the person referred to in point (b);

(d) the period during which the advertisement was presented;

(e) whether the advertisement was intended to be presented specifically to one or more particular groups of recipients of the service and if so, the main parameters used for that purpose including where applicable the main parameters used to exclude one or more of such particular groups;

(f) the commercial communications published on the very large online platforms and identified pursuant to Article 26(2);

(g) the total number of recipients of the service reached and, where applicable, aggregate numbers broken down by Member State for the group or groups of recipients that the advertisement specifically targeted.

3. As regards paragraph 2, points (a), (b) and (c), where a provider of very large online platform or of very large online search engine has removed or disabled access to a specific advertisement based on alleged illegality or incompatibility with its terms and conditions, the repository shall not include the information referred to in those points. In such case, the repository shall include, for the specific advertisement concerned, the information referred to in Article 17(3), points (a) to (e), or Article 9(2), point (a)(i), as applicable.

The Commission may, after consultation of the Board, the relevant vetted researchers referred to in Article 40 and the public, issue guidelines on the structure, organisation and functionalities of the repositories referred to in this Article.

Article 45: Codes of Conduct

1. The Commission and the Board shall encourage and facilitate the drawing up of voluntary codes of conduct at Union level to contribute to the proper application of this Regulation, taking into account in particular the specific challenges of tackling different

types of illegal content and systemic risks, in accordance with Union law in particular on competition and the protection of personal data.

2. Where significant systemic risk within the meaning of Article 34(1) emerge and concern several very large online platforms or very large online search engines, the Commission may invite the providers of very large online platforms concerned or the providers of very large online search engines concerned, and other providers of very large online platforms, of very large online search engines, of online platforms and of other intermediary services, as appropriate, as well as relevant competent authorities, civil society organisations and other relevant stakeholders, to participate in the drawing up of codes of conduct, including by setting out commitments to take specific risk mitigation measures, as well as a regular reporting framework on any measures taken and their outcomes.

3. When giving effect to paragraphs 1 and 2, the Commission and the Board, and where relevant other bodies, shall aim to ensure that the codes of conduct clearly set out their specific objectives, contain key performance indicators to measure the achievement of those objectives and take due account of the needs and interests of all interested parties, and in particular citizens, at Union level. The Commission and the Board shall also aim to ensure that participants report regularly to the Commission and their respective Digital Services Coordinators of establishment on any measures taken and their outcomes, as measured against the key performance indicators that they contain. Key performance indicators and reporting commitments shall take into account differences in size and capacity between different participants.

4. The Commission and the Board shall assess whether the codes of conduct meet the aims specified in paragraphs 1 and 3, and shall regularly monitor and evaluate the achievement of their objectives, having regard to the key performance indicators that they might contain. They shall publish their conclusions.

APPENDIX

The Commission and the Board shall also encourage and facilitate regular review and adaptation of the codes of conduct.

In the case of systematic failure to comply with the codes of conduct, the Commission and the Board may invite the signatories to the codes of conduct to take the necessary action.

Code of Conduct on Disinformation

Transparency obligations for AI systems

Commitment 15. Relevant Signatories that develop or operate AI systems and that disseminate AI-generated and manipulated content through their services (e.g. deepfakes) commit to take into consideration the transparency obligations and the list of manipulative practices prohibited under the Artificial Intelligence Act.

In order to satisfy Commitment 15:

Measure 15.1. Relevant Signatories will establish or confirm their policies in place for countering prohibited manipulative practices for AI systems that generate or manipulate content, such as warning users and proactively detect such content.

QRE 15.1.1: In line with EU and national legislation, relevant Signatories will report on their policies in place for countering prohibited manipulative practices for AI systems that generate or manipulate content.

Measure 15.2. Relevant Signatories will establish or confirm their policies in place to ensure that the algorithms used for detection, moderation and sanctioning of impermissible conduct and content on their services are trustworthy, respect the rights of end-users and do not constitute prohibited manipulative practices impermissibly distorting their behaviour in line with Union and Member State's legislation.

QRE 15.2.1: Relevant Signatories will report on their policies and actions to ensure that the algorithms used for detection, moderation and sanctioning of impermissible conduct and content on their services are trustworthy, respect the rights of end-users and do not constitute prohibited manipulative practices in line with Union and Member States legislation.

EU Copyright Directive

Article 4: Exception or Limitation for text and Data Mining

1. Member States shall provide for an exception or limitation to the rights provided for in Article 5(a) and Article 7(1) of Directive 96/9/EC, Article 2 of Directive 2001/29/EC, Article 4(1)(a) and (b) of Directive 2009/24/EC and Article 15(1) of this Directive for reproductions and extractions of lawfully accessible works and other subject matter for the purposes of text and data mining.

2. Reproductions and extractions made pursuant to paragraph 1 may be retained for as long as is necessary for the purposes of text and data mining.

3. The exception or limitation provided for in paragraph 1 shall apply on condition that the use of works and other subject matter referred to in that paragraph has not been expressly reserved by their rightholders in an appropriate manner, such as machine-readable means in the case of content made publicly available online.

EU Cyber Resilience Act

Article 12: High-risk AI Systems

1. Without prejudice to the requirements relating to accuracy and robustness set out in Article 15 of Regulation (EU) 2024/1689, products with digital elements which fall within the scope of this Regulation and which are classified as high-risk AI systems pursuant to Article 6 of that Regulation shall be deemed to comply with the cybersecurity requirements set out in Article 15 of that Regulation where:

APPENDIX

   (a) those products fulfil the essential cybersecurity requirements set out in Part I of Annex I;

   (b) the processes put in place by the manufacturer comply with the essential cybersecurity requirements set out in Part II of Annex I; and

   (c) the achievement of the level of cybersecurity protection required under Article 15 of Regulation (EU) 2024/1689 is demonstrated in the EU declaration of conformity issued under this Regulation.

2. For the products with digital elements and cybersecurity requirements referred to in paragraph 1 of this Article, the relevant conformity assessment procedure provided for in Article 43 of Regulation (EU) 2024/1689 shall apply. For the purposes of that assessment, notified bodies which are competent to control the conformity of the high-risk AI systems under Regulation (EU) 2024/1689 shall also be competent to control the conformity of high-risk AI systems which fall within the scope of this Regulation with the requirements set out in Annex I to this Regulation, provided that the compliance of those notified bodies with the requirements laid down in Article 39 of this Regulation has been assessed in the context of the notification procedure under Regulation (EU) 2024/1689.

3. By way of derogation from paragraph 2 of this Article, important products with digital elements as listed in Annex III to this Regulation, which are subject to the conformity assessment procedures referred to in Article 32(2), points (a) and (b), and Article 32(3) of this Regulation and critical products with digital elements as listed in Annex IV to this Regulation which are required to obtain a European cybersecurity certificate pursuant to Article 8(1) of this Regulation or, absent that, which are subject to the conformity assessment procedures referred to in Article 32(3) of this Regulation, and which are classified as high-risk AI systems pursuant to Article 6 of Regulation (EU) 2024/1689, and to which the conformity assessment procedure based on

internal control as referred to in Annex VI to Regulation (EU) 2024/1689 applies, shall be subject to the conformity assessment procedures provided for in this Regulation in so far as the essential cybersecurity requirements set out in this Regulation are concerned.

4. Manufacturers of products with digital elements as referred to in paragraph 1 of this Article may participate in the AI regulatory sandboxes referred to in Article 57 of Regulation (EU) 2024/1689.

Annex I: Essential Cybersecurity Requirements

Part I Cybersecurity Requirements Relating to the Properties of Products with Digital Elements

(1) Products with digital elements shall be designed, developed and produced in such a way that they ensure an appropriate level of cybersecurity based on the risks.

(2) On the basis of the cybersecurity risk assessment referred to in Article 13(2) and where applicable, products with digital elements shall:

  (a) be made available on the market without known exploitable vulnerabilities;

  (b) be made available on the market with a secure by default configuration, unless otherwise agreed between manufacturer and business user in relation to a tailor-made product with digital elements, including the possibility to reset the product to its original state;

  (c) ensure that vulnerabilities can be addressed through security updates, including, where applicable, through automatic security updates that are installed within an appropriate timeframe enabled as a default setting, with a clear and easy-to-use opt-out mechanism, through the notification of available updates to users, and the option to temporarily postpone them;

APPENDIX

(d) ensure protection from unauthorised access by appropriate control mechanisms, including but not limited to authentication, identity or access management systems, and report on possible unauthorised access;

(e) protect the confidentiality of stored, transmitted or otherwise processed data, personal or other, such as by encrypting relevant data at rest or in transit by state of the art mechanisms, and by using other technical means;

(f) protect the integrity of stored, transmitted or otherwise processed data, personal or other, commands, programs and configuration against any manipulation or modification not authorised by the user, and report on corruptions;

(g) process only data, personal or other, that are adequate, relevant and limited to what is necessary in relation to the intended purpose of the product with digital elements (data minimisation);

(h) protect the availability of essential and basic functions, also after an incident, including through resilience and mitigation measures against denial-of-service attacks;

(i) minimise the negative impact by the products themselves or connected devices on the availability of services provided by other devices or networks;

(j) be designed, developed and produced to limit attack surfaces, including external interfaces;

(k) be designed, developed and produced to reduce the impact of an incident using appropriate exploitation mitigation mechanisms and techniques;

(l) provide security related information by recording and monitoring relevant internal activity, including the access to or modification of data, services or functions, with an opt-out mechanism for the user;

(m) provide the possibility for users to securely and easily remove on a permanent basis all data and settings and, where such data can be transferred to other products or systems, ensure that this is done in a secure manner.

Part II Vulnerability Handling Requirements

Manufacturers of products with digital elements shall:

(1) identify and document vulnerabilities and components contained in products with digital elements, including by drawing up a software bill of materials in a commonly used and machine-readable format covering at the very least the top-level dependencies of the products;

(2) in relation to the risks posed to products with digital elements, address and remediate vulnerabilities without delay, including by providing security updates; where technically feasible, new security updates shall be provided separately from functionality updates;

(3) apply effective and regular tests and reviews of the security of the product with digital elements;

(4) once a security update has been made available, share and publicly disclose information about fixed vulnerabilities, including a description of the vulnerabilities, information allowing users to identify the product with digital elements affected, the impacts of the vulnerabilities, their severity and clear and accessible information helping users to remediate the vulnerabilities; in duly justified cases, where manufacturers consider the security risks of publication to outweigh the security benefits, they may delay making public information regarding a fixed vulnerability until after users have been given the possibility to apply the relevant patch;

(5) put in place and enforce a policy on coordinated vulnerability disclosure;

(6) take measures to facilitate the sharing of information about potential vulnerabilities in their product with digital elements as well as in third-party components contained in that product, including by providing a contact address for the reporting of the vulnerabilities discovered in the product with digital elements;

(7) provide for mechanisms to securely distribute updates for products with digital elements to ensure that vulnerabilities are fixed or mitigated in a timely manner and, where applicable for security updates, in an automatic manner;

(8) ensure that, where security updates are available to address identified security issues, they are disseminated without delay and, unless otherwise agreed between a manufacturer and a business user in relation to a tailor-made product with digital elements, free of charge, accompanied by advisory messages providing users with the relevant information, including on potential action to be taken.

Annex V: EU Declaration of Conformity

The EU declaration of conformity referred to in Article 28, shall contain all of the following information:

1. Name and type and any additional information enabling the unique identification of the product with digital elements

2. Name and address of the manufacturer or its authorised representative

3. A statement that the EU declaration of conformity is issued under the sole responsibility of the provider

4. Object of the declaration (identification of the product with digital elements allowing traceability, which may include a photograph, where appropriate)

5. A statement that the object of the declaration described above is in conformity with the relevant Union harmonisation legislation

6. References to any relevant harmonised standards used or any other common specification or cybersecurity certification in relation to which conformity is declared

7. Where applicable, the name and number of the notified body, a description of the conformity assessment procedure performed and identification of the certificate issued

8. Additional information:

   Signed for and on behalf of:

   (place and date of issue):

   (name, function) (signature):

Annex VI: Simplified EU Declaration of Conformity

The simplified EU declaration of conformity referred to in Article 13(20) shall be provided as follows:

> Hereby, ... [name of manufacturer] declares that the product with digital elements type ... [designation of type of product with digital element] is in compliance with Regulation (EU) 2024/2847 ([1]).
>
> The full text of the EU declaration of conformity is available at the following internet address: ...

EU Data Act

Article 6: Obligations of Third Parties Receiving Data at the Request of the User

1. A third party shall process the data made available to it pursuant to Article 5 only for the purposes and under the conditions agreed with the user and subject to Union and national law on the protection of personal data including the rights of the data subject insofar as personal data are concerned. The third party shall erase the data when they are no longer necessary for the agreed purpose, unless otherwise agreed with the user in relation to non-personal data.

2. The third party shall not:

    (b) notwithstanding Article 22(2), points (a) and (c), of Regulation (EU) 2016/679, use the data it receives for the profiling, unless it is necessary to provide the service requested by the user;

NIS 2 Directive

Article 21: Cybersecurity Risk-Management Measures

1. Member States shall ensure that essential and important entities take appropriate and proportionate technical, operational and organisational measures to manage the risks posed to the security of network and information systems which those entities use for their operations or for the provision of their services, and to prevent or minimise the impact of incidents on recipients of their services and on other services.

    Taking into account the state-of-the-art and, where applicable, relevant European and international standards, as well as the cost of implementation, the measures referred to in the first subparagraph shall ensure a level of security of network and information systems appropriate to the risks posed. When assessing the proportionality of those measures, due account shall be taken of the degree of the entity's exposure to risks, the entity's size and the likelihood of occurrence of incidents and their severity, including their societal and economic impact.

2. The measures referred to in paragraph 1 shall be based on an all-hazards approach that aims to protect network and information systems and the physical environment of those systems from incidents, and shall include at least the following:

    (a) policies on risk analysis and information system security;

    (b) incident handling;

(c) business continuity, such as backup management and disaster recovery, and crisis management;

(d) supply chain security, including security-related aspects concerning the relationships between each entity and its direct suppliers or service providers;

(e) security in network and information systems acquisition, development and maintenance, including vulnerability handling and disclosure;

(f) policies and procedures to assess the effectiveness of cybersecurity risk-management measures;

(g) basic cyber hygiene practices and cybersecurity training;

(h) policies and procedures regarding the use of cryptography and, where appropriate, encryption;

(i) human resources security, access control policies and asset management;

(j) the use of multi-factor authentication or continuous authentication solutions, secured voice, video and text communications and secured emergency communication systems within the entity, where appropriate.

3. Member States shall ensure that, when considering which measures referred to in paragraph 2, point (d), of this Article are appropriate, entities take into account the vulnerabilities specific to each direct supplier and service provider and the overall quality of products and cybersecurity practices of their suppliers and service providers, including their secure development procedures. Member States shall also ensure that, when considering which measures referred to in that point are appropriate, entities are required to take into account the results of the coordinated security risk assessments of critical supply chains carried out in accordance with Article 22(1).

4. Member States shall ensure that an entity that finds that it does not comply with the measures provided for in paragraph 2 takes, without undue delay, all necessary, appropriate and proportionate corrective measures.

5. By 17 October 2024, the Commission shall adopt implementing acts laying down the technical and the methodological requirements of the measures referred to in paragraph 2 with regard to DNS service providers, TLD name registries, cloud computing service providers, data centre service providers, content delivery network providers, managed service providers, managed security service providers, providers of online market places, of online search engines and of social networking services platforms, and trust service providers.

The Commission may adopt implementing acts laying down the technical and the methodological requirements, as well as sectoral requirements, as necessary, of the measures referred to in paragraph 2 with regard to essential and important entities other than those referred to in the first subparagraph of this paragraph.

When preparing the implementing acts referred to in the first and second subparagraphs of this paragraph, the Commission shall, to the extent possible, follow European and international standards, as well as relevant technical specifications. The Commission shall exchange advice and cooperate with the Cooperation Group and ENISA on the draft implementing acts in accordance with Article 14(4), point (e).

Those implementing acts shall be adopted in accordance with the examination procedure referred to in Article 39(2).

General Product Safety Regulation

Recital (2): Directive 2001/95/EC needs to be revised and updated in light of the developments related to new technologies and online selling, to ensure consistency with developments in Union harmonisation legislation and in standardisation legislation, to ensure a better functioning of product safety recalls as well as to ensure a clearer framework for food-imitating products hitherto regulated by Council Directive 87/357/EEC ([4]). In the interest of clarity, Directives 2001/95/EC and 87/357/EEC should be repealed and replaced by this Regulation.

Recital (25): New technologies might pose new risks to consumers' health and safety or change the way the existing risks could materialise, such as an external intervention hacking the product or changing its characteristics. New technologies might substantially modify the original product, for instance through software updates, which should then be subject to a new risk assessment if that substantial modification were to have an impact on the safety of the product.

Recital (26): Specific cybersecurity risks affecting the safety of consumers, as well as protocols and certifications, can be dealt with by sectoral legislation. However, it should be ensured that, in cases where such sectoral legislation does not apply, the relevant economic operators and national authorities take into consideration risks linked to new technologies, when designing the products and assessing them respectively, in order to ensure that changes introduced in the product do not jeopardise its safety.

Product Liability Directive

Recital (37):

In order to ensure that injured persons have an enforceable claim for compensation where a manufacturer of a product is established outside the Union, it should be possible to hold the importer of that product and the authorised representative of the manufacturer, appointed in relation to specified tasks under Union legislation, for example under product safety and market surveillance legislation, liable. Market surveillance has shown that supply chains sometimes involve economic operators whose novel form means that they do not fit easily into traditional supply chains under the existing legal framework. Such is the case, in particular, with fulfilment service providers, which perform many of the same functions as importers but which might not always correspond to the traditional definition of importer in Union law. Fulfilment service providers play an increasingly significant role as economic operators, enabling and facilitating access to the Union market for products from third countries. That shift in relevance is already reflected in the product safety and market surveillance framework, in particular Regulations (EU) 2019/1020 ([12]) and (EU) 2023/988 ([13]) of the European Parliament and of the Council. Therefore, it should be possible to hold fulfilment service providers liable, but given the subsidiary nature of their role, they should be liable only where no importer or authorised representative is established in the Union. In the interests of channelling liability in an effective manner towards manufacturers, importers, authorised representatives and fulfilment service providers, it should be possible to hold distributors liable only where they fail to promptly identify a relevant economic operator established in the Union.

APPENDIX

Recital (48):

National courts should presume the defectiveness of a product or the causal link between the damage and the defectiveness, or both, where, notwithstanding the defendant's disclosure of information, it would be excessively difficult for the claimant, in particular due to the technical or scientific complexity of the case, to prove the defectiveness or the causal link, or both. They should do so taking into account all the circumstances of the case. In such cases, imposing the usual standard of proof as required under national law, which often calls for a high degree of probability, would undermine the effectiveness of the right to compensation. Therefore, given that manufacturers have expert knowledge and are better informed than the injured person, and in order to maintain a fair apportionment of risk while avoiding a reversal of the burden of proof, that claimant should be required to demonstrate, where the claimant's difficulties relate to proving defectiveness, only that it is likely that the product was defective, or, where the claimant's difficulties relate to proving the causal link, only that the defectiveness of the product is a likely cause of the damage. Technical or scientific complexity should be determined by national courts on a case-by-case basis, taking into account various factors. Those factors should include the complex nature of the product, such as an innovative medical device; the complex nature of the technology used, such as machine learning; the complex nature of the information and data to be analysed by the claimant; and the complex nature of the causal link, such as a link between a pharmaceutical or food product and the onset of a health condition or a link that, in order to be proven, would require the claimant to explain the inner workings of an AI system. The assessment of excessive difficulties should also be made by national courts on a case-by-case basis. While a claimant should provide arguments to demonstrate excessive difficulties, proof of such difficulties should not be required. For example, in a claim concerning an AI system, the claimant should, for the court to decide that excessive difficulties exist, neither be required to explain the AI system's specific characteristics nor how those characteristics make it harder to establish the causal link. The defendant should have the possibility of contesting all elements of the claim, including the existence of excessive difficulties.

Article 8: Economic Operators Liable for Defective Products

1. Member States shall ensure that the following economic operators are liable for damage in accordance with this Directive:

    (a) the manufacturer of a defective product;

    (b) the manufacturer of a defective component, where that component was integrated into, or inter-connected with, a product within the manufacturer's control and caused that product to be defective, and without prejudice to the liability of the manufacturer referred to in point (a); and

    (c) in the case of a manufacturer of a product or a component established outside the Union, and without prejudice to the liability of that manufacturer:

    　(i) the importer of the defective product or component;

    　(ii) the authorised representative of the manufacturer; and

    　(iii) where there is no importer established within the Union or authorised representative, the fulfilment service provider.

The liability of the manufacturer referred to in the first subparagraph, point (a), shall also cover any damage caused by a defective component where it was integrated into, or inter-connected with, a product within that manufacturer's control.

Article 9: Disclosure of Evidence

1. Member States shall ensure that, at the request of a person who is claiming compensation in proceedings before a national court for damage caused by a defective product (the 'claimant') and who has presented facts and evidence sufficient to support the plausibility of the claim for compensation, the defendant is required to disclose relevant evidence that is at the defendant's disposal, subject to the conditions set out in this Article.

APPENDIX

2. Member States shall ensure that, at the request of a defendant that has presented facts and evidence sufficient to demonstrate the defendant's need for evidence for the purposes of countering a claim for compensation, the claimant is required, in accordance with national law, to disclose relevant evidence that is at the claimant's disposal.

3. Member States shall ensure that the disclosure of evidence pursuant to paragraphs 1 and 2, and in accordance with national law, is limited to what is necessary and proportionate.

4. Member States shall ensure that, when determining whether the disclosure of evidence requested by a party is necessary and proportionate, national courts consider the legitimate interests of all parties concerned, including third parties, in particular in relation to the protection of confidential information and trade secrets.

5. Member States shall ensure that, where a defendant is required to disclose information that is a trade secret or an alleged trade secret, national courts are empowered, upon a duly reasoned request of a party or on their own initiative, to take the specific measures necessary to preserve the confidentiality of that information when it is used or referred to in the course of or after the legal proceedings.

6. Member States shall ensure that, where a party is required to disclose evidence, national courts are empowered, upon a duly reasoned request of the opposing party or where the national court concerned deems it appropriate and in accordance with national law, to require such evidence to be presented in an easily accessible and easily understandable manner, if such presentation is deemed proportionate by the national court in terms of costs and effort for the required party.

7. This Article does not affect national rules relating to the pre-trial disclosure of evidence, where such rules exist.

Article 10: Burden of Proof

1. Member States shall ensure that a claimant is required to prove the defectiveness of the product, the damage suffered and the causal link between that defectiveness and that damage.

2. The defectiveness of the product shall be presumed where any of the following conditions are met:

    (a) the defendant fails to disclose relevant evidence pursuant to Article 9(1);

    (b) the claimant demonstrates that the product does not comply with mandatory product safety requirements laid down in Union or national law that are intended to protect against the risk of the damage suffered by the injured person; or

    (c) the claimant demonstrates that the damage was caused by an obvious malfunction of the product during reasonably foreseeable use or under ordinary circumstances.

3. The causal link between the defectiveness of the product and the damage shall be presumed where it has been established that the product is defective and that the damage caused is of a kind typically consistent with the defect in question.

4. A national court shall presume the defectiveness of the product or the causal link between its defectiveness and the damage, or both, where, despite the disclosure of evidence in accordance with Article 9 and taking into account all the relevant circumstances of the case:

    (a) the claimant faces excessive difficulties, in particular due to technical or scientific complexity, in proving the defectiveness of the product or the causal link between its defectiveness and the damage, or both; and

    (b) the claimant demonstrates that it is likely that the product is defective or that there is a causal link between the defectiveness of the product and the damage, or both.

5. The defendant shall have the right to rebut any of the presumptions referred to in paragraphs 2, 3 and 4.

APPENDIX

UK Data Use and Access Act

Section 80: Automated Decision-making

(1) For Article 22 of the UK GDPR (automated individual decision-making, including profiling) substitute—

"Section 4A Automated individual decision-making

Article 22A Automated Processing and Significant Decisions

1. For the purposes of Articles 22B and 22C—

    (a) a decision is based solely on automated processing if there is no meaningful human involvement in the taking of the decision, and

    (b) a decision is a significant decision, in relation to a data subject, if—

    (i) it produces a legal effect for the data subject, or

    (ii) it has a similarly significant effect for the data subject.

2. When considering whether there is meaningful human involvement in the taking of a decision, a person must consider, among other things, the extent to which the decision is reached by means of profiling.

Article 22B Restrictions on Automated Decision-making

1. A significant decision based entirely or partly on processing described in Article 9(1) (processing of special categories of personal data) may not be taken based solely on automated processing, unless one of the following conditions is met.

2. The first condition is that the decision is based entirely on processing of personal data to which the data subject has given explicit consent.

3. The second condition is that—

(a) the decision is—

    (i) necessary for entering into, or performing, a contract between the data subject and a controller, or

    (ii) required or authorised by law, and

(b) point (g) of Article 9(2) applies.

4. A significant decision may not be taken based solely on automated processing if the processing of personal data carried out by, or on behalf of, the decision-maker for the purposes of the decision is carried out entirely or partly in reliance on Article 6(1)(ea).

Article 22C Safeguards for Automated Decision-making

1. Where a significant decision taken by or on behalf of a controller in relation to a data subject is—

    (a) based entirely or partly on personal data, and

    (b) based solely on automated processing,

    the controller must ensure that safeguards for the data subject's rights, freedoms and legitimate interests are in place which comply with paragraph 2 and any regulations under Article 22D(3).

2. The safeguards must consist of or include measures which—

    (a) provide the data subject with information about decisions described in paragraph 1 taken in relation to the data subject;

    (b) enable the data subject to make representations about such decisions;

    (c) enable the data subject to obtain human intervention on the part of the controller in relation to such decisions;

    (d) enable the data subject to contest such decisions

APPENDIX

China's Algorithmic Recommendations Provisions

Chapter II: Regulation of Information Services

Article 9:

The providers of algorithmic recommendation services shall strengthen the management of information security, establishing and completing a pool of characteristics used to identify illegal and negative content, and improve standards, rules, and procedures for inclusion in the pool. Where it is discovered that algorithmically generated or synthesized information is not conspicuously labeled, transmission may continue only after making a conspicuous label.

Where unlawful information is discovered, transmission shall be immediately stopped, and measures shall be employed to eliminate it or otherwise address it, stop the spread of the information, store relevant records, and report to the internet information departments and relevant departments. Where negative information is discovered, it shall be addressed in accordance with the relevant provisions on the management of the internet information content ecology.

Article 12:

The providers of algorithmic recommendation services are encouraged to comprehensively use strategies such as for eliminating duplicate content and for fragmentation and intervention, and optimize the transparency and explainability of rules for searches, sorting, selections, pushing, and displays, to avoid producing a negative impact on users, and to prevent and reduce contention and disputes.

Article 13:

Where the providers of algorithmic recommendation services provide Internet news information services, they shall obtain Internet news information service permits in accordance with law, regulate the carrying out Internet news information collection and publication services, forwarding services, and transmission platform services, and must not generate or synthesize fake news information or transmit news information from units that are not within the scope provided by the state.

Article 14:
The providers of algorithmic recommendation services must not use algorithms to register fake accounts, illegal trade accounts, manipulate user accounts, or give false likes, comments, or forwards; and must not use algorithms to interfere with information presentation such as by blocking information, making excessive recommendations, manipulating the order of top content lists or search results, or controlling hot searches or selections, influencing online public opinion or evading oversight and management.

Chapter III: Protection of User's Rights and Interests

Article 16:
The providers of algorithmic recommendation services shall inform users in a conspicuous fashion of the circumstances of the algorithmic recommendation services provided, and display the algorithmic recommendation services' basic principles, intended purposes, main operation mechanisms, and so forth in an appropriate manner.

Article 17:
The providers of algorithmic recommendation services shall provide users with options not targeting their individual characteristics or provide users with convenient options to close algorithmic recommendation services. Where users select to close algorithmic recommendation services, the algorithmic recommendation service providers shall immediately stop providing those services.

Article 21:
Where the providers of algorithmic recommendation services market goods or provide services to consumers, they shall protect the consumers' rights to fair transactions and must not use algorithms to unreasonably differentiate terms of transaction prices or other transaction conditions, or carry out other unlawful conduct, based on consumers' preferences, transaction habits, or other traits.

Article 22:
The providers of algorithmic recommendation services shall set up convenient and effective portals for user appeals and public complaints or reports, clarifying the process for handling them and time limits for giving feedback, to promptly accept and address them, and give feedback on the outcomes.

APPENDIX

China's Deep Synthesis Provisions

Chapter II: Ordinary Provisions

Article 6:

Deep synthesis services must not be used by any organization or individual to produce, reproduce, publish, or transmit information that is prohibited by laws or administrative regulations, or to engage in activities that are prohibited by laws and administrative regulations such as those that endanger the national security and interests, harm the image of the nation, harm the societal public interest, disturb economic or social order, or harm the lawful rights and interests of others.

Deep synthesis service providers and users must not use deep synthesis services to produce, reproduce, publish, or transmit fake news information. Where news information that is produced and published based on deep syntheses services is reprinted, The news information published by the source unit of Internet news information shall be reproduced according to law.

Article 10:

Deep synthesis service providers shall strengthen the management of deep synthesis content and employ technical measures or manual methods to conduct reviews of the data inputted by users and synthesis outcomes.

Deep synthesis service providers shall establish and complete a pool of characteristics used to identify illegal and negative content, and improve standards, rules, and procedures for inclusion in the pool, and record and store related network logs.

Where deep synthesis service providers discover illegal or negative information, they shall employ measures to address it in accordance with law, store related records, and promptly make a report to the telecommunications department or relevant departments in charge; and take measures in accordance with laws and agreements against the related deep synthesis service users, such as giving warnings, restricted functions, service suspensions, and account closures.

Article 11:
Deep synthesis service providers shall establish and complete mechanisms for dispelling rumors, and where it is discovered that deep synthesis information services were used to produce, reproduce, publish, or transmit false information, they shall promptly employ measures to dispel the rumors, store related records, and make a report to the internet information departments and relevant departments in charge.

Article 12:
Deep synthesis service providers shall set up convenient portals for user appeals, public complaints, and reports, and shall publish the process for handling them and the time limits for responses, promptly accepting and handling them, and giving feedback on the outcome.

Chapter III: Data and Technical Management Specifications

Article 14:
Deep synthesis service providers and technical supporters shall strengthen the management of training data, employ necessary measures to ensure the security of training data, and where training data includes personal information, they shall comply with relevant provisions on the protection of personal information.

Where deep synthesis service providers and technical supports provide functions for editing biometric information such as faces and voices, they shall prompt the users of the deep synthesis service to notify the individuals whose personal information is being edited and obtain their independent consent in accordance with law.

Article 16:
Deep synthesis service providers shall employ technical measures to attach symbols to information content produced or edited by their services' users that do not impact users' usage, and store log information in accordance with laws, administrative regulations, and relevant state provisions.

Article 17:
Where deep synthesis service providers provide the following deep synthesis services which might cause confusion or mislead the public, they shall make a conspicuous label in a reasonable position or location on information content they generate or edit, alerting the public of the deep synthesis generation:

APPENDIX

(1) services such as smart dialogue or smart writing, etc., which simulate natural persons to generate or edit texts;

(2) speech generation services such as voice synthesis and imitations or editing services that significantly change personal identification characteristics;

(3) services that generate images or video of virtual persons such as face generation, face swapping, face manipulation, and gesture manipulation, or editing services that significantly change personal identification characteristics;

(4) Generation or editing services such as realistic immersive scenes;

(5) Other services that have functions that generate or significantly alter information content.

Where deep synthesis service providers provide deep synthesis services other than those provided for in the preceding paragraph, they shall provide functions for prominently labeling, and alert deep synthesis service users that they may make prominent labels.

China's Generative AI Interim Measures
Chapter I: General Provisions

Article 4:
The provision and use of generative AI services shall comply with the requirements of laws and administrative regulations, respect social mores, ethics, and morality, and obey the following provisions:

(1) Uphold the Core Socialist Values; content that is prohibited by laws and administrative regulations such as that inciting subversion of national sovereignty or the overturn of the socialist system, endangering national security and interests or harming the nation's image, inciting separatism or undermining national unity and social stability, advocating terrorism or extremism, promoting ethnic hatred and ethnic discrimination, violence and obscenity, as well as fake and harmful information;

APPENDIX

(2) During processes such as algorithm design, the selection of training data, model generation and optimization, and the provision of services, effective measures are to be employed to prevent the creation of discrimination such as by race, ethnicity, faith, nationality, region, sex, age, profession, or health;

(5) Based on the characteristics of the service type, employ effective measures to increase transparency in generative AI services and to increase the accuracy and reliability of generated content.

Article 7:

The providers of generative AI services (hereinafter "providers") shall carry out pre-training, optimization training, and other activities handling training data in accordance with law, and comply with the following provisions:

(1) Use data and foundational models that have lawful sources;

(2) Where intellectual property rights are involved, the intellectual property rights that are lawfully enjoyed by others must not be infringed;

(3) Where personal information is involved, the consent of the personal information subject shall be obtained or it shall comply with other situations provided by laws and administrative regulations;

(4) Employ effective measures to increase the quality of training data, and increase the truth, accuracy, objectivity, and diversity of training data;

Article 8:

When manual tagging is conducted in the course of researching and developing generative AI technology, the providers shall formulate clear, specific, and feasible tagging rules that meet the requirements of these Measures; carry out assessments of the quality of data tagging, with spot checks to verify the accuracy of tagging content; and conduct necessary training for tagging personnel to increase their awareness of legal compliance and oversee and guide them to carry out tagging efforts in a standardized way.

APPENDIX

Chapter III Service Specifications

Article 10:
Providers shall clarify and disclose the user groups, occasions, and uses of their services, guide users' scientific understanding and lawful use of generative AI technology, and employ effective measures to prevent minor users from overreliance or addiction to generative AI services.

Article 11:
Providers shall fulfill confidentiality obligations towards information that is input by users, and users' usage records, in accordance with law; they must not collect unnecessary personal information, must not illegally retain user input information and usage records from which users' identities can be determined, and must not illegally provide user input information and usage records to others.

Providers shall lawfully and promptly accept and address requests from individuals such as to access, reproduce, modify, supplement, or delete their personal information.

Article 12:
Providers shall label generated content such as images and video in accordance with the Provisions on the Administration of Deep Synthesis Internet Information Services.

Article 14:
Where providers discover illegal content they shall promptly employ measures to address it such as stopping generation, stopping transmission, and removal, employ measures such as model optimization training to make corrections and report to the relevant departments in charge.

Where providers discover that users are using generative AI services to engage in illegal activities, they shall employ measures in accordance with laws and agreements to address it, including warnings, limiting functions, and suspending or concluding the provision of services, and store the relevant records and report to the relevant departments in charge.

Article 15:
Providers shall establish and complete mechanisms for making complaints and reports, setting up easy complaint and reporting portals, disclosing the process for handling them and the time limits for giving responses, and promptly accepting and handling complaints and reports from the public and giving feedback on the outcome.

Article 18:
Where users discover that generative AI services do not comply with laws, administrative regulations, or these Measures, they have the right to make a complaint or report to the relevant departments in charge.

China's Synthetic Content Labeling Measures

Article 4:

Where the generative or synthesis services provided by service providers fall within the situations of the first paragraph of Article 17 of the Provisions on the Administration of Deep Synthesis Internet Information Services, explicit labels shall be added to the generated synthetic content in accordance with the following requirements:

(1) Add labels such as text notifications, or notifications using common symbols, at appropriate positions in the beginning, end, or middle of text, or add conspicuous notification labels in interactive scenario interfaces or beside text;

(2) Add labels such as voice notifications or audio and rhythmic notifications at appropriate positions in the beginning, end, or middle of audio, or add conspicuous notification labels in interactive scenario interfaces;

(3) Add conspicuous notification labels in appropriate places in images;

(4) Add conspicuous notification labels to video starting screens of at appropriate positions around the video playback area; conspicuous notification labels may be added to the end and middle of the video at appropriate locations;

(5) When presenting virtual scenes, conspicuous notification labels shall be added in appropriate positions on the starting screen, and conspicuous notification labels can be added in appropriate positions during the ongoing virtual scene services;

(6) Explicit labels that are effective in giving conspicuous notice should be added in other generation and synthesis service scenarios based on the characteristics of the applications. When service providers provide functions such as for downloading, reproducing, or exporting generated synthetic content, they shall ensure that the files contain explicit labels that satisfy these requirements.

APPENDIX

Article 5:
Service providers shall add implicit labels to the metadata of generated synthetic content files in accordance with Article 16 of the Provisions on the Administration of Deep Synthesis Internet Information Services; the implicit labels are to include production factor information such as the generated synthetic content's attribute information, the service providers' name or code, and the content reference number.

Service providers are encouraged to add implicit labels to generated synthetic content in forms such as digital watermarks.

"File Metadata" refers to descriptive information embedded in the file header according to a specific encoding format, which is used to record information content such as the file source, attributes, and uses.

Colorado SB-205

6-1-1702. Developer Duty to Avoid Algorithmic Discrimination Required Documentation

(1) On and after February 1, 2026, a developer of a high-risk artificial intelligence system shall use reasonable care to protect consumers from any known or reasonably foreseeable risks of algorithmic discrimination arising from the intended and contracted uses of the high-risk artificial intelligence system. In any enforcement action brought on or after February 1, 2026, by the Attorney General pursuant to section 6-1-1706, there is a rebuttable presumption that a developer used reasonable care as required under this section if the developer complied with this section and any additional requirements or obligations as set forth in rules promulgated by the Attorney General pursuant to section 6-1-1707.

(2) On and after February 1, 2026, and except as provided in subsection (6) of this section, a developer of a high-risk artificial intelligence system shall make available to the deployer or other developer of the high-risk artificial intelligence system:

(a) A general statement describing the reasonably foreseeable uses and known harmful or inappropriate uses of the high-risk artificial intelligence system;

(b) Documentation disclosing: (I) High-level summaries of the type of data used to train the high-risk artificial intelligence system; (II) Known or reasonably foreseeable limitations of the high-risk artificial intelligence system, including known or reasonably foreseeable risks of algorithmic discrimination arising from the intended uses of the high-risk artificial intelligence system; (III) The purpose of the high-risk artificial intelligence system; (IV) The intended benefits and uses of the high-risk artificial intelligence system; and (V) All other information necessary to allow the deployer to comply with the requirements of section 6-1-1703;

(c) Documentation describing: (I) How the high-risk artificial intelligence system was evaluated for performance and mitigation of algorithmic discrimination before the high-risk artificial intelligence system was offered, sold, leased, licensed, given, or otherwise made available to the deployer; (II) The data governance measures used to cover the training datasets and the measures used to examine the suitability of data sources, possible biases, and appropriate mitigation; (III) The intended outputs of the high-risk artificial intelligence system; (IV) The measures the developer has taken to mitigate known or reasonably foreseeable risks of algorithmic discrimination that may arise from the reasonably foreseeable deployment of the high-risk artificial intelligence system; and (V) How the high-risk artificial intelligence system should be used, not be used, and be monitored by an individual when the high-risk artificial intelligence system is used to make, or is a substantial factor in making, a consequential decision; and

(d) Any additional documentation that is reasonably necessary to assist the deployer in understanding the outputs and monitor the performance of the high-risk artificial intelligence system for risks of algorithmic discrimination.

(3) (a) Except as provided in subsection (6) of this section, a developer that offers, sells, leases, licenses, gives, or otherwise makes available to a deployer or other developer a high-risk

APPENDIX

artificial intelligence system on or after February 1, 2026, shall make available to the deployer or other developer, to the extent feasible, the documentation and information, through artifacts such as model cards, dataset cards, or other impact assessments, necessary for a deployer, or for a third party contracted by a deployer, to complete an impact assessment pursuant to section 6-1-1703 (3).

(b) A developer that also serves as a deployer for a high-risk artificial intelligence system is not required to generate the documentation required by this section unless the high-risk artificial intelligence system is provided to an unaffiliated entity acting as a deployer.

(4) (a) On and after February 1, 2026, a developer shall make available, in a manner that is clear and readily available on the developer's website or in a public use case inventory, a statement summarizing: (I) The types of high-risk artificial intelligence systems that the developer has developed or intentionally and substantially modified and currently makes available to a deployer or other developer; and (II) How the developer manages known or reasonably foreseeable risks of algorithmic discrimination that may arise from the development or intentional and substantial modification of the types of high-risk artificial intelligence systems described in accordance with subsection (4)(a)(I) of this section.

(b) A developer shall update the statement described in subsection (4)(a) of this section: (I) As necessary to ensure that the statement remains accurate; and (II) No later than ninety days after the developer intentionally and substantially modifies any high-risk artificial intelligence system described in subsection (4)(a)(I) of this section.

(5) On and after February 1, 2026, a developer of a high-risk artificial intelligence system shall disclose to the Attorney General, in a form and manner prescribed by the Attorney General, and to all known deployers or other developers of the high-risk artificial intelligence system, any known or reasonably foreseeable risks

of algorithmic discrimination arising from the intended uses of the high-risk artificial intelligence system without unreasonable delay but no later than ninety days after the date on which: (a) The developer discovers through the developer's ongoing testing and analysis that the developer's high-risk artificial intelligence system has been deployed and has caused or is reasonably likely to have caused algorithmic discrimination; or (b) The developer receives from a deployer a credible report that the high-risk artificial intelligence system has been deployed and has caused algorithmic discrimination.

(6) Nothing in subsections (2) to (5) of this section requires a developer to disclose a trade secret, information protected from disclosure by state or federal law, or information that would create a security risk to the developer.

(7) On and after February 1, 2026, the Attorney General may require that a developer disclose to the Attorney General, no later than ninety days after the request and in a form and manner prescribed by the Attorney General, the statement or documentation described in subsection (2) of this section. The Attorney General may evaluate such statement or documentation to ensure compliance with this part 17, and the statement or documentation is not subject to disclosure under the "Colorado open records act", part 2 of article 72 of title 24. In a disclosure pursuant to this subsection (7), a developer may designate the statement or documentation as including proprietary information or a trade secret. To the extent that any information contained in the statement or documentation includes information subject to attorney-client privilege or work-product protection, the disclosure does not constitute a waiver of the privilege or protection.

APPENDIX

6-1-1703. Deployer Duty to Avoid Algorithmic Discrimination Risk Management Policy and Program

(1) On and after February 1, 2026, a deployer of a high-risk artificial intelligence system shall use reasonable care to protect consumers from any known or reasonably foreseeable risks of algorithmic discrimination. In any enforcement action brought on or after February 1, 2026, by the Attorney General pursuant to section 6-1-1706, there is a rebuttable presumption that a deployer of a high-risk artificial intelligence system used reasonable care as required under this section if the deployer complied with this section and any additional requirements or obligations as set forth in rules promulgated by the Attorney General pursuant to section 6-1-1707.

(2) (a) On and after February 1, 2026, and except as provided in subsection (6) of this section, a deployer of a high-risk artificial intelligence system shall implement a risk management policy and program to govern the deployer's deployment of the high-risk artificial intelligence system. The risk management policy and program must specify and incorporate the principles, processes, and personnel that the deployer uses to identify, document, and mitigate known or reasonably foreseeable risks of algorithmic discrimination. The risk management policy and program must be an iterative process planned, implemented, and regularly and systematically reviewed and updated over the life cycle of a high-risk artificial intelligence system, requiring regular, systematic review and updates. A risk management policy and program implemented and maintained pursuant to this subsection (2) must be reasonable considering: (I) (a) The guidance and standards set forth in the latest version of the "Artificial Intelligence Risk Management Framework" published by the National Institute of Standards and Technology in the United States Department of Commerce, Standard ISO/IEC

APPENDIX

42001 of the International Organization for Standardization, or another nationally or internationally recognized risk management framework for artificial intelligence systems, if the standards are substantially equivalent to or more stringent than the requirements of this part 17; or (b) Any risk management framework for artificial intelligence systems that the Attorney General, in the Attorney General's discretion, may designate; (II) The size and complexity of the deployer; (III) The nature and scope of the high-risk artificial intelligence systems deployed by the deployer, including the intended uses of the high-risk artificial intelligence systems; and (IV) The sensitivity and volume of data processed in connection with the high-risk artificial intelligence systems deployed by the deployer.

(b) A risk management policy and program implemented pursuant to subsection (2)(a) of this section may cover multiple high-risk artificial intelligence systems deployed by the deployer.

(3) (a) Except as provided in subsections (3)(d), (3)(e), and (6) of this section: (I) A deployer, or a third party contracted by the deployer, that deploys a high-risk artificial intelligence system on or after February 1, 2026, shall complete an impact assessment for the high-risk artificial intelligence system; and (II) On and after February 1, 2026, a deployer, or a third party contracted by the deployer, shall complete an impact assessment for a deployed high-risk artificial intelligence system at least annually and within ninety days after any intentional and substantial modification to the high-risk artificial intelligence system is made available.

(b) An impact assessment completed pursuant to this subsection (3) must include, at a minimum, and to the extent reasonably known by or available to the deployer: (I) A statement by the deployer disclosing the purpose, intended use cases, and deployment context of, and benefits afforded by, the high-risk artificial intelligence system; (II) An analysis of whether the deployment of the high-risk artificial intelligence system poses any known or reasonably foreseeable risks of algorithmic discrimination and, if so, the nature of the algorithmic discrimination and the steps that have been taken to mitigate the risks; (III) A description of the categories of data the high-risk artificial intelligence system processes as inputs and the outputs the high-risk artificial intelligence system produces; (IV) If the deployer used data to customize the high-risk artificial intelligence system, an overview of the categories of data the deployer used to customize the high-risk artificial intelligence system; (V) Any metrics used to evaluate the performance and known limitations of the high-risk artificial intelligence system; (VI) A description of any transparency measures taken concerning the high-risk artificial intelligence system, including any measures taken to disclose to a consumer that the high-risk artificial intelligence system is in use when the high-risk artificial intelligence system is in use; and (VII) A description of the post-deployment monitoring and user safeguards provided concerning the high-risk artificial intelligence system, including the oversight, use, and learning process established by the deployer to address issues arising from the deployment of the high-risk artificial intelligence system.

(c) In addition to the information required under subsection (3)(b) of this section, an impact assessment completed pursuant to this subsection (3) following an intentional and substantial modification to a high-risk artificial intelligence system on or after February 1, 2026, must include a statement disclosing the extent to which the high-risk artificial intelligence system was used in a manner that was consistent with, or varied from, the developer's intended uses of the high-risk artificial intelligence system.

(d) A single impact assessment may address a comparable set of high-risk artificial intelligence systems deployed by a deployer.

(e) If a deployer, or a third party contracted by the deployer, completes an impact assessment for the purpose of complying with another applicable law or regulation, the impact assessment satisfies the requirements established in this subsection (3) if the impact assessment is reasonably similar in scope and effect to the impact assessment that would otherwise be completed pursuant to this subsection (3).

(f) A deployer shall maintain the most recently completed impact assessment for a high-risk artificial intelligence system as required under this subsection (3), all records concerning each impact assessment, and all prior impact assessments, if any, for at least three years following the final deployment of the high-risk artificial intelligence system.

(g) On or before February 1, 2026, and at least annually thereafter, a deployer, or a third party contracted by the deployer, must review the deployment of each high-risk artificial intelligence system deployed by the deployer to ensure that the high-risk artificial intelligence system is not causing algorithmic discrimination.

(4) (a) On and after February 1, 2026, and no later than the time that a deployer deploys a high-risk artificial intelligence system to make, or be a substantial factor in making, a consequential decision concerning a consumer, the deployer shall: (I) Notify the consumer that the deployer has deployed a high-risk artificial intelligence system to make, or be a substantial factor in making, a consequential decision before the decision is made; (II) Provide to the consumer a statement disclosing the purpose of the high-risk artificial intelligence system and the nature of the consequential decision; the contact information for the deployer; a description, in plain language, of the high-risk artificial intelligence system; and instructions on how to access the statement required by subsection (5)(a) of this section; and (III) Provide to the consumer information, if applicable, regarding the consumer's right to opt out of the processing of personal data concerning the consumer for purposes of profiling in furtherance of decisions that produce legal or similarly significant effects concerning the consumer under section 6-1-1306 (1)(a)(I)(c).

APPENDIX

(b) On and after February 1, 2026, a deployer that has deployed a high-risk artificial intelligence system to make, or be a substantial factor in making, a consequential decision concerning a consumer shall, if the consequential decision is adverse to the consumer, provide to the consumer: (I) A statement disclosing the principal reason or reasons for the consequential decision, including: (a) The degree to which, and manner in which, the high-risk artificial intelligence system contributed to the consequential decision; (b) The type of data that was processed by the high-risk artificial intelligence system in making the consequential decision; and (c) The source or sources of the data described in subsection (4)(b)(I)(b) of this section; (II) An opportunity to correct any incorrect personal data that the high-risk artificial intelligence system processed in making, or as a substantial factor in making, the consequential decision; and (III) An opportunity to appeal an adverse consequential decision concerning the consumer arising from the deployment of a high-risk artificial intelligence system, which appeal must, if technically feasible, allow for human review unless providing the opportunity for appeal is not in the best interest of the consumer, including in instances in which any delay might pose a risk to the life or safety of such consumer.

(c) (I) Except as provided in subsection (4)(c)(ii) of this section, a deployer shall provide the notice, statement, contact information, and description required by subsections (4)(a) and (4)(b) of this section: (a) Directly to the consumer; (b) In plain language; (c) In all languages in which the deployer, in the ordinary course of the deployer's business, provides contracts, disclaimers, sale announcements, and other information to consumers; and (d) In a format that is accessible to consumers with disabilities. (II) If the deployer is unable to provide the notice, statement, contact information, and description required by subsections (4)(a) and (4)(b) of this section directly to the consumer, the deployer shall make the notice, statement, contact information, and description available in a manner that is reasonably calculated to ensure that the consumer receives the notice, statement, contact information, and description.

(5) (a) On and after February 1, 2026, and except as provided in subsection (6) of this section, a deployer shall make available, in a manner that is clear and readily available on the deployer's website, a statement summarizing: (I) The types of high-risk artificial intelligence systems that are currently deployed by the deployer; (II) How the deployer manages known or reasonably foreseeable risks of algorithmic discrimination that may arise from the deployment of each high-risk artificial intelligence system described pursuant to subsection (5)(a)(I) of this section; and (III) In detail, the nature, source, and extent of the information collected and used by the deployer.

(b) A deployer shall periodically update the statement described in subsection (5)(a) of this section.

(6) Subsections (2), (3), and (5) of this section do not apply to a deployer if, at the time the deployer deploys a high-risk artificial intelligence system and at all times while the high-risk artificial intelligence system is deployed: (a) The deployer: (I) Employs fewer than fifty full-time equivalent employees; and (II) Does not use the deployer's own data to train the high-risk artificial intelligence system; (b) The high-risk artificial intelligence system: (I) Is used for the intended uses that are disclosed to the deployer as required by section 6-1-1702 (2)(a); and (II) Continues learning based on data derived from sources other than the deployer's own data; and (c) The deployer makes available to consumers any impact assessment that: (I) The developer of the high-risk artificial intelligence system has completed and provided to the deployer; and (II) Includes information that is substantially similar to the information in the impact assessment required under subsection (3)(b) of this section.

(7) If a deployer deploys a high-risk artificial intelligence system on or after February 1, 2026, and subsequently discovers that the high-risk artificial intelligence system has caused algorithmic discrimination, the deployer, without unreasonable delay, but no later than ninety days after the date of the discovery, shall send to the Attorney General, in a form and manner prescribed by the Attorney General, a notice disclosing the discovery.

APPENDIX

(8) Nothing in subsections (2) to (5) and (7) of this section requires a deployer to disclose a trade secret or information protected from disclosure by state or federal law. To the extent that a deployer withholds information pursuant to this subsection (8) or section 6-1-1705 (5), the deployer shall notify the consumer and provide a basis for the withholding.

(9) On and after February 1, 2026, the Attorney General may require that a deployer, or a third party contracted by the deployer, disclose to the Attorney General, no later than ninety days after the request and in a form and manner prescribed by the Attorney General, the risk management policy implemented pursuant to subsection (2) of this section, the impact assessment completed pursuant to subsection (3) of this section, or the records maintained pursuant to subsection (3)(f) of this section. The Attorney General may evaluate the risk management policy, impact assessment, or records to ensure compliance with this part 17, and the risk management policy, impact assessment, and records are not subject to disclosure under the "Colorado Open Records Act", part 2 of article 72 of title 24. In a disclosure pursuant to this subsection (9), a deployer may designate the statement or documentation as including proprietary information or a trade secret. To the extent that any information contained in the risk management policy, impact assessment, or records include information subject to attorney-client privilege or work-product protection, the disclosure does not constitute a waiver of the privilege or protection.

6-1-1704. Disclosure of an Artificial Intelligence System to Consumer

(1) On and after February 1, 2026, and except as provided in subsection (2) of this section, a deployer or other developer that deploys, offers, sells, leases, licenses, gives, or otherwise

makes available an artificial intelligence system that is intended to interact with consumers shall ensure the disclosure to each consumer who interacts with the artificial intelligence system that the consumer is interacting with an artificial intelligence system.

(2) Disclosure is not required under subsection (1) of this section under circumstances in which it would be obvious to a reasonable person that the person is interacting with an artificial intelligence system.

Texas Responsible AI Governance Act

Subchapter B. Duties and Prohibitions on use of Artificial Intelligence

Sec. 552.051. Disclosure to Consumers

(a) In this section, "health care services" means services related to human health or to the diagnosis, prevention, or treatment of a human disease or impairment provided by an individual licensed, registered, or certified under applicable state or federal law to provide those services.

(b) A governmental agency that makes available an artificial intelligence system intended to interact with consumers shall disclose to each consumer, before or at the time of interaction, that the consumer is interacting with an artificial intelligence system.

(c) A person is required to make the disclosure under Subsection (b) regardless of whether it would be obvious to a reasonable consumer that the consumer is interacting with an artificial intelligence system.

APPENDIX

(d) A disclosure under Subsection (b): (1) must be clear and conspicuous; (2) must be written in plain language; and (3) may not use a dark pattern, as that term is defined by Section 541.001.

(e) A disclosure under Subsection (b) may be provided: (1) by using a hyperlink to direct a consumer to a separate Internet web page; or (2) for an artificial intelligence system related to health care services, as part of any waivers or forms signed by a patient at the start of service.

Sec. 552.052. Manipulation of Human Behavior

A person may not develop or deploy an artificial intelligence system in a manner that intentionally aims to incite or encourage a person to: (1) commit physical self-harm, including suicide; (2) harm another person; or (3) engage in criminal activity.

Sec. 552.053. Social Scoring

A governmental entity may not use or deploy an artificial intelligence system that evaluates or classifies a natural person or group of natural persons based on social behavior or personal characteristics, whether known, inferred, or predicted, with the intent to calculate or assign a social score or similar categorical estimation or valuation of the person or group of persons that results or may result in: (1) detrimental or unfavorable treatment of a person or group of persons in a social context unrelated to the context in which the behavior or characteristics were observed or noted; (2) detrimental or unfavorable treatment of a person or group of persons that is unjustified or disproportionate to the nature or gravity of the observed or noted behavior or characteristics; or (3) the infringement of any right guaranteed under the United States Constitution, the Texas Constitution, or state or federal law.

Sec. 552.054. Capture of Biometric Data

(a) In this section, "biometric data" means data generated by automatic measurements of an individual's biological characteristics. The term includes a fingerprint, voiceprint, eye retina or iris, or other unique biological pattern or characteristic that is used to identify a specific individual. The term does not include a physical or digital photograph or data generated from a physical or digital photograph, a video or audio recording or data generated from a video or audio recording, or information collected, used, or stored for health care treatment, payment, or operations under the Health Insurance Portability and Accountability Act of 1996 (42 U.S.C. Section 1320d et seq.).

(b) A governmental entity may not develop or deploy an artificial intelligence system for the purpose of uniquely identifying a specific individual using biometric data or the targeted or untargeted gathering of images or other media from the Internet or any other publicly available source without the individual's consent, if the gathering would infringe on any right of the individual under the United States Constitution, the Texas Constitution, or state or federal law.

(c) A violation of Section 503.001 is a violation of this section.

Sec. 552.055. Political Viewpoint Discrimination

(a) A person may not develop or deploy an artificial intelligence system with the intent for the artificial intelligence system to: (1) limit an individual's ability to express beliefs or opinions or receive the expression of another individual's beliefs or opinions based solely on the individual's political beliefs, opinions, or affiliations; or (2) otherwise infringe on an individual's freedom of association or ability to freely express the individual's beliefs or opinions.

(b) A person may not use an artificial intelligence system on an interactive computer service, as defined by Section 323.001, to intentionally: (1) block, ban, remove, deplatform, demonetize, debank, de-boost, restrict, or otherwise limit an individual; (2) engage in behavior described by Subsection (a); or (3) modify or manipulate content posted by an individual for the purpose of censoring the individual's political speech.

APPENDIX

(c) Subsection (b) applies regardless of whether the interactive computer service is automated or overseen by an individual.

(d) This section does not apply to speech that: (1) is illegal under state or federal law; (2) constitutes a credible threat of violence or incitement to imminent lawless action; (3) contains material that is obscene, as defined by Section 43.21, Penal Code; (4) contains a deep fake video produced or distributed in violation of Section 21.165, Penal Code; (5) violates intellectual property rights; or (6) violates a developer's or deployer's publicly available terms of service.

(e) This section shall be construed in a manner consistent with applicable federal law, including 47 U.S.C. Section 230 and the United States Constitution.

Sec. 552.056. Unlawful Discrimination

(a) In this section: (1) "Insurance entity" means: (A) an entity described by Section 82.002(a), Insurance Code; (B) a fraternal benefit society regulated under Chapter 885, Insurance Code; or (C) the developer of an artificial intelligence system used by an entity described by Paragraph (A) or (B). (2) "Protected class" means a group or class of persons with a characteristic, quality, belief, or status protected from discrimination by state or federal civil rights laws, and includes race, color, national origin, sex, age, religion, or disability.

(b) A person may not develop or deploy an artificial intelligence system with the intent to unlawfully discriminate against a protected class in violation of state or federal law.

(c) For purposes of this section, a disparate impact is not sufficient by itself to demonstrate an intent to discriminate.

(d) This section does not apply to an insurance entity for purposes of providing insurance services if the entity is subject to applicable statutes regulating unfair discrimination, unfair methods of competition, or unfair or deceptive acts or practices related to the business of insurance.

Sec. 552.057. Certain Sexually Explicit Videos, Images, And Child Pornography

(a) A person may not develop or distribute an artificial intelligence system with the sole intent of producing, assisting or aiding in producing, or distributing: (1) visual material in violation of Section 43.26, Penal Code; or (2) deep fake videos or images in violation of Section 21.165, Penal Code.

(b) A court determining the sole intent of a person under this section shall consider marketing materials or terms of use associated with the artificial intelligence system.

New York City Local Law No. 144

Section 1. Chapter 5 of title 20 of the administrative code of the city of New York is amended by adding a new subchapter 25 to read as follows:

Subchapter 25. Automated Employment Decision Tools

§ 20-870 Definitions.

For the purposes of this subchapter, the following terms have the following meanings:

Automated employment decision tool. The term "automated employment decision tool" means any computational process, derived from machine learning, statistical modeling, data analytics, or artificial intelligence, that issues simplified output, including a score, classification, or recommendation, that is used to substantially assist or replace discretionary decision making for making employment decisions that impact natural persons. The term "automated employment decision tool" does not include a tool that does not automate, support, substantially assist or replace discretionary decision-making processes and that does not materially impact natural persons, including, but not limited to, a junk email filter, firewall, antivirus software, calculator, spreadsheet, database, data set, or other compilation of data.

APPENDIX

Bias audit. The term "bias audit" means an impartial evaluation by an independent auditor. Such bias audit shall include but not be limited to the testing of an automated employment decision tool to assess the tool's disparate impact on persons of any Component 1 category required to be reported by employers pursuant to subsection (c) of Section 2000e-8 of Title 42 of the United States Code as specified in Part 1602.7 of Title 29 of the Code of Federal Regulations.

Employment decision. The term "employment decision" means to screen candidates for employment or employees for promotion within the city.

§ 20-871 Requirements for automated employment decision tools.

- a. In the city, it shall be unlawful for an employer or an employment agency to use an automated employment decision tool to screen a candidate or employee for an employment decision unless:

    1. Such tool has been the subject of a bias audit conducted no more than one year prior to the use of such tool; and

    2. A summary of the results of the most recent bias audit of such tool as well as the distribution date of the tool to which such audit applies has been made publicly available on the website of the employer or employment agency prior to the use of such tool.

- b. **Notices required.** In the city, any employer or employment agency that uses an automated employment decision tool to screen an employee or a candidate who has applied for a position for an employment decision shall notify each such employee or candidate who resides in the city of the following:

    1. That an automated employment decision tool will be used in connection with the assessment or evaluation of such employee or candidate that resides in the city. Such notice shall be made no less than ten business days before such use and allow a candidate to request an alternative selection process or accommodation;

    2. The job qualifications and characteristics that such automated employment decision tool will use in the assessment of such candidate or employee. Such notice shall be made no less than 10 business days before such use; and

3. If not disclosed on the employer or employment agency's website, information about the type of data collected for the automated employment decision tool, the source of such data and the employer or employment agency's data retention policy shall be available upon written request by a candidate or employee. Such information shall be provided within 30 days of the written request. Information pursuant to this section shall not be disclosed where such disclosure would violate local, state, or federal law, or interfere with a law enforcement investigation.

Utah AI Policy Act

13-2-12. Generative Artificial Intelligence -- Impact on Liability for Violation of Consumer Protection Law

(1) As used in this section: (a) "Generative artificial intelligence" means an artificial system that: (i) is trained on data; (ii) interacts with a person using text, audio, or visual communication; and (iii) generates non-scripted outputs similar to outputs created by a human, with limited or no human oversight. (b) "License" means a state-granted authorization for a person to engage in a specified occupation: (i) based on the person meeting personal qualifications established under state law; and (ii) where state law requires the authorization before the person may lawfully engage in the occupation for compensation. (c) "Regulated occupation" means an occupation regulated by the Department of Commerce that requires a person to obtain a license or state certification to practice the occupation. (d) "State certification" means a state-granted authorization given to a person to use the term "state certified" as part of a designated title related to engaging in a specified occupation: (i) based on the person meeting personal qualifications established under state law; and (ii) where state

law prohibits a noncertified person from using the term "state certified" as part of a designated title but does not otherwise prohibit a noncertified person from engaging in the occupation for compensation.

(2) It is not a defense to the violation of any statute administered and enforced by the division, as described in Section 13-2-1, that generative artificial intelligence: (a) made the violative statement; (b) undertook the violative act; or (c) was used in furtherance of the violation.

(3) A person who uses, prompts, or otherwise causes generative artificial intelligence to interact with a person in connection with any act administered and enforced by the division, as described in Section 13-2-1, shall clearly and conspicuously disclose to the person with whom the generative artificial intelligence interacts, if asked or prompted by the person, that the person is interacting with generative artificial intelligence and not a human.

(4) (a) A person who provides the services of a regulated occupation shall prominently disclose when a person is interacting with a generative artificial intelligence in the provision of regulated services. (b) Nothing in this section permits a person to provide the services of a regulated occupation through generative artificial intelligence without meeting the requirements of the regulated occupation.

(5) A disclosure described in Subsection (4)(a) shall be provided: (a) verbally at the start of an oral exchange or conversation; and (b) through electronic messaging before a written exchange.

California Bot Act

SECTION 1. Chapter 6 (commencing with Section 17940) is added to Part 3 of Division 7 of the Business and Professions Code, to read:

Chapter 6. Bots

17940. For purposes of this chapter: (a) "Bot" means an automated online account where all or substantially all of the actions or posts of that account are not the result of a person. (b) "Online" means appearing on any public-facing Internet Web site, Web application, or digital application, including a social network or publication. (c) "Online platform" means any public-facing Internet Web site, Web application, or digital application, including a social network or publication, that has 10,000,000 or more unique monthly United States visitors or users for a majority of months during the preceding 12 months. (d) "Person" means a natural person, corporation, limited liability company, partnership, joint venture, association, estate, trust, government, governmental subdivision or agency, or other legal entity or any combination thereof.

17941. (a) It shall be unlawful for any person to use a bot to communicate or interact with another person in California online, with the intent to mislead the other person about its artificial identity for the purpose of knowingly deceiving the person about the content of the communication in order to incentivize a purchase or sale of goods or services in a commercial transaction or to influence a vote in an election. A person using a bot shall not be liable under this section if the person discloses that it is a bot. (b) The disclosure required by this section shall be clear, conspicuous, and reasonably designed to inform persons with whom the bot communicates or interacts that it is a bot.

17942. (a) The duties and obligations imposed by this chapter are cumulative with any other duties or obligation imposed by any other law. (b) The provisions of this chapter are severable. If any provision of this chapter or its application is held invalid, that invalidity shall not affect other provisions or applications that can be given effect without the invalid provision or application. (c) This chapter does not impose a duty on service providers of online platforms, including, but not limited to, Web hosting and Internet service providers.

17943. This chapter shall become operative on July 1, 2019.

California Artificial Intelligence Training Data Transparency Act

SECTION 1. Title 15.2 (commencing with Section 3110) is added to Part 4 of Division 3 of the Civil Code, to read:

APPENDIX

Title 15.2. Artificial Intelligence Training Data Transparency

3110. For purposes of this title, the following definitions shall apply: (a) "Artificial intelligence" means an engineered or machine-based system that varies in its level of autonomy and that can, for explicit or implicit objectives, infer from the input it receives how to generate outputs that can influence physical or virtual environments. (b) "Developer" means a person, partnership, state or local government agency, or corporation that designs, codes, produces, or substantially modifies an artificial intelligence system or service for use by members of the public. For purposes of this subdivision, "members of the public" does not include an affiliate as defined in subparagraph (A) of paragraph (1) of subdivision (c) of Section 1799.1a, or a hospital's medical staff member. (c) "Generative artificial intelligence" means artificial intelligence that can generate derived synthetic content, such as text, images, video, and audio, that emulates the structure and characteristics of the artificial intelligence's training data. (d) "Substantially modifies" or "substantial modification" means a new version, new release, or other update to a generative artificial intelligence system or service that materially changes its functionality or performance, including the results of retraining or fine tuning. (e) "Synthetic data generation" means a process in which seed data are used to create artificial data that have some of the statistical characteristics of the seed data. (f) "Train a generative artificial intelligence system or service" includes testing, validating, or fine tuning by the developer of the artificial intelligence system or service.

3111. On or before January 1, 2026, and before each time thereafter that a generative artificial intelligence system or service, or a substantial modification to a generative artificial intelligence system or service, released on or after January 1, 2022, is made publicly available to Californians for use, regardless of whether the terms of that use include compensation, the developer of the system or service shall post on the developer's internet website documentation regarding the data used by the developer to train the generative artificial intelligence system or service, including, but not be limited to, all of the following: (a) A high-level summary of the datasets used in the development of the generative artificial intelligence system or service, including, but not limited to: (1) The sources or owners of the datasets. (2) A description of how the datasets further the intended purpose of the artificial intelligence system or service. (3) The number of data points included in the datasets, which may be in general ranges, and with estimated figures for dynamic datasets. (4) A description of the types of data points within the datasets. For purposes of this paragraph, the following definitions apply: (A) As applied to datasets that include labels, "types of data points" means the types of labels used. (B) As applied to datasets without labeling, "types of data points" refers to the general characteristics. (5) Whether the datasets include any data protected by copyright, trademark, or patent, or whether the datasets are entirely in the public domain. (6) Whether the datasets were purchased or licensed by the developer. (7) Whether the datasets include personal information, as defined in subdivision (v) of Section 1798.140. (8) Whether the datasets include aggregate consumer information, as defined in subdivision (b) of Section 1798.140. (9) Whether there was any cleaning, processing, or other modification to the datasets by the developer, including the intended purpose of those efforts in relation to the artificial intelligence system or service. (10) The time period during which the data in the datasets were collected, including a notice if the data collection is ongoing. (11) The dates the datasets were first used during the development of the artificial intelligence system or service. (12) Whether the generative artificial intelligence system or service used or continuously uses synthetic data generation in its development. A developer may include a description of the functional need or desired purpose of the synthetic data in relation to the intended purpose of the system or service. (b) A developer shall not be required to post documentation regarding the data used to train a generative artificial intelligence system or service for any of the following: (1) A generative artificial intelligence system or service whose sole purpose is to help ensure security and integrity. For purposes of this paragraph, "security and integrity" has the same meaning as defined in subdivision (ac) of Section 1798.140, except as applied to any developer or user and not limited to businesses, as defined in subdivision (d) of that section. (2) A generative artificial intelligence system or service whose sole purpose is the operation of aircraft in the national airspace. (3) A generative artificial intelligence system or service developed for national security, military, or defense purposes that is made available only to a federal entity.

California AI Transparency Act

Section 1. Chapter 25 (commencing with Section 22757) is added to Division 8 of the Business and Professions Code, to read:

APPENDIX

Chapter 25. AI Transparency Act

22757. This chapter shall be known as the California AI Transparency Act.

22757.1. As used in this chapter: (a) "Artificial intelligence" or "AI" means an engineered or machine-based system that varies in its level of autonomy and that can, for explicit or implicit objectives, infer from the input it receives how to generate outputs that can influence physical or virtual environments. (b) "Covered provider" means a person that creates, codes, or otherwise produces a generative artificial intelligence system that has over 1,000,000 monthly visitors or users and is publicly accessible within the geographic boundaries of the state. (c) "Generative artificial intelligence system" or "GenAI system" means an artificial intelligence that can generate derived synthetic content, including text, images, video, and audio, that emulates the structure and characteristics of the system's training data. (d) "Latent" means present but not manifest. (e) "Manifest" means easily perceived, understood, or recognized by a natural person. (f) "Metadata" means structural or descriptive information about data. (g) "Personal information" has the same meaning as defined in Section 1798.140 of the Civil Code. (h) "Personal provenance data" means provenance data that contains either of the following: (1) Personal information. (2) Unique device, system, or service information that is reasonably capable of being associated with a particular user. (i) "Provenance data" means data that is embedded into digital content, or that is included in the digital content's metadata, for the purpose of verifying the digital content's authenticity, origin, or history of modification. (j) "System provenance data" means provenance data that is not reasonably capable of being associated with a particular user and that contains either of the following: (1) Information regarding the type of device, system, or service that was used to generate a piece of digital content. (2) Information related to content authenticity.

22757.2. (a) A covered provider shall make available an AI detection tool at no cost to the user that meets all of the following criteria: (1) The tool allows a user to assess whether image, video, or audio content, or content that is any combination thereof, was created or altered by the covered provider's GenAI system. (2) The tool outputs any system provenance data that is detected in the content. (3) The tool does not output any personal provenance data that is detected in the content. (4) (A) Subject to subparagraph (B), the tool is publicly accessible. (B) A covered provider may impose reasonable limitations on access to the tool to prevent, or respond to, demonstrable risks to the security or integrity of its GenAI system. (5) The tool allows a user to upload content or provide a uniform resource locator (URL) linking to online content. (6) The tool supports an application programming interface that allows a user to invoke the tool without visiting the covered provider's internet website. (b) A covered provider shall collect user feedback related to the efficacy of the covered provider's AI detection tool and incorporate relevant feedback into any attempt to improve the efficacy of the tool. (c) A covered provider shall not do any of the following: (1) (A) Except as provided in subparagraph (B), collect or retain personal information from users of the covered provider's AI detection tool. (B) (i) A covered provider may collect and retain the contact information of a user who submits feedback pursuant to subdivision (b) if the user opts in to being contacted by the covered provider. (ii) User information collected pursuant to clause (i) shall be used only to evaluate and improve the efficacy of the covered provider's AI detection tool. (2) Retain any content submitted to the AI detection tool for longer than is necessary to comply with this section. (3) Retain any personal provenance data from content submitted to the AI detection tool by a user.

22757.3. (a) A covered provider shall offer the user the option to include a manifest disclosure in image, video, or audio content, or content that is any combination thereof, created or altered by the covered provider's GenAI system that meets all of the following criteria: (1) The disclosure identifies content as AI-generated content. (2) The disclosure is clear, conspicuous, appropriate for the medium of the content, and understandable to a reasonable person. (3) The disclosure is permanent or extraordinarily difficult to remove, to the extent it is technically feasible. (b) A covered provider shall include a latent disclosure in AI-generated image, video, or audio content, or content that is any combination thereof, created by the covered provider's GenAI system that meets all of the following criteria: (1) To the extent that it is technically feasible and reasonable, the disclosure conveys all of the following information, either directly or through a link to a permanent internet website: (A) The name of the covered provider. (B) The name and version number of the GenAI system that created or altered the content. (C) The time and date of the content's creation or alteration. (D) A unique identifier. (2) The disclosure is detectable by the covered provider's AI detection tool. (3) The disclosure is consistent with widely accepted industry standards. (4) The disclosure is permanent or extraordinarily difficult to remove, to the extent it is technically feasible. (c) (1) If a covered provider licenses its GenAI system to a third party, the covered provider shall require by contract that the licensee maintain the system's capability to include a disclosure required by subdivision (b) in content the system creates or alters. (2) If a covered provider knows that a third-party licensee modified a licensed GenAI system such that it is no longer capable of including a disclosure required by subdivision (b) in content the system creates or alters, the covered provider shall revoke the license within 96 hours of discovering the licensee's action. (3) A third-party licensee shall cease using a licensed GenAI system after the license for the system has been revoked by the covered provider pursuant to paragraph (2).

22757.4. (a) (1) A covered provider that violates this chapter shall be liable for a civil penalty in the amount of five thousand dollars ($5,000) per violation to be collected in a civil action filed by the Attorney General, a city attorney, or a county counsel. (2) A prevailing plaintiff in an action brought pursuant to this subdivision shall be entitled to all reasonable attorney's costs and fees. (b) Each day that a covered provider is in violation of this chapter shall be deemed a discrete violation. (c) For a violation by a third-party licensee of paragraph (3) of subdivision (c) of Section 22757.3, the Attorney General, a county counsel, or a city attorney may bring a civil action for both of the following: (1) Injunctive relief. (2) Reasonable attorney's fees and costs.

22757.5. This chapter does not apply to any product, service, internet website, or application that provides exclusively non-user-generated video game, television, streaming, movie, or interactive experiences.

22757.6. This chapter shall become operative on January 1, 2026.

Affordable Care Act

Sec. 1557. Nondiscrimination

(a) In General

Except as otherwise provided for in this title (or an amendment made by this title), an individual shall not, on the ground prohibited under:

- **Title VI of the Civil Rights Act of 1964** (42 U.S.C. 2000d et seq.)
- **Title IX of the Education Amendments of 1972** (20 U.S.C. 1681 et seq.)
- **The Age Discrimination Act of 1975** (42 U.S.C. 6101 et seq.)
- **Section 504 of the Rehabilitation Act of 1973** (29 U.S.C. 794)

be excluded from participation in, be denied the benefits of, or be subjected to discrimination under, any health program or activity, any part of which is receiving Federal financial assistance, including credits, subsidies, or contracts of insurance, or under any program or activity that is administered by an Executive Agency or any entity established under this title (or amendments). The enforcement mechanisms provided for and available under such title VI, title IX, section 504, or such Age Discrimination Act shall apply for purposes of violations of this subsection.

American Disabilities Act
Sec. 12112. Discrimination

(a) General rule

No covered entity shall discriminate against a qualified individual on the basis of disability in regard to job application procedures, the hiring, advancement, or discharge of employees, employee compensation, job training, and other terms, conditions, and privileges of employment.

(b) Construction

As used in subsection (a) of this section, the term "discriminate against a qualified individual on the basis of disability" includes—

(5) (A) not making reasonable accommodations to the known physical or mental limitations of an otherwise qualified individual with a disability who is an applicant or employee, unless such covered entity can demonstrate that the accommodation would impose an undue hardship on the operation of the business of such covered entity; or (B) denying employment opportunities to a job applicant or employee who is an otherwise qualified individual with a disability, if such denial is based on the need of such covered entity to make reasonable accommodation to the physical or mental impairments of the employee or applicant;

APPENDIX

(6) using qualification standards, employment tests or other selection criteria that screen out or tend to screen out an individual with a disability or a class of individuals with disabilities unless the standard, test or other selection criteria, as used by the covered entity, is shown to be job-related for the position in question and is consistent with business necessity; and

(d) Medical examinations and inquiries

(1) In general The prohibition against discrimination as referred to in subsection (a) of this section shall include medical examinations and inquiries.

(2) Preemployment (A) Prohibited examination or inquiry Except as provided in paragraph (3), a covered entity shall not conduct a medical examination or make inquiries of a job applicant as to whether such applicant is an individual with a disability or as to the nature or severity of such disability. (B) Acceptable inquiry A covered entity may make preemployment inquiries into the ability of an applicant to perform job-related functions.

(3) Employment entrance examination A covered entity may require a medical examination after an offer of employment has been made to a job applicant and prior to the commencement of the employment duties of such applicant, and may condition an offer of employment on the results of such examination, if— (A) all entering employees are subjected to such an examination regardless of disability; (B) information obtained regarding the medical condition or history of the applicant is collected and maintained on separate forms and in separate medical files and is treated as a confidential medical record, except that— (i) supervisors and managers may be informed regarding necessary restrictions on the work or duties of the employee and necessary accommodations; (ii) first aid and safety personnel may be informed, when appropriate, if the disability might require emergency treatment; and (iii) government officials investigating compliance with this chapter shall be provided relevant information on request; and (C) the results of such examination are used only in accordance with this subchapter.

(4) Examination and inquiry (A) Prohibited examinations and inquiries A covered entity shall not require a medical examination and shall not make inquiries of an employee as to whether such employee is an individual with a disability or as to the nature or severity of the disability, unless such examination or inquiry is shown to be job-related and consistent with business necessity. (B) Acceptable examinations and inquiries A covered entity may conduct voluntary medical examinations, including voluntary medical histories, which are part of an employee health program available to employees at that work site. A covered entity may make inquiries into the ability of an employee to perform job-related functions. (C) Requirement Information obtained under subparagraph (B) regarding the medical condition or history of any employee are subject to the requirements of subparagraphs (B) and (C) of paragraph (3).

Title XII, Civil Rights Act

Section 2000e-16, Employment by Federal Government

(a) Discriminatory practices prohibited; employees or applicants for employment subject to coverage

All personnel actions affecting employees or applicants for employment (except with regard to aliens employed outside the limits of the United States) in:

- military departments as defined in section 102 of title 5
- executive agencies as defined in section 105 of title 5 (including employees and applicants for employment who are paid from nonappropriated funds)
- the United States Postal Service and the Postal Rate Commission
- those units of the Government of the District of Columbia having positions in the competitive service

APPENDIX

- and in those units of the legislative and judicial branches of the Federal Government having positions in the competitive service, and in the Library of Congress

shall be made free from any discrimination based on race, color, religion, sex, or national origin.

(b) Equal Employment Opportunity Commission; enforcement powers; issuance of rules, regulations, etc.; annual review and approval of national and regional equal employment opportunity plans; review and evaluation of equal employment opportunity programs and publication of progress reports; consultations with interested parties; compliance with rules, regulations, etc.; contents of national and regional equal employment opportunity plans; authority of Librarian of Congress

Except as otherwise provided in this subsection, the Equal Employment Opportunity Commission shall have authority to enforce the provisions of subsection (a) of this section through appropriate remedies, including reinstatement or hiring of employees with or without back pay, as will effectuate the policies of this section, and shall issue such rules, regulations, orders and instructions as it deems necessary and appropriate to carry out its responsibilities under this section.

The Equal Employment Opportunity Commission shall:

1. be responsible for the annual review and approval of a national and regional equal employment opportunity plan which each department and agency and each appropriate unit referred to in subsection (a) of this section shall submit in order to maintain an affirmative program of equal employment opportunity for all such employees and applicants for employment;

2. be responsible for the review and evaluation of the operation of all agency equal employment opportunity programs, periodically obtaining and publishing (on at least a semiannual basis) progress reports from each such department, agency, or unit; and

3. consult with and solicit the recommendations of interested individuals, groups, and organizations relating to equal employment opportunity.

The head of each such department, agency, or unit shall comply with such rules, regulations, orders, and instructions which shall include a provision that an employee or applicant for employment shall be notified of any final action taken on any complaint of discrimination filed by him thereunder.

The plan submitted by each department, agency, and unit shall include, but not be limited to:

1. provision for the establishment of training and education programs designed to provide a maximum opportunity for employees to advance so as to perform at their highest potential; and

2. a description of the qualifications in terms of training and experience relating to equal employment opportunity for the principal and operating officials of each such department, agency, or unit responsible for carrying out the equal employment opportunity program and of the allocation of personnel and resources proposed by such department, agency, or unit to carry out its equal employment opportunity program.

With respect to employment in the Library of Congress, authorities granted in this subsection to the Equal Employment Opportunity Commission shall be exercised by the Librarian of Congress.

(c) Civil action by employee or applicant for employment for redress of grievances; time for bringing of action; head of department, agency, or unit as defendant

Within 90 days of receipt of notice of final action taken by a department, agency, or unit referred to in subsection (a) of this section, or by the Equal Employment Opportunity Commission upon an appeal from a decision or order of such department, agency, or unit on a complaint of discrimination based on race, color, religion, sex or national origin, brought pursuant to subsection (a) of this section, Executive Order 11478 or any

APPENDIX

succeeding Executive orders, or after one hundred and eighty days from the filing of the initial charge with the department, agency, or unit or with the Equal Employment Opportunity Commission on appeal from a decision or order of such department, agency, or unit until such time as final action may be taken by a department, agency, or unit, an employee or applicant for employment, if aggrieved by the final disposition of his complaint, or by the failure to take final action on his complaint, may file a civil action as provided in section 2000e-5 of this title, in which civil action the head of the department, agency, or unit, as appropriate, shall be the defendant.

(d) Section 2000e-5(f) through (k) of this title applicable to civil actions

The provisions of section 2000e-5(f) through (k) of this title, as applicable, shall govern civil actions brought hereunder, and the same interest to compensate for delay in payment shall be available as in cases involving nonpublic parties.

(e) Government agency or official not relieved of responsibility to assure nondiscrimination in employment or equal employment opportunity

Nothing contained in this Act shall relieve any Government agency or official of its or his primary responsibility to assure nondiscrimination in employment as required by the Constitution and statutes or of its or his responsibilities under Executive Order 11478 relating to equal employment opportunity in the Federal Government.

Index

A

Accountability, 65, 66, 76, 112, 143, 144
    assurance, 33
        impact assessment, 41, 42
        internal audits, 42
        monitoring, measurement, analysis, and evaluation, 42
        risk assessment, 41, 42
    concepts, 31
    contestability, 33
    and fairness, 145
    principle, 31, 32
    provisions
        assurance, 35
        contestability, 37, 38
        high-risk AI systems, 35
        traceability, 40, 41
    reporting
        of concerns, 43
        external, 43
    traceability, 33, 34, 43–46
Accuracy, 127, 128, 161–163
Affordable Care Act, 29, 262, 263
AI, *see* Artificial intelligence (AI)
Algorithmic exceptionalism, 3
Algorithmic recommendations provisions, 58, 81, 102, 119
    information services, 230, 231
    user's rights and interests, 231, 232
Allocation of roles and responsibilities, 90, 91

Americans with Disabilities Act, 29, 100, 263–265
Anonymization, 85
Anti-discrimination laws, 22
Article 50(4), 57
Artificial intelligence (AI), 35
    algorithmic bias, 3
    Article 3, 149
    attacks, 53
    category of controls, 13
    clause/requirement, 11, 12
    disciplines, 4, 5
    economic risks, 1
    governance, 5–7
    insecure, 50–52
    ISO 42001 certification, 17–19
    job redistribution, 1
    legal compliance, 4
    policy, 60
    political divisiveness, 5
    privacy and fairness, 145
    safety, 50
    security, 49, 50, 145
    supportive relationships, 143–146
    system impact assessment and process, 24, 25
    system verification and validation, 64, 65
    technical deficiencies, 2
    training data transparency, 258, 259
    transparency, 145

INDEX

Assurance, 33
Authorization, 72
Automated decision-making
    Article 22B restrictions, 228, 229
    Article 22C Safeguards, 229
    processing and significant
        decisions, 228
Automated employment decision
    tools, 253-255
Automated individual decision-making,
    204, 205
Automated processing, 228
Automatically generated logs, 164
Automation bias, 3, 53

B

Bias audit, 254
Biometric data, 250
Black box problem, 109, 110
Bots, 257, 258
Burden of proof, 227

C

California AI Transparency Act, 115,
    116, 259-262
California Artificial Intelligence Training
    Data Transparency Act, 115,
    258, 259
California Bot Act, 29, 116, 257, 258
California Consumer Privacy Act, 81
California Generative AI Training Data
    Transparency Act, 29
California Transparency Act, 29
CE marking, 182
Certificates, 177
Civil Rights Act, 29

Clauses, 11, 12
    and controls, 146
    ISO 42001 and the law, 19-29
Code of Conduct on Disinformation, 212
Codes of conduct, 57, 210-212
Colorado SB-205
    developer duty to avoid algorithmic
        discrimination, 238-248
    disclosure, 248
Colorado SB 205, 29, 82, 101, 116, 117
Common specifications,
    commission, 172-174
Communication, 123, 124
    of information, 89
Conformity assessment, 35, 36, 149,
    175-177, 179-181
Consequential decision, 38
Consistency, 128, 129
Consumer protection law, 255, 256
Contestability, 33
Cultural diversity, 147
Customer relationships, 46, 125
Cyberattacks, 53
Cybersecurity, 161-163
Cybersecurity requirements
    products with digital elements,
        215, 216
    vulnerability, 217, 218
Cybersecurity risk-management
    measures, 220-222

D

Data acquisition, 43, 62
Data collection limitation, 73
Data governance
    acquisition, 62, 86, 87, 103, 134, 135
    Article 10, 153-155

INDEX

Clause 6.1.2, 131
management, 61, 62
management processes, 87, 103, 133
provenance, 134, 135
quality, 86, 87, 104, 132–134
resources, 104, 134, 135
preparation, 87, 88, 135
Data lineage, 33
Data management, 61, 62
Data minimization, 72, 73
Data poisoning, 51
Data protection impact assessment, 205–207
Data protection rules, 147
Data provenance, 33
Data quality, 75, 132, 133
Decision-making, 38, 193, 194
Decision-making process, 98
Deepfakes, 56
Deep Synthesis Provisions, 58, 119
Deep synthesis services, 81
    data and technical management specifications, 233, 234
    ordinary provisions, 232, 233
DEI, *see* Diversity, equity, and inclusion (DEI)
Demographic parity, 94
Deployer-consumer disclosure, 117
Deployers, 184–186
Deployers of high-risk AI systems, 166–170
Deployment, 98
Derogation, 179–181
Developer duty, 238–248
Differential privacy, 86
Digital Services Act, 29, 57, 58, 115
    categories, 208
    codes of conduct, 210–212
    fairness, 100

online advertising transparency, 209, 210
recommender system transparency, 208, 209
Discrimination, 263–265
Diversity, equity, and inclusion (DEI), 146
Documentation, 13, 23, 24, 163, 164
developer duty, 238–248

E

Economic operators, 225
Emotional contagion, 2
Employment, 265–268
Encryption, 85
Equal access, 147
Equal opportunity, 95
EU Artificial Intelligence (AI) Act, 5, 28, 34, 35, 37, 42, 53–55, 130
deepfakes, 56
fairness, 99–101
general-purpose AI models, 188–191
high-risk (*see* High-risk AI systems)
manipulation and deception, 56
post-market monitoring, 190–194
principles, 147
prohibited AI practices, 149
Recital (106), 148
Recital (108), 148
Recital (110), 148, 149
transparency, 112–115
transparency obligations, 184–186
EU Copyright Directive, 213
EU Cyber Resilience Act, 29, 54, 55
high-risk AI systems, 213–215
EU Data Act, 29
obligations of third parties, 219
privacy, 79

271

INDEX

EU declaration of conformity, 181, 182, 218, 219
Exception/limitation for text and data mining, 213
Explainability, 109, 111
    See also Transparency
External accountability
    allocation of responsibilities, 45, 46
    control over processes, 44
    customer relationships, 46
    supplier relationships, 45, 46
External reporting, 65, 90, 106, 139

F

Fair Information Principles, 71
Fairness, 147
    assurance
        internal audits, 105
        risk assessment, 105
    automatic AI systems, 93
    bias, 96
        data, 97
        development, 97
        subconscious, 97
    data governance, 103, 104
    demographic parity, 94
    deployment, 98
    Digital Services Act, 100
    equal opportunity, 95
    equal treatment, 93
    EU Artificial Intelligence (AI) Act, 99–101
    group, 93
    sufficiency, 95, 96
    team diversity, 102
    transparency and accountability, 106
File Metadata, 238

Fundamental rights impact assessment, 36, 37

G

GDPR, *see* General Data Protection Regulation (GDPR)
Gender equality, 147
General Data Protection Act, 28
General Data Protection Regulation (GDPR), 79–82, 115, 197, 198
General Product Safety Regulation (GPSR), 222, 223
General-purpose AI models, 54
    Article 53(1), 194, 195
    obligations for providers, 186–188
    systemic risk, 188, 189, 195, 196
Generative AI Interim, 59
Generative AI Interim Measures, 81, 102, 119, 131
    general provisions, 234, 235
    service specifications, 236
Generative artificial intelligence, 53, 255, 256
GPSR, *see* General Product Safety Regulation (GPSR)

H

Harmonised standards, 171, 172
Harmonized approach, 16
Health Insurance Portability and Accountability Act (HIPAA), 81
High-risk AI systems, 213–215
    accuracy, robustness and cybersecurity, 161–163
    certificates, 171–184
    compliance with requirements, 150
    conformity assessment, 171–184

data and data governance, 153–155
　　human oversight, 159, 160
　　information to deployers, 157
　　obligations of providers, 162–170
　　post-market monitoring, 190, 191
　　presumption of conformity, 174
　　record-keeping, 156, 157
　　registration, 171–184
　　risk management system, 151–154
　　standards, 171–184
　　technical documentation, 155, 156
　　transparency, 157–159
High-risk artificial intelligence system, 37
HIPAA, *see* Health Insurance Portability and Accountability Act (HIPAA)
Human autonomy, 32, 33
Human-in-the-loop approach, 63
Human-on-the-loop, 32, 33
Human oversight, 159, 160

I, J, K

ICT, *see* Information and communications technology (ICT)
IEC, *see* International Electrotechnical Commission (IEC)
Impact assessments, 41, 42, 61, 83, 84
　　data protection, 205–207
　　fairness, 105
　　for high-risk AI systems, 169, 170
　　requirements, 16
Implementation Guidance
　　B.2.2, 23
　　B.2.3, 60
　　B.3.2, 24, 44
　　B.4.3, 120, 134
　　B.5.2, 25, 61
　　B.6.1.2, 102
　　B.6.2.3, 63
　　B.6.2.4, 137
　　B.6.2.6, 138
　　B.6.2.7, 140
　　B.6.2.8, 25
　　B.7.2, 61, 120
　　B.7.3, 25, 43, 87, 103, 120
　　B.7.4, 104, 132
　　B.8.2, 121, 140
　　B.8.4, 65
　　B.9.2, 26
　　B.9.4, 27, 89, 124, 139
　　B.10.2, 45
　　B.10.3, 45
　　B.10.4, 46, 125
Incident reporting, 65, 88, 89, 125
Individual participation, 75
Inference, 74
Information and communications technology (ICT), 10
Information security policy, 61
Information technology (IT), 10
Integrated privacy-specific approach
　　AI policy, 83
　　impact assessments, 83, 84
　　privacy by design, 84–86
Integrated security-specific approach
　　artificial intelligence (AI) policy, 60
　　high-level framework, 60
　　Impact assessments, 61
　　ISO 27001, 60
Intended use, 89
Internal accountability, 44
Internal audits, 23, 42, 105
International Electrotechnical Commission (IEC), 9, 10
International Organization for Standardization (ISO), 9, 10

INDEX

ISO 42001 and the law
    artificial intelligence (AI)
        determining and documenting, 25
        life cycle, 25
        policy and documentation, 23, 24
        responsible and intended systems, 26, 27
        system impact assessment, 24, 25
    direct contribution, 27
    employee awareness, 22, 23
    implementation and certification, 27
    implementation process, 21
    indirect contribution, 28, 29
    interested parties, 21, 22
    internal audits, 23
    legal status, 19, 20
    organization's objectives, 21
    reporting to stakeholders, 26
    risks and opportunities, 22
    roles and responsibilities, 24
ISO 42001 certification, 50, 60, 61, 65, 146
ISO/IEC 42001:2023
    clauses, 11, 12
    controls, 12, 13
    harmonized approach, 16
    organizations, 9, 10
    process approach, 14, 15
    risk-based approach, 15, 16
    solution, 16, 17
    standard, 10, 11
IT, *see* Information technology (IT)
Iterative process, 37

L

Lawfulness of processing, 198–201
Leadership, 12

Legal compliance, 4
Legal provisions, 38

M

Machine learning (ML), 10, 131
ML, *see* Machine learning (ML)
Model cards, 122
Model inversion, 52
Model poisoning, 52

N

New York City Local Law 144, 101, 118, 119
    automated employment decision tools, 253–255
NIS 2 Directive, 55, 220–222
Non-binding frameworks, 7
Non-compliance finding, 22
Nondiscrimination, 262, 263
Notified bodies, 178, 179

O

Obligations of providers and deployers, 189
    Article 16, 162, 163
    automatically generated logs, 164
    corrective actions and duty of information, 164, 165
    documentation, 163, 164
    high-risk AI systems, 165–169
    impact assessment, 169, 170
    See also General-purpose AI models
Online advertising transparency, 209, 210
Opacity, 110
Openness, 74, 75
Overfitting, 129

P, Q

Personal data, 70, 201–203
Personal data, information and access to automated individual decision-making, 204, 205
    data subject, 204
    right of access, 204
Personal Information Protection Law (PIPL), 80
Personality profiles, 2
PIPL, *see* Personal Information Protection Law (PIPL)
Plan-Do-Check-Act cycle, 14, 15
Post-market monitoring
    high-risk AI systems, 190, 191
    individual decision-making, 193, 194
    sharing of information, 191–193
Privacy, 69
    accountability, 76
    breaches, 70, 71
    data governance, 86–88
    Data minimization, 72, 73
    data quality, 75
    discrimination, 69, 70
    individual participation, 75
    organizations, 70
    purpose specification, 72
    security safeguards, 72
    transparency and accountability, 88–90
    use limitation
        inference, 74
        openness, 74, 75
        secondary use, 73
        web-scraping, 74
Processing of personal data, 201–203
Product Liability Directive (PLD), 56, 223–225
Products with digital elements, 215, 216
Prohibited AI practices, 149
Providers, 184–186
Pseudonymization, 85

R

Record-keeping, 13, 156, 157
Registration, 183, 184
Reporting of serious incidents, 191–193
Risk assessment, 36, 41, 42, 105, 131
Risk-based approach, 15, 16
Risk management, 12
    policy, 35
    system, 151–154
Robustness, 144, 147, 161–163
    accuracy, 127, 128, 130
    consistency, 128, 129
    data governance, 131–135
    documentation and information, 140
    documentation, system and computing resource, 136, 137
    operational safeguards
        intended use, 139
        system operation and monitoring, 138
        system verification and validation, 137
    reliability, 127
    system technical documentation, 140
Role-specific trainings, 23

S

"Safe harbor" provisions, 27
Security and privacy, 143

INDEX

Security and safety
    assurance measures, 64, 65
    data governance, 61–63
    integrated security-specific
        approach, 60
    operational safeguards
        system deployment, 63
        system design and development, 63
        system infrastructure, 63
    provisions
        artificial intelligence (AI)
            safety, 55, 56
        manipulation, disinformation and
            deepfakes, 56–60
        measures for labeling, 59, 60
        security, 53–55
    transparency and
        accountability, 65, 66
Security safeguards, 72
Service providers, 238
Simplified EU declaration of
    conformity, 219
Skepticism, 1
Social scoring, 250
Socio-technical context, 42
Stakeholders, 1, 2, 6, 7, 10–12, 15, 148
    reporting to, 26
Standardisation, 171, 172
Supplier relationships, 45, 46, 66, 106, 139
Symbiotic relationship, 20, 21
Synthetic content labeling measures
    requirements, 237, 238
    service providers, 237
Synthetic Content Labeling Measures, 119
System and computing resources, 136, 137
System cards, 123
System deployment, 63
System documentation, 106

T

Team diversity, 102
Technical documentation, 155, 156
Testing method, 65
Texas Responsible AI Governance Act, 29,
    82, 101, 117, 118
    biometric data, 250
    health care services, 249, 250
    human behavior, 250
    political discrimination, 251, 252
    sexually explicit videos, 253
    social scoring, 250
    unlawful discrimination, 252
The Council of Europe Framework
    Convention on Artificial
    Intelligence, 19
The New York City Local Law 144, 29
Title VII of the Civil Rights Act, 100
Title XII, Civil Rights Act, 265–268
Traceability
    of input, 33, 39
        data acquisition, 43
    of output, 34, 40
        external accountability, 44–46
        internal accountability, 44
        roles and responsibilities, 44
Transparency, 33, 43, 65, 66, 110, 143,
    144, 157–159
    Article 53(1), point (b), 196, 197
    black box problem, 109, 110
    consequences
        accountability, 112
        erosion of trust, 112
    data governance
        acquisition, 120
        management
            processes, 120

provenance, 120
resources, 120
Digital Services Act, 115
disclosure
communication, 124
customer relationships, 125
incident reporting, 125
intended use, 124
EU Artificial Intelligence (AI) Act, 112–115
non-technical documentation, 121–124
technical documentation, 121
US state laws, 115–117
Transparency obligations, 184–186

U, V

UK Data Use and Access Act
automated decision-making, 228, 229
privacy, 80, 81
Union harmonisation
legislation, 150
Unpredictability, 128
Use policy, 123
Utah AI Policy Act, 29, 118, 255, 256

W, X, Y, Z

Watermarks label, 124
Web-scraping, 74

GPSR Compliance

The European Union's (EU) General Product Safety Regulation (GPSR) is a set of rules that requires consumer products to be safe and our obligations to ensure this.

If you have any concerns about our products, you can contact us on

ProductSafety@springernature.com

In case Publisher is established outside the EU, the EU authorized representative is:

Springer Nature Customer Service Center GmbH
Europaplatz 3
69115 Heidelberg, Germany